An Economic History of Ireland since 1660

L. M. CULLEN

B. T. Batsford Ltd London

© L. M. Cullen 1972
First published 1972
Reprinted 1976: first paperback edition
ISBN 0 7134 1382 4

Printed and bound in Great Britain by
Billing & Sons Limited, Guildford, London and Worcester
for the publishers
B. T. Batsford Ltd
4 Fitzhardinge Street, London W1H OAH

Contents

Preface   IV

1 The Irish Economy: Agriculture in a
European Setting 1660–1689   7

2 War, Legislation and Stagnation 1689–1730   26

3 Markets and Harvests 1730–1793   50

4 Land and Industry 1730–1793   77

5 Economic Structure and Rural Crisis 1793–1851   100

6 The Emergence of Modern Ireland 1851–1921   134

7 Stagnation and Growth in Ireland 1922–1971   171

Bibliographical Note   188

Note on Primary Sources   196

Index   203

Preface

The aim of this book is to outline the main features of Irish economic history since 1660. Only in recent decades has study of the subject begun to emerge from the shadow of political preoccupations or interests. It was in fact political events which gained intellectual and general acceptance for a view of the economic background reflecting the dominant political themes—the land question and home rule—of the second half of the nineteenth century. The general histories of Froude (1872–4) and Lecky (1892) reflected this climate of opinion, and from a conservative standpoint lent authority to the nationalist version of Irish history. Between them Froude and Lecky created an intellectual framework beyond which the first accounts of Irish economic history did not venture. Thus, the accepted view, popular and scholarly, of the past was drawn from the preoccupations of the second half of the century and of the early twentieth. A handful of eighteenth-century writings such as Swift's and Hely-Hutchinson's and a few recurrent themes in the literature of the eighteenth century were given a disproportionate significance in accounts of the eighteenth-century antecedents. Modern dilemmas—political and economic—are less intertwined in their historical background than has often been assumed, a point necessary to make because by an inversion economic interests are sometimes asserted today as a cause of political divergencies or conflicts within the island. If anything, such an inversion underestimates the strength of political, religious or racial forces in their own right in Irish history.

Irish economic history as a study is still in its infancy, so much

so that the only major advance in relation to it has been archival.
The accumulation of material in archives and libraries or its cata-
loguing in institutions such as the National Library where ten or
fifteen years ago the absence of listing made it virtually inaccessible,
will facilitate study of the subject in the 1970s. The arrangement
of archives in southern Ireland is not comparable with the north
whose archival facilities are two generations ahead of the primitive
facilities in the south. But the surveying of material in recent decades
by the Irish Manuscripts Commission, the growth of a large collection of material of economic and social interest in the National
Library, and the establishment of the Cork Archives Council, are
in themselves major advances.

A general book at this stage is necessarily tentative, its conclusions
subject to modification. In a short book, moreover, it is not possible
to cover all aspects equally. The reader who wants a broader introduction to the social background should refer to L. M. Cullen, *Life
in Ireland* (London, 1968) and, for trade unions, to J. W. Boyle,
Leaders and workers (Cork, 1966). For a fuller coverage of economic
and social issues since 1920, north and south, the reader should
consult F. S. L. Lyons, *Ireland since the Famine* (London, 1971).

I am greatly indebted to a large number of individuals for assistance in the study underlying this book. I should like to record a
special indebtedness to Mr Kenneth Darwin, former deputy keeper
of the Public Records of Northern Ireland, Mr Brian Trainor, his
successor, and Mr W. H. Crawford also of the Public Record Office
of Northern Ireland, for encouragement and practical assistance. I
am also indebted to Miss Agnes Carroll, Cloneevin, Co. Louth; Mr
P. J. White, Meath county librarian; Mr John Stokes, Messrs
Hardman, Winder and Stokes, Dublin; Mr Alexander Findlater,
Dublin; Mrs Olive Goodbody, Society of Friends, Dublin; Mrs
Amy Monahan, Castletown, Co. Carlow; Captain R. C. Prior-
Wandesforde, Carlow; Professor Conor O'Malley, Galway; Mr
Richard Hilliard, Killarney; Mr T. V. Jackson, Rayleigh, Essex;
Mrs Christine Frame, University of Durham; and the late Dr
Raymond G. Cross, Brackenstown House, Co. Dublin, for material
and information put at my disposal; and to many others for help
and guidance in many ways.

Trinity College, Dublin   L. M. CULLEN
9 September 1971

Note on Dates

Where a year is referred to in the text it usually refers to all or part of a calendar year ending in December. The insertion of a hyphen indicates a period of time covering all or part of two or more years, a vertical stroke a twelve-month period terminating other than in December. Thus, e.g. ' 1777 ' is intended to signify all or part of a year terminating in December 1777; ' 1777–8 ' indicates a period of time covering all or part of the years 1777 and 1778; ' 1777/8 ' signifies a twelve-month year ending in the course of 1778, usually though not invariably the Irish fiscal year ending 25 March. The fiscal year terminating on 25 March was usual only from the end of the first decade of the eighteenth century. Before that, fiscal returns were usually though not invariably made in respect of a year ending 25 December.

I

The Irish Economy
Agriculture in a European Setting
1660-1689

The Irish economy in the sixteenth century was an underdeveloped one. Its exports revealed its character. Fish and hides were the main items in shipments outwards from its ports, evidence of the unsophisticated nature of the island's production. Fish were the harvest of its rivers and of the rich fishing grounds off its coasts. Skins and hides came from the wild animal life of the forests as well as from the domesticated herds of cattle and flocks of sheep. In all probability, the population at the outset of the century was scarcely a million. It was, it seems likely, not much larger a century later, some probable rise in numbers in the first half of the century being more or less offset by a reduction in population through war losses and more substantially through plague or famine during the military campaigns of the closing two decades of the century. It was a primitive country, thinly settled, the people themselves underemployed. Woodlands occupied perhaps an eighth of the country around 1600. Woodland growth was strongest below the 500-foot line, hence woodlands covered rich ground and alluvial valleys that could be turned to pastoral or arable use. The wolf, extinct in England by 1500, was still present in Ireland, a further testimony to the relatively lightly settled nature of the country.

The first half of the seventeenth century, however, witnessed a rapid transition in Irish agricultural life. Previously, it seems, the hides of cattle were more important in trade than the meat itself.

Meat was consumed locally at low prices, only the hides entered into trade extensively, and they rather than cattle or beef featured in the country's export trade. However, from the early years of the seventeenth century, exports of cattle, formerly negligible, grew rapidly. In 1621, a year of particularly low prices, imports of Irish cattle were a sufficient threat to warrant the introduction in the House of Commons in London by the English interests affected of a bill intended to exclude them. The bill did not proceed further, imports were already well established and the interests affected were unable to command general support for the proposed exclusion. Wool exports increased too, like cattle overshadowing the formerly important categories of fish and hides. They amounted to 160,000 stone *per annum* by the late 1630s. Very significantly too, exports of butter, unimportant in the sixteenth century, were the third most important export by 1641. A rise in exports of cattle, wool and butter is consistent with more extensive settlement of the countryside and a growing population. It is likely, allowing for natural increase in population, freedom from war and from major calamity, and some net immigration, that the population of the island was of the order of one and a half million by 1641. At a later date Petty in fact suggested retrospectively a figure of this magnitude.

Settlement entailed the destruction of woodland. The process, made attractive by settlement, of cutting down the forests was quickened by the rapid growth of the iron industry from the early decades of the seventeenth century. Its shifting locations swiftly consumed woodlands, and at one time or another the industry was conducted on some 90 sites within the country. The Earl of Cork was an early entrepreneur establishing furnaces along the banks of the rivers in co. Cork. In 1672, according to Sir William Petty, 1,000 tons of iron a year were produced : some 10 iron furnaces and above 20 forges and bloomeries were at work. Petty himself established the industry at Kenmare in 1670. The process of deforestation created valuable though impermanent exports – timber, barrel-staves and iron smelted by charcoal. Such exports would not outlive the forests, and showed signs of falling off long before the end of the century. At one stage more iron had been exported than imported. More significant by far, even in the seventeenth century itself, was the rise in exports of products produced from the land won from the forests. Cattle, wool and butter were already the most significant exports by 1641 : of the three only wool had been a substantial export two generations previously. The altered pattern of land use may have been behind the rapid rise of the ports of the south-west in the first half of the seventeenth century. Previously they had been overshadowed by Galway and by Dublin and Drogheda. But the three principal ports of the south-west – Cork, Youghal and Kinsale – seem to have expanded very rapidly as exports of wool, cattle and butter grew, suggesting very considerable advances in the potentially rich pastoral hinterland which they served.

From a woodland society Ireland was emerging as an agricultural region with a substantial agricultural surplus. Overseas markets were, however, few, and not always stable. All of Europe was agricultural, hence largely self-sufficient in years of normal conditions. The absence of outlets was reinforced by the slow growth of population in Europe at large in the seventeenth century. Spain, which had offered a market for Irish products in the sixteenth century, was in the throes of demographic difficulties, its population falling sharply after each of three great waves of plague around 1600, 1650 and again in 1676-85. The consequence of this situation in Europe was that long-term prospects did not appear good for communities with an agricultural surplus. The problem was in part one of a grain surplus throughout Europe. But a grain surplus could lead to a surplus of livestock as low grain prices encouraged farmers everywhere to concentrate a little more on livestock, whose prices appeared relatively more favourable. Such a trend would have serious implications for an exporter of livestock and livestock products like Ireland. However, the agricultural crisis was a feature more of the second half than of the first half of the century. Moreover, as far as Ireland was concerned, its emergence was concealed by war between 1641 and 1652 and by the aftermath of war. The prolonged wars disrupted but did not destroy economic life. The most serious effects were evident between 1650 and 1653, and were more directly the effect of plague than of war. Plague, making its appearance in 1650, killed hundreds of thousands; war destroyed crops and cattle; famine occurred in 1652. The price of corn soared from under 12s a quarter to 50s in 1653. Plague, and to a lesser extent famine, killed far more than war had done. Petty estimated plague deaths at 412,500. The population was reduced probably to around a million.

The early 1650s was a period of crisis – war, plague, famine. The population fell sharply although not as sharply as some contemporary and later accounts have suggested. The loss of livestock left lands understocked : cattle and sheep had even to be imported to build up stocks again. The Cromwellian Plantation, which followed the wars and which replaced many of the former landlords by the soldiery or by the Adventurers who had financed the military expeditions to Ireland, created uncertainty about land title. Underpopulation combined with the uncertainty engendered by a massive change in the title to land led to a dramatic fall in the purchase price of land. In 1653, land fetched 2s 6d an acre compared with 30s in 1641. The low level of economic activity was reflected in the customs revenue as well : as high as £50,000 or £60,000 a year in the 1630s, it was under £12,000 as late as 1656.

However, the country was set for recovery. The severity of the economic contraction was to a large extent caused by the consequences of plague and famine. Once plague and famine passed, economic conditions began to look up. The population below the level of proprietor – and non-proprietors were the vast majority – were not removed in the course of implementing the Plantation; the new owners themselves were eager to manage their estates in a businesslike way. The customs farm which yielded under £12,000 clear in 1656 was set for above three times the amount within a year or two; it reached £51,535 in 1659/60. Agricultural prices were at the time more favourable than later in the century; exports rose rapidly. Not only did exports recover, but their volume rose above preceding levels : exports of beef, cattle and sheep were of record proportions in the early 1660s. This was a somewhat exceptional situation, because it was achieved despite the fact that agriculture elsewhere, through some switch to livestock production, was already somewhat better balanced than previously. In fact, although the volume of Irish exports rose to a record level, signs of marketing difficulties are evident in the pattern of exports. Between 1641 and 1665 exports of cattle increased only by 25 per cent; butter exports actually fell; exports of sheep rose dramatically but at the expense of wool exports. Instead of increasing its output of wool, Ireland was helping to stock English sheeplands – on the whole a less lucrative business than trade in wool itself. Nevertheless, despite some evidence of unfavourable trends, the overall volume of Irish agricultural exports had risen at a time when local supplies of livestock and livestock products were expanding elsewhere and when as a consequence trade in agricultural products was likely to remain rather stagnant.

Several factors explain Ireland's position. The fact that the surplus was in livestock rather than in grain helped, as the problems in tillage emerged earlier and more acutely than in pastoral farming. Ireland's insular position was relevant, although not that much because the significance of its insular position lay exclusively in its proximity to two rising markets for livestock or livestock products – the English market, and the transatlantic trade.

The most important feature by far in the growth of Irish trade was the English market, which took cattle, sheep, wool and some of the butter and beef exported. The English market was stimulated by two outstanding developments – the continued growth of London as a city and hence as a market in its own right, and the expansion of the woollen industry. The London market was supplied with grain from close at hand, but the cattle fattened in the counties around London were drawn in from farther afield, from the west, from Wales, and from Scotland as well as from Ireland. It was the emergence of this far-flung trade in livestock that was responsible for the growth of Irish cattle exports and for live cattle becoming the island's largest single export. The internal significance of the cattle trade was as great as its external. The export trade was served by cattle fairs. Cattle fairs drew business interests together and gave to the country its first semblance of effective economic unity. Next in importance was the trade in wool and sheep. This was geared to the expanding English woollen industry. As the demand for wool grew, English sheep numbers increased sharply. Ireland's role in sheep farming was subject to English requirements: rising sheep numbers in England were reflected, as the trade figures suggest, in a fall in wool exports and in a rise in exports of young sheep to help stock expanding English sheepwalks in the late 1650s and 1660s.

The progress of transatlantic trade in the seventeenth century created an alternative market for some of Ireland's output of pastoral products. The transatlantic market for beef or butter was a small one before mid-century. But its foundations were already being laid with the progress of English and French colonisation in the West Indies at that time. Between 1609 and 1632 English settlers took over Barbados, Antigua, Nevis and Monserrat; in 1655 Jamaica was seized from Spain. The French settled Martinique and Guadaloupe in 1635, and step by step French settlers ousted the Spaniards from the western half of the Spanish island of Hispaniola, establishing in the land taken over the French colony of St Domingue. Once plantations of sugar expanded rapidly from the 1650s, the economic significance of the colonial possessions in the West Indies immediately became obvious. Labour was scarce in the plantation islands; negro slaves were imported from Africa. It was more economic to employ this scarce and expensive labour force to produce sugar and to rely on cheap imports to feed the inhabitants. One of the main foodstuffs imported from Europe was beef, heavily salted so that it would preserve in the long and slow voyage across the warm waters of the middle Atlantic. Some of the beef was carried direct from Ireland; much of it was first shipped from Ireland to European ports and thence carried across the Atlantic. So important was this trade that, even when the English Navigation Act of 1663 required all goods for the English colonies to be shipped from England and Wales, an exception was made for salted provisions (as well as for servants and horses). The growing trade across the Atlantic also created an ancillary demand for beef and butter to feed the crews of the rising number of merchant and naval vessels in the Atlantic. The market was small to start with but largely as a result of its rapid expansion in the late 1650s and early 1660s, exports of salt beef from Ireland were twice as large in 1665 as in 1641. They more than doubled again by 1683. There was, however, little demand for Irish beef for consumption in Europe. Europe was more or less self-sufficient. In fact, because of enhanced self-sufficiency in Europe, butter exports had fallen between 1641 and 1665. There was little compensating colonial demand for butter at the time, although one was to grow later as the colonies became much more populous. Galway, which had formerly been closely linked to southern Europe as a market, to some extent compensated for the decline in that market by participation in the rising trade with the West Indies. Galway families, such as the Blakes, settled in Barbados and Monserrat as merchants and planters. There was an active trade in provisions from Galway to the West Indies. The business interests of the Galway merchants in the West Indies facilitated their entry into the growing traffic in tobacco from the American mainland to Ireland as well.

Thus, Irish export trade had recovered remarkably well from the dislocation of the early 1650s. But once recovery was complete, future growth in trade appeared less certain. The customs revenue which rose rapidly from the low levels of the mid-1650s stagnated in the early 1660s, rising only from £51,535 in 1659/60 to £55,597 in 1662/3. Clearly, the impetus for further expansion seemed limited. In fact, the early 1660s proved to be years of crisis. Low grain prices in Europe in the 1650s had already helped to orientate farmers towards livestock. Prices of livestock fell in the early 1660s. Poor Irish fairs were simply a reflection of bad market conditions in England. Low or indifferent prices for cattle and sheep in England, however, led to an outcry against imports from Ireland. In 1663 an act was passed placing a prohibitive duty on cattle or sheep imported from Ireland between 1 July and 20 December. The act came into effect in 1664. Cattle could still be imported before July, and in this way the trade continued through 1664, 1665 and 1666. As prices continued low, a bill proposing the total exclusion of Irish cattle and sheep was introduced in the English Commons in 1665; parliament was prorogued, however, before it could have passed through all its stages. The following year a bill was introduced again to exclude Irish cattle, sheep, beef and pork and passed into law in January 1667.

Between 1664 and 1667 the economic situation deteriorated. Before 1663 Irish currency had exchanged for English at the rate of Irish £104 or £102 to English £100, at times even at par. In 1666, however, the premium of Irish pounds paid to acquire English £100 rose to £5 or £6 per cent. This signifies that Irish money exchanged less favourably against English money than formerly, a reflection of a deteriorating economic situation. This situation was, however, by no means caused solely by the act of 1663 or by that of 1667. The prices of goods unaffected by the acts also fell. War was a factor in pushing the prices of Irish exports down and hence making the exchange rates more adverse. Between 1665 and 1667, as part of the king's dominions, Ireland was at war with France and Holland. War dislocated the country's foreign trade; at home disease killed many animals in 1665, the tenants in consequence faring badly, in extreme cases even abandoning their farms. War and livestock losses combined to make it a disastrous year. The customs revenue fell in the year ended March 1666 by one-fifth.* The difficulties in marketing livestock had been evident even in the early months of the year when imports were still free from the prohibitive impost. In June 1665, Thomas Herbert, agent for the Kerry estate of Lord Herbert, noted a net proceed from the sale of 52 steers and 260 sheep on the English market of only £120; at one time the steers alone would have realised £160. In the first half of the same year some Irish drovers had failed to find a market at Carlisle for the cattle they had taken across and had to bring them as far as Norfolk before selling them. The causes of the economic difficulties of the mid-sixties were too complex to justify ascribing them simply to the Cattle Acts. In fact, despite the passage of the total prohibition of cattle imports from Ireland in January 1667, Irish economic conditions showed signs of recovery by the autumn of that year. Nor was the act of 1667 any more effective than that of 1663 in improving conditions in England. It was reported from Lord Herbert's Welsh estates as late as April 1668 that 'it is hard to get in rents. Some of Lord Herbert's tenants of the highest degree are behind three years, some two.' The Irish customs revenue rose in each of the years ending March 1667 and 1668. In 1668 the revenue was 6 per cent above the level of 1664.

In fact, the worst years were tied up with adverse domestic weather conditions. A bad winter followed by a bad spring in 1671 was disastrous, perhaps even more so than 1665, for livestock. The fall in livestock numbers reduced the export trade; customs revenue fell sharply and the decline in the country's exports was reflected in a worsening of the exchanges in 1671. A setback such as this would ordinarily be temporary. The outbreak of war in early 1672 helped to make the crisis more prolonged than it would otherwise have been. In fact, the economic crisis in these years was far more acute than in the years of the passing of the Cattle Acts. The effects of the war between early 1672 and early 1674 were particularly severe. Dutch privateers were exceptionally active, preying even on traffic at the mouth of Dublin Bay. The wool trade with England, the branch of trade least subject to wartime disruption despite the attentions of privateers, fared best. Trade with the continent in salted beef and butter suffered disastrously: cattle during these

* Continuous customs and imported excise data exist in a sole source for 1660-9. The data are apparently incomplete as the 1664 and 1668 figures do not agree with fuller figures available elsewhere for those two years, perhaps by omitting customs on exports. Assuming consistency in the omissions, they should reflect general trends in the level of economic activity.

years were worth little more than the value of the hides and tallow. Peace in early 1674, however, made it possible for Irish overseas trade to recover. The customs duties amounted to £93,825 in 1675/6 and to £121,390 in the year 1679/80. In fact, one of the most serious of the results of the Cattle Acts was not so much the obvious result of reducing trade as of limiting the outlets least subject to harassment in time of war, and thus making the Irish economy more vulnerable to the effects of war by enhanced dependence on outlets on continental Europe which suffered immediately and directly from hostilities. The wool trade was able to survive hostilities much better, and hence was able to respond to altered market conditions in the second half of the 1660s readily, reaching record proportions at the beginning of the 1670s. In 1673, Sir William Temple's opinion was that ' the wool of Ireland seems not to be capable [of] any [further] increase.'

In the assessment of the Cattle Acts, conditions before and after the Acts must be looked into. The price of beef bore up well in the early 1660s, reflecting the rising colonial demand, while the price of cattle for the English market fell. This explains why some Irish landowners were not unduly dismayed by the passage of the acts of 1663 and 1667. They saw in discouragement of the cattle trade the possibility of switching production from unprofitable trade in young cattle to beef, in which the profit was larger and the price trend firmer. In this they were oversanguine. The trade in beef was badly disrupted by the war. Moreover, they overestimated the potential market which existed. While the market for beef had grown and continued to grow, it expanded rather slowly, and larger Irish supplies ensured that prices remained low even in years of peace. If the English market had remained open to Irish cattle, the existence of the English market for livestock as an alternative market, while of declining remunerativeness, might have moderated the fall in prices. The rising trade in beef, however, was not large enough to absorb all the cattle on offer. Hence, livestock farming declined in the 1670s and 1680s. Total exports of beef and of cattle converted into beef equivalent in 1665 were much greater than exports of beef in 1669 or 1683. In this sense the Cattle Acts contributed to Irish marketing problems. However, judging by the course of exchange between Dublin and London, the balance of payments worsened alarmingly only in war years or in years such as 1671 when Irish foreign trade reflected livestock losses. In 1671 and in the following two years the rates of exchange – the premium of Irish pounds commanded by £100 English – soared to 10 per cent, and on occasion to as high as 15 per cent. Once the war years were left behind, the exchange improved sharply. In the remainder of the 1670s and in the 1680s it averaged 7 per cent. If the premium before 1665 was, say, 3 per cent, the worsening in the exchanges consequent on the Cattle Acts amounted only to 4 per cent. This would suggest that the worsening in the exchange was limited, amounting to a modest devaluation of the Irish currency. One reason for this perhaps unexpected result is that English sheep-lands, understocked because English agriculture had difficulty in making good fully the deficiency in breeding cattle and sheep, created a soaring demand for Irish wool in the late 1660s and early 1670s. This development was significant not only in the short term but in the long term because it set back by as much as a generation the long-term trend for domestic wool supply in England to expand to the detriment of the Irish wool producer. The impact of the Cattle Acts has tended to be overestimated by linking the Cattle Acts directly with the plight of the Irish economy in 1671, 1672 and 1673 and the very high course of exchange in those years. Moreover, the worsening in the exchanges was in many ways simply a facet of the deteriorating situation of agriculturists generally in Europe. To a large extent it reflected the worsening in the terms of trade of a country with a large agricultural surplus at a time when the supply of agricultural goods everywhere tended to rise. The situation had its positive aspects too. The cost of exchange in remitting money from Ireland to England made living outside Ireland less attractive to potential absentees. The high exchange also led some absentee landlords to participate directly in the expansion of the country's foreign trade: by marketing produce from Ireland overseas they hoped to avoid the high premium necessary to purchase bills of exchange. In this way, almost para-doxically, the unfavourable economic situation directed capital and enterprise from an unexpected source – absentee landlords – into trade at a time of real crisis in the economy.

The Cattle Acts reflected the agricultural crisis which was general in rural Europe in these decades. They did not spring from English policy towards Ireland. They were promoted in Parliament by the members from districts which raised young cattle for feeding in the fattening counties closer to the London market. Thus, there was a sharp division or conflict of interest between different regions in England about the proposed measures. Members of Parliament from breeding counties regarded Irish cattle as cheap and dangerous competition; members from fattening counties regarded them as a competitive and desirable import and feared a rise in their costs if Irish cattle were excluded. A prolonged and sharp debate took place on the bill proposing a total exclusion in 1666. Those in favour of the measure had little confidence that they could rely on the willingness of the administration to implement it; for that reason Irish cattle and sheep were declared in the bill to be a 'nuisance' so as to preclude the possibility of the king's royal prerogative being exercised to admit cattle and sheep from Ireland. The measure was a temporary one, and on the eve of its expiring in May 1679 the debate was taken up again in Parliament on the merits of continuing the prohibition. The conflict of interest was as before; the case for the admission of Irish cattle was pleaded both in the commons and in writings or tracts. Some of the west-of-England ports, dependent on Anglo-Irish trade, had views which were in conflict with the interests of the local agricultural community. In April 1679 the Society of Merchant Venturers in Bristol had urged the city representatives in the Commons to seek a freeing of the importation of Irish cattle; in the same month one of the Chester members voted against the bill to continue the prohibition, writing to the Mayor of the city: ' I have had a hard bout about the bringing of Irish cattle; we sait untill 4 o'clock in the afternoone; I thought I should be pulled in peices of my countrey men and the rest of my acquaintance for deviding in the house agt. them, for the good of the citty.' The progress of the bill was held up by the abrupt prorogation of Parliament: in consequence, Irish cattle entered freely in the remainder of the year and during 1680. The prohibition was finally restored only in an act of November 1680, which entered into effect the following February. The influx of Irish cattle during the twenty months in which the prohibition had lapsed stirred up fears of Irish competition among the agricultural interest. Butter had not been excluded in 1667; before and after 1667 only small quantities of Irish butter were sent to England. Now, however, it also was excluded. This exclusion was not of economic significance; it illustrates, however, the attitude of the English agricultural interest in a period of low prices and crisis in agriculture.

Whatever happened about price trends in beef and cattle, unreassuring throughout the period, before as well as after the Cattle Acts, prices of wool, tallow, hides and butter were on the whole satisfactory. The export trade in these commodities was behind the substantial growth in population and consumption in Ireland at this time. The population may have been in excess of two million in the 1680s. Imports grew significantly too. Valued at £336,437 in 1665, they amounted to £433,040 in 1681. The rise in economic activity is reflected in customs duties as well. The yield of £93,825 in 1675/6 had increased to £117,504 in 1681/2 and to £138,880 in 1686. The most striking single index of increasing consumption is the rise in tobacco imports. Tobacco was already widely consumed among adults, male and female, in the 1660s. Imports rose from 1,817,775 lb in 1665 to a figure not exceeding 2,400,000 lb in the closing years of the 1670s; they rose again in the first half of the 1680s to 3,312,451 lb in 1686. Thus in less than twenty years tobacco consumption had almost doubled. These twenty years were the most important period in the history of tobacco consumption in Ireland : over the whole eighteenth century, the consumption only doubled. The Navigation Laws did not adversely affect Irish consumption of colonial produce. Such produce could be freely imported direct to Ireland until 1671. The act of 1671 prohibited the direct importation of enumerated products, including items such as sugar and tobacco. Nevertheless, imports continued to rise through the 1670s. It is true, of course, that the act, while not harming the consumer, may have adversely affected the Irish importer who had relied on direct imports. However, such harm was probably limited. Though the prohibition had lapsed in 1680 and was not restored until 1685 the port of Galway, which had close ties with the Americas, continued to languish. Moreover, throughout the period, there was widespread evasion of the Navigation Acts, and this must have softened any possible impact on Irish business interests.

The growth of trade in the Restoration was accompanied by a significant change in the structure of the economy. The structural development was closely tied up with greater centralisation. As long as the volume of trade in Ireland had been small and growing slowly, no port had been outstanding. Each port handled the trade of a narrow hinterland, and the narrowness of the hinterland served by a port ensured that the contrast between ports in volume of business was not very striking. This explains why many ports, of limited importance in modern times, seemed relatively so much more important in medieval or early modern times. As late as the 1650s Galway was regarded as the second port of the island. Once trade grew, however, the best-situated ports grew at the expense of less well-situated ports. Cork, well up the Lee, expanded at the expense of Youghal and Kinsale, both estuarine and hence less well situated from the point of view of serving a growing hinterland. Trade moved from Carrickfergus at the head of Belfast Lough to Belfast which gave direct access to the Lagan corridor. Above all, Dublin grew disproportionately in the seventeenth century. Visitors were impressed by its wealth and extent. By the 1680s it had a population of around 60,000. The size and expansion of the city were primarily responsible for the rapid development of the traffic in coal from England to Ireland at this time. A corollary of Dublin's growth was the dominating position it was acquiring in Irish inland and foreign trade. In the six years 1664-9, Dublin accounted for 40 per cent of the customs revenue. A contemporary, noting this feature, commented: ' it lying in Ireland as ye center of a semi-cercle much of ye importacons especially those from England are carryed out of Dublin and Leinster itself even into the other 3 provinces'. Dublin merchants also purchased commodities as far afield as Belfast for export. In addition to their role in commodity trade, they provided foreign exchange facilities for merchants in many lesser centres. In the south, Cork was emerging as the most important port. Its impact was most evident on ports close at hand, but was felt even farther afield. In 1668 Waterford had a greater export trade than Cork; in the 1680s there were even complaints of a decline of trade in Waterford. Galway declined relatively; its trade also decayed in absolute terms: even the lapse in 1680 of the prohibition on the direct importation of enumerated products from the colonies did not help to restore its fortunes. Its decay was attributed by a contemporary in 1686 to the road from the town being bad. It is doubtful whether its road was worse than those elsewhere. But the contemporary in question was not far wrong. The trade on the road was declining, and the reason was simply the growing activity of Dublin merchants as buyers and sellers in what had once been Galway's exclusive hinterland.

So, some of the indices of prosperity existed in Ireland in the Restoration period: a rise in living standards and an evolving economic structure. The price of land rose from three years' purchase in the difficult years of the 1650s to 12 years' purchase or even more. In money terms land was about 30s an acre in 1673; 40s in 1683. Rents rose too. Petty's estimate of the total rental in 1672 was £900,000, in 1687 £1,200,000. The rise in the price of land or in rentals was obviously of benefit to landowners and landlords. How did the ordinary people fare? The land system itself had of course been fundamentally altered. Many of the old owners had been dispossessed; some were restored to their lands at the Restoration, but a large number of the old proprietors never made good their claim to their former estates. Some of the dispossessed proprietors became tenants, a few became tories. Resentment of the land settlement was in part behind their actions. But their activities went beyond that to mere banditry. In one sense they were the last flowering in an age of growing administrative effectiveness of a medieval tradition of lawlessness. In another sense they were modern, preying not only indiscriminately on the settled community but on the rich pickings which the growth in traffic on the roads offered. The active banditry in the wild lands between Dundalk and Newry is to no small degree simply a reflection of the temptation to lawlessness offered by the rapidly growing flow of goods and cash on the road between Dublin and Belfast, in consequence of the spreading tentacles of Dublin's economic role. The upheaval in landownership did not directly affect the ordinary people, tenants or labourers, at all. In fact, the 1650s proved a decade of remarkable prosperity for them. Agricultural prices in the 1650s were higher than they were to be in subsequent decades; at the same time rents were dramatically low, and depopulation meant that tenants were eagerly sought after by landlords and encouraged to stay. The new system was less arbitrary than the old one; the relationship between tenant and landlord was a commercial one; especially when rents were low or prices high, this was infinitely preferable to the arbitrary dominion of the old proprietors. At a later date Petty commented on the favourable condition of the people in the 1650s; even a native commentator, unlikely to concede any benefit to Cromwellian rule, admitted that never had the ordinary people been better-off or more insolent.

The culmination of Restoration prosperity was reached in the first half of the 1680s. The customs revenue reached its peak in the year 1686. To some extent this was simply a consequence of relatively favourable weather conditions and lack of interruption of trade by war. In the 1670s, there had been bad weather conditions in 1670/1, 1674 and 1678. In addition, there had been war from 1672 to 1674; in 1678 rumours of war had almost the same effect. Merchants in the south reduced their foreign trade, withdrew their monies from London, and exchange rates in April were as high as 11 per cent. Things improved in the autumn; the exchange was two or three per cent ' and was falling till news of the Popist plot arrived, which startles and amazes the English in this kingdom, and trade is worse than before, though then bad '. The next seven years were relatively favourable. They were free from internal or external political crises or alarm. Weather conditions were relatively favourable also : in particular livestock were not, except in 1684, decimated by disease and consequent loss. At the same time foreign markets were relatively buoyant. In particular exports of butter soared, and prices were at times remarkably high. So much did the butter trade advance that its importance as the major earner of foreign exchange was expressly recognised in a government proclamation in 1685. The butter trade was, however, a vulnerable one. Its rapid progress was heavily dependent on the French market, especially the Flanders market. However, the rapid growth of this market in the late 1670s and early 1680s was primarily a consequence of a sequence of unfavourable years in French agriculture generally, its animal husbandry in particular. Irish foreign trade was thus doubly vulnerable. Livestock might be decimated by animal disease with serious economic consequences as in 1671 and 1684. Favourable foreign markets could not be counted on indefinitely. French livestock production with a reversal of weather conditions recovered steeply in the second half of the 1680s, and – a rare phenomenon in France – prices of meat and butter fell sharply. Less remunerative foreign markets were quickly reflected in internal conditions in Ireland. Customs revenue fell heavily from its peak in 1686. In 1688 a high duty was placed on Irish beef imported for home consumption in France as opposed to reshipment to the colonies. Low prices and high Irish imports combined led to a fairly high French impost on Irish butter in 1687 and to its being increased in 1688. An alarming cattle distemper in 1688, killing livestock in great numbers in Ireland, added to the emerging economic difficulties. At the same time, the political stability of the first half of the decade was being quickly undermined, after 1685. Protestant merchants were disquieted by the strong Catholic sympa-

thies of King James' Irish administration. Some moved their effects
to England; the exchange rose to 14 per cent in February 1687.
Petty's *Treatise of Ireland*, written in 1687, describes the economic
effects of this alarm. Prices fell sharply; rents fell from 3s 6d to
2s 6d, and the purchase price of land from as much as 14 years'
rent to 10 years. This was a temporary development, but the
deteriorating situation in 1688 was reflected in an exodus of merchants and capital in 1689. So, by 1689 the three factors making
for economic advance – favourable markets abroad, freedom from
animal disease at home, and political stability – had all broken
down. When in March 1689 the values of coins current in Ireland
were reset, the par of exchange was in effect established at Irish
£108 6s 8d = English £100. This represented, in effect, a further
devaluation of the Irish currency, if one regards the former par as
being in the region of Irish £107.

Up to 1686 an upward trend had been clearly evident in the
Irish economy. At relatively stable or even declining valuations, the
value of exports had risen from £402,389 in 1665 to £570,343,
in 1683. In others words, exports had risen by 42 per cent, and as
prices had fallen somewhat the rise in volume was somewhat sharper
still. With a rise in population, rents rose substantially as well. The
increase in the volume of production suggests, however, that tenants
did not forgo all the advantages they had gained. In some respects
Irish countrypeople were well off. Sir William Petty thought them
better clothed than the country people in France or the poor in
most European countries. Another index of the diffusion of prosperity is the extent of horse ownership. Petty stated that the poorest
rode on horseback. This is an imprecise and – if taken literally – an
exaggerated statement. But elsewhere he indicated that one-third
of the cabins possessed a garron for tillage. Grain prices were low,
but tillage was widespread, and grain in the form of oatcakes,
supplemented from August to May by potatoes, was important in
the diet. Housing conditions were bad, although this reflected the
survival of traditional standards more than poverty. The chimney
was becoming common at this time. It was often making its appearance in popular housing for the first time. According to Petty's
calculations, one-fifth of the cabins had a chimney. Petty's estimate
of population in 1672 – regarded as an underestimate – suggested
that there were 300,000 English and Scottish in Ireland, and some
800,000 Irish. It may be assumed that the English and Scottish

lived above the meanest condition. Petty's calculations seem to imply that about a quarter of the 800,000 Irish lived above that level as well. These calculations would suggest that 500,000 out of the population of 1,100,000 calculated by Petty lived above subsistence level, a proportion which would certainly bear favourable comparison with the social structure of other European countries at that time.

If so many inhabitants of the countryside lived in poverty, it was largely because they were underemployed. Agriculture did not create a great amount of agricultural employment for labourers. Wages themselves at 4d a day were inadequate even though prices were low. The smaller farmers themselves were underoccupied on their holdings, and low prices in good years and disastrous losses of crops or animals in a bad season helped to ensure that their position remained precarious. Employment in subsidiary activities such as spinning and weaving was very useful because the income from such work usefully supplemented the meagre or precarious income from agriculture. Knowledge of cloth-making was widespread, but the number engaged in production for the market was limited. Petty estimated a mere 30,000 workers (including their wives) in the woollen industry. Temple and Petty commented on the extent to which country people were unoccupied and on the opportunities this presented for promoting the textile industry. The industry was small to start with, but it increased significantly during the Restoration. Exports rose substantially. The most valuable single textile export was frieze. This cloth was the same as country people wove for themselves, and hence country weavers could easily supply the market. Other branches of the industry – old and new drapery – required more specialised skills. Although they too were a cottage industry, limitations of skill slowed down the progress of the industry.

Exports of Woollens	1641	1665	1683	1687
Drapery, new (pieces)	–	224	5,659	11,360
Drapery, old (pieces)	506	32	75	103
Frieze (yards)	279,722	444,381	753,189	1,129,716

Significantly, too, imports of cloth were relatively small, and through the expansion of the domestic industry, fell off sharply in the 1680s.

Imports of Woollens from England (in yards)

	1665	1684	1687
Drapery, old	12,030	23,533	11,469
Drapery, new	133,864	173,304	74,747

Petty had commented in 1672 that the value added to Irish exports by processing or manufacture in Ireland was not above £8,000 a year. The situation was better in the 1680s. In 1687 the value of old and new drapery exported was £23,029; with the addition of frieze the figure came to £79,515.

The linen industry in 1665 was relatively small. The export of yarn was smaller than in 1641. The spinning of yarn for export in the 1630s was largely a feature of the hinterland of the ports of Dundalk and Drogheda with little yarn exported from any of the Ulster ports save Derry. The poor condition of the trade in the mid-1660s does not suggest that the pattern had greatly changed in the interval. Its subsequent advance must have been modest; by comparison with 1669 the export figures for 1683 suggest some degree of setback. The industry grew significantly in the 1680s, however. Its growth at this time is reflected in an extension of the export activity of the industry into Ulster. Areas in which the industry was later to become a staple, such as Lurgan, date their advance to this period. An influx of Scots and north English into the thinly peopled north was responsible for its rapid development in the 1680s.

Exports of Linen Cloth and Yarn

	1641	1665	1669	1683	1686
Linen yarn (cwt)	2,921	3,477	4,625	3,677	5,992
Linen cloth (yards)		14,750	51,100	23,136	131,568

Previously, Ulster had been the most backward of the four provinces. Rents had been lower than in the other provinces. No port in Ulster was among the first seven ports in the 1660s. The better-populated condition of the province in the 1680s, the quickening of economic activity in the province in the same decade, and the influx of immigrants and capital into it, was reflected in the significant role acquired by Belfast in the 1680s. So impressed were some contemporaries by the rapidity of Belfast's growth that they described it as the second or third town in Ireland. As early as 1688, Dr William Sacheverell described Belfast as ' the second town in Ireland, well built, full of people, and of great trade '. This was an exaggeration, but the north's economic position had in fact improved dramatically in the last two decades of the century. Belfast itself had by 1700 become the fourth port in Ireland.

The changes in the Irish economy in the second half of the century were significant : growth in the volume of trade, a change in its structure with Dublin's pre-eminence becoming more marked, and late in the century a significant advance in the formerly backward north-east. Low prices, however, lay like a shadow across the economy : prices fell in the second half of the 1680s, and its advance was halted. The only off-setting advantage was the fact that low costs advantaged the manufacturer. Just as the low price of land in the north – lower than elsewhere in Ireland – attracted Scottish or English immigrants in the 1680s, low costs gave a competitive edge to exports of linen and woollens. Industrial advance was more significant in the 1680s than in any other comparable period in the seventeenth century. Agricultural prices, however, effectively determined living standards in Ireland. Prosperity was determined too by peace, and war loomed again on the horizon in 1689.

War, Legislation and Stagnation
1689-1730

The Irish economy was vulnerable in the 1680s. Through the growth in its foreign trade, it was dependent on foreign markets. The country's ability to sell abroad in turn depended both on the buoyancy of these markets and on the level of animal stocks within Ireland. Reduced supplies in Ireland or enlarged output overseas both affected Irish economic prospects sharply. Abnormal livestock mortality was the central feature in determining these prospects. Livestock disease in Ireland decimated the base of the export trade; livestock disease overseas suddenly increased foreign demand for Irish beef or butter. The heavy dependence of market conditions on the level of mortality emphasises that in normal years the market for livestock products was restricted. This was in part a consequence of basic self-sufficiency, in part a consequence of some diversification of agriculture caused by greater livestock production encouraged by low cereal prices. Difficult conditions in Flanders and in France had concealed the underlying weakness of the market in the 1670s and early 1680s. From 1685 conditions in France – which took 43 per cent of total Irish exports in 1683, for instance – improved dramatically. As a result of enlarged supplies, prices fell sharply. Low prices made the substantial imports from Ireland undesirable. Irish beef imported for domestic consumption in France was subjected to a prohibitive impost in 1688. Irish butter was subject to a fairly stiff duty in 1687, and the duty was increased the following year.

Thus at the end of the 1680s low prices were evidence of poor economic prospects. These prospects – dark in themselves – were

to be overtaken by prolonged war from 1689 to 1697 which disrupted or hampered access to many foreign markets. In 1667 trade
had been permitted with enemy countries to help the country overcome the effects of the closure of the cattle trade. In this war, however, restrictions on foreign trade were tight. At the outset, trade
was embargoed with the parts of Ireland under Jacobite control.
Even when the campaigns in Ireland had ended, stricter control
remained and licences were required in trade with the West Indies,
and bonds had to be entered for any ships sailing to friendly or
neutral countries. The intention was to prevent fraudulent shipment to hostile ports in Spain or France. Evasion softened the
impact of wartime restriction, but privateering vessels, seizing merchant ships often indiscriminately, discouraged trade as well.

The setback caused by the closing, complete or partial, of markets
was made more serious by the destruction wrought in the military
campaigns in Ireland between 1689 and 1691. The destruction
was by no means as extensive as in the early 1650s. Ulster ceased
to be a theatre of military operations after July 1689; the rest of
the eastern half of the island a year later. Arable cultivation was
not greatly upset; neither famine nor plague decimated the civilian
population. Livestock numbers were, however, sadly depleted,
either by destruction, sheer plundering or acquisition for victualling
the army. In consequence of shortage for home requirements,
exports of beef, butter and pork were prohibited in September 1691
for six months. In January 1692 the Privy Council of Ireland petitioned the British Treasury for leave for some time to transport
animals, mares, cows, hogs and sheep from England and Scotland
duty free. The customs revenue from exports from Ireland was
lower in 1692 and 1693 than it had been in the war years 1690 and
1691. The recovery in exports was somewhat long drawn out;
even in 1696 the volume of exports of beef and wool was less than
half prewar levels, approaching them for the first time in 1697.

Nevertheless, economic recovery took place more quickly in the
1690s than the export figures suggest. One reason for this is that
cereal production was not unduly disrupted by the campaigns and
that subsequent harvests were well above average in a decade in
which harvest failure was quite common in Europe. Severe famine
was experienced in France in 1693, and in Scotland in 1698-9.
Less dramatic shortages were experienced elsewhere. In January
1694 the corporation of Bristol sought permission to import Irish

grain free of duty. In 1696 Bristol again sought such permission, because of the dearth, and grain also flowed to Scotland. Exports to Scotland were responsible in late 1696 for a sharp rise in prices in Ireland and for the imposition of a temporary ban on shipment for fear of shortage. In 1698-9, a disastrous year in Scotland, the outflow from Ireland to Scotland was enormous. Despite the embargo on trade with France, Irish grain found its way there during the French famine of 1693-4 and in 1696. Good harvests favoured the Irish countryman. They also meant that the authorities favoured the export of grain : the English Treasury had no objection to the export of grain from Ireland, on account of the great abundance of corn, after the harvest of 1694. Shortages elsewhere helped to ensure that, despite good Irish harvests, prices remained high. Good harvests and high prices together spelled prosperity for the countryman. A contemporary writing from Dublin in September 1699 spoke of

> the great failure of corne in Europe for a year or two past, which gave the countery an opportunity of raising theire corne to a very high price, which because we could not import any from abroad, we were not able to bring down ye rates which were not rais'd through any scarcity at home; this has enriched ye plowman who always heretofore sold his corne to pay his rent . . . this sort of people are in a better condition than ever I know them to be. They are generally ye native Irish for its rare to heare of an Englishman ever able to pay his rent by ye plow.

Another factor facilitating early recovery was an inflow of capital. The proceeds of duties on imports were at a comparatively high level in 1691, and in 1692 they were the largest recorded since the new tariff had been introduced in 1662. Compared with the meagre level of exports, imports of tobacco were enormous in both years, the 1692 figure of 3,962,132 lb being the largest recorded to that date and not exceeded in any subsequent year in the decade. The rise in customs duties and in the consumption of commodities such as tobacco reflected the inflow of capital. Before and during the campaigns, there had been a heavy exodus of Protestants and their effects from the country. Already in 1691 there was a substantial drift back too the areas under Williamite control. The process accelerated in 1692, the first year of peace. However, to the extent that the capital inflow was a consequence of repatriation it was temporary in nature. Official opinion itself in Ireland anticipated that the customs revenue from imports would fall in 1693 : ' because the greatest part of the people belonging to this kingdom are already returned and provided with all sorts of apparell and other necessaries, which must lessen the importation for some time '. This anticipation was borne out by events. The revenue from imports fell very sharply in 1693, and the 1691 level was not surpassed until 1697. However, though it fell from the peak of 1691 and 1692 there is evidence of a continuing capital inflow in the 1690s. Much of it was the consequence of an influx of Scots into the north-east. This had already been evident in the 1680s. It accelerated in the 1690s. The north-east fared better than the rest of the island in the military campaigns. Loss of livestock was less than in the rest of the country. In consequence, its foreign trade recovered more quickly than else-where. Its merchants did well out of provisioning the Williamite armies. Once the war had ended the better condition of the north-east admitted of the resumption of its trade more quickly, and the profits made in provisioning the armies financed the extension of its foreign trade. Belfast successfully maintained illegal trade links with France during the war years, a natural consequence of surplus there and dearth in France, and connived at officially because some channels with the enemy were welcome as possible intelligence. The war years enhanced the importance that Belfast had already acquired in the preceding decade. Cheap lands and the relatively quick economic recovery attracted many Scots to Ulster. Difficult economic conditions in Scotland added to the extent of the migra-tion. One contemporary estimated that 30,000 had already come to the north since the Revolution in 1689 and that a further 20,000 arrived during the famine of 1698-9 in Scotland. These figures are not to be taken as precise : they do, however, reflect contemporary opinion. The rapid influx of Scottish dissenters at this time explains why contemporaries such as bishop King were alarmed about the future of their community in the island in 1699.

However, this capital inflow is not sufficient of itself to explain the economic recovery of the 1690s. The most obvious channel of the inflow was that from Scotland into Ulster. This was a rather special inflow accounted for by exceptionally cheap land in the north and by abnormally poor harvests and economic conditions in Scotland in that decade. Moreover, much of the capital inflow financed consumption rather than investment. This may be seen in the high level of tobacco imports in 1692. In 1694 and 1695 imports of tobacco and customs duties on imports both rose sharply while the value of total English exports to Ireland – which would include capital goods as well as highly taxed consumer goods – actually fell in 1694. We can detect in this development the consequence of the exceptionally good harvest of 1694. A good harvest increased the real income of many of the ordinary people who had an exceptionally high propensity to spend rather than save. If some of the capital inflow of the 1690s flowed into investment and if some of this investment took place outside Ulster, we have to look to other factors to account for the situation. The most relevant of these was the monetary situation. The scarcity of money in the early 1690s was reflected in a high nominal valuation of coins. The guinea, worth 21s 6d in England, exchanged for 24s in Ireland. Emigrants to Ireland or repatriates therefore stood to gain from the disposal of the coins they brought with them. The outflow of coin to Ireland was, however, likely to be hampered by the inadequacies of the currency supply in England itself. This is a reason why the capital outflow to Ireland fell off so abruptly in 1693, and why the value of the guinea in Ireland was increased in May 1695 to 26s. In June 1695 the value of the guinea in England soared to 30s. The high price of guineas in England actually caused an outflow of guineas from Ireland to England. Bills on London were in no demand because debts there could be settled so advantageously by the export of guineas. In consequence bills had to be offered in Ireland for much less than their nominal value in England. The credit inflation dismayed English merchants jealous of any competition. Merchants were alarmed by the disparity in costs between England and Ireland: John Cary and other merchants of Bristol wrote in December 1695 that ' they supply all ye West Indies wth. provisions and have beat us out of that trade by the exchange, wch. is now near 30 p.ct., they will in a short time furnish Spain, Portugall, and other places on the continent, with all sorts of woollen manufactures '.

In fact, Cary and his colleagues were mistaken if they made the assumption that the exchange had uniformly favoured Ireland in the course of previous months, and that this was the basis of the competitiveness of Irish agricultural produce at that time. During the second half of 1695, far from there being a large premium in Irish money from the sale of a bill of exchange in Dublin, the customary situation was reversed with bills of exchange where purchased for Irish money giving a premium in sterling. This reflected the attractiveness of remitting funds from Ireland in guineas and hence the lack of demand by remitters in Dublin for bills of exchange. Bills of exchange could find a purchaser only if they offered a similar premium, and hence, although slowly, the premium on guineas reflected itself in the emergence of a similar premium on bills of exchange. The growing shortage of money in Ireland moderated the rise in prices in contrast to the inflationary situation in England, a development intensified by the fact that in 1696 the supply of animal products had recovered sufficiently to leave for the first time in six years a significant surplus for export : in 1695 beef exports almost doubled. Indeed, in terms of competitive advantage on the exchange, the effective cost of English goods to the Irish buyer had fallen in consequence of the premium in sterling commanded by guineas or bills of exchange in Dublin. This – in addition to the good harvest of 1694 – accounts for the high level of tobacco imports in 1695 and the sizeable inflow of dutiable goods generally in 1695. As for woollens the exchanges in the second half of 1695 handicapped rather than favoured Irish exports. Because a foreign buyer, remitting a bill from London to Dublin, realised in the sale of the bill a much smaller sum in Irish currency than the nominal sterling value of the bill, the effective cost of Irish cloth to the foreign purchaser had in fact risen. Exports of new drapery from Ireland were lower in 1695 than in the two preceding years, and imports from England rose.

Irish goods acquired a competitive advantage again on the exchanges only when the currency situation in England became more normal. In April 1696 the guinea was reduced to 22s in England while it still stood at 26s in Ireland. Thus, coin commanded a higher price in Ireland than in England; this was in turn reflected in a premium of Irish £15 to £17 acquired by £100 sterling remitted to Ireland by bill of exchange. On the Irish side, the premium on bills of exchange was at first slow in rising to the level dictated by the disparity in the price of the guinea in the two countries. This reflected the expectation or apprehension of merchants that the value of the guinea would be reduced. In consequence, given the certain premium that guineas yielded, coin rather than bills was remitted to Ireland, the flow of specie was reversed, and guineas poured into Ireland.

The Cork merchant and banking house of Edward and Joseph Hoare in November 1696 advised an English merchant to remit by specie rather than by bill: 'if you have any business this way, it would be most yor advantage, to send mo: in yor ships to come wth. convoy, or order yr. mo: to be sent from Lond: to Holly-head, and so in ye packett boats to Dublin wch. is of late much practised.' By June 1697 Mary Ffingall wrote from Liège that 'my son writes that money was never so plentiful in Ireland as now'. A continuing inflow of these proportions suggests a favour-able balance of payments. This is seen in the fact that bills of exchange on Dublin, which, purchased with bank notes instead of specie, commanded a premium of £1 Irish in August 1696, exchanged at par in London by October of the same year. Despite the high valuation of money, prices remained moderate in 1696 and 1697. This meant that the competitive advantage to the foreigner was not reduced by rising costs in Ireland. This stimu-lated the foreign demand for butter in 1696, for beef in 1697. It also encouraged exports of woollen cloth. A merchant in Youghal, Abraham Lawton, had noted in a letter as early as 14 August 1696 that 'ye manufactury of this land cometh on very well and trading increaseth. We have a pretty trade to Flanders and Holland . . . there is 2 men in Cork yt. buy at least 100 peeces of serge a week, wch. they send to Holland, are better approved of yn. they that go from Tapsome. Their advantage is great in ye exch. now.' Some artisans in the industry were attracted to Ireland, and some foreign capital – notably Huguenot – was invested in the industry in co. Cork. Exports of new drapery doubled in 1696, and doubled again in 1697. In 1698 they soared to 23,286 pieces of cloth. The success of the industry was thus substantial. Moreover, even before cloth had acquired its competitive advantage, it had improved its position in the home market: between 1693 and 1696 imports of new drapery had been halved.

In fact, the progress of the industry should not be exaggerated. For all the rapid recovery of the industry exports of new drapery were only double the exports of 1687. The total value of cloth exports did not rise as sharply as exports of new drapery would suggest. The value of exports of cloth (old and new drapery and frieze) in 1687 had been £79,515; in 1698 the corresponding figure was £101,713. The relative value of cloth had in all probability fallen between 1687 and 1698. In 1698 total exports amounted to £996,305, cloth accounting for 10 per cent of the total. In 1687 exports must certainly have been below £600,000, and hence cloth could have accounted for more than 13 per cent. In 1683, a year in which the value of total exports was high (£570,343) and the value of cloth relatively low (£49,201), the proportion was already 9 per cent. The reason for this was the decline in the exports of frieze. They had been at a peak in 1687 when 1,129,716 yards had been exported. In 1698 the total was only 666,901 yards. The most immediate reason for this had been the decline in the French market. The French, badly clothed and with an indifferent textile industry, had offered a ready market for Irish frieze in the 1680s. Since 1687 high duties had changed all that; in 1698 exports of frieze to France were insignificant. Moreover, the relatively rapid growth of exports in 1697 and 1698 was not unprecedented; between 1683 and 1687 they had doubled as well. In any event, the rapid rate of growth of exports in 1697 and 1698 was powerfully stimulated by a short-term advantage which Ireland enjoyed in the rate of exchange.

This was not likely to be a continuing advantage; the high nominal value of money was likely to be reflected sooner or later in a rise in the price of commodities and of lands, and hence in costs generally. The rise in prices in 1696 and 1697 was moderated by the sharp rise at that time in domestic supply, which for the first time since 1689 was near normal. But once recovery was complete the moderating effect of further increases in supply no longer operated, and prices were likely to rise rapidly if demand remained strong. In fact, peace in Europe in 1697 helped to boost foreign demand strongly. The price of wool for the English market rose sharply after a slump in 1696-7, and beef for the continental market also rose; as did butter, more sharply but less permanently. As prices rose and foreign prospects appeared to augur better, rents and the purchase price of land rose further. As prices rose the situation in Ireland became inflationary. When the value of the guinea was further reduced in England in February 1699, it seemed likely that the value of money in Ireland would be reduced shortly. Expecting a fall in the nominal value of coins in their possession, people became anxious to convert coin as quickly as it came into their possession into goods or land. The price of lands and rent, both low in the first half of the 1690s, were now rising very sharply. In September 1699 a contemporary in Dublin noted:

' I am of opinion that land is at ye higth [*sic*] for rent and purchase for people are so eager to part with theire mony, that through feare of a loss by reducing it to its former denomination they are ready to throw it away.' Rising prices and rents meant a reduction in the large margin of competitive advantage that Irish goods enjoyed in 1696. In other words, the competitive advantage that Irish exports enjoyed in 1696 was impermanent by nature, and hence the future increase of exports of woollens could not be projected at the rate of new drapery in 1697 and 1698.

It was at this stage, in 1699, that the English Parliament prohibited the export of woollen goods from Ireland. Low prices in Ireland had alarmed the merchants in Bristol as far back as 1695. At that time they instructed their representatives in Parliament to raise the issue. Their alarm was exaggerated. Ireland's substantial advantage in terms of low costs was a consequence, first, of the low level of economic activity there in the first half of the nineties and then of the substantial advantage in exchange from 1696 which reduced the price of Irish commodities, though rising internally, to foreign purchasers. These advantages were bound to be temporary. By the middle of the 1690s prices of land were already beginning to recover. The competitive advantage which Ireland enjoyed in the exchanges was also likely to be temporary for the reasons which have been outlined. It was, however, common for contemporaries to complain about foreign competition and to demand that something be done to protect English commercial interests. Contemporaries, always prone to be alarmist about the danger of outsiders taking away the foreign trade of England, were not likely to see Ireland's substantial cost advantages in the middle of the 1690s as something transitory and which did not require drastic action. A bill to exclude Irish woollens from foreign trade came before Parliament in 1697, and again in 1698. Another bill was introduced at the end of 1698, and became law in 1699. It forbade the export of woollen cloth from Ireland overseas. It did not prohibit exports to England, but the duties there were prohibitive as far as drapery was concerned.

The act which passed through Parliament in 1699 was not, however, the consequence of official English policy towards Ireland. The measure had been promoted by the merchants of Bristol and the various interests in the woollen industry in the south-west of England. It by no means commanded unanimous support and the issue dragged on through three years in Parliament. Moreover, the English authorities had hoped that the pressure for such a measure might be satisfied by a compromise step in which the Irish Parliament would impose additional duties on the export of cloth from Ireland. At the beginning of 1699 an act was at last passed by the Irish Parliament imposing a duty of 20 per cent on exports of old drapery and 10 per cent on new drapery. These rates, however, were much less than English official opinion thought necessary to equalise the costs of English and Irish cloth. It was scarcely likely in those circumstances that the measure would satisfy the English woollen interest. The proposal to prohibit Irish exports of cloth was therefore taken up vigorously in 1699, and became law in the same year. The statute represented a victory for the vested interests concerned. The English government itself had taken no initiative in the matter until pressure had been brought to bear by Bristol, Exeter and other ports of the south-west, and even at that stage the official efforts had been directed towards a compromise arrangement. At the time the economic significance of the proposal for the prohibition of exports of woollens seemed fairly limited even to people in Ireland. This was certainly true of the merchant community who regarded it as harmful but not disruptive of the economy at large. The greatest indignation was stirred up by religious or political considerations. Bishop King of Derry was alarmed at the fact that the prohibition would affect members of the Church of Ireland disproportionately, and would thus strengthen the growing Presbyterian interest in the north which caused him so much concern. Others such as William Molyneux were angered by the constitutional inferiority of the Irish Parliament to the English. Molyneux wrote a book early in 1698, *The case of Ireland's being bound by Acts of Parliament in England stated*, refuting the proposition that the English Parliament could legislate for the Irish. The real significance of the act, then and later, rested in its constitutional implications. The high-handed nature of the act, and the fact that the proposals culminating in its passing had called forth the clearest statement of Ireland's claim to constitutional equality with its sister kingdom, gave the act a prominence which no other measure of an economic character enjoyed.

In 1720 the celebrated *Sixth of George the First* was passed, confirming the right of the English Parliament to bind Ireland by legislation. The ferment this act had caused was overtaken in 1722 by the violent controversy over Wood's Halfpence. A patent was granted in July 1722 to William Wood, an English ironmaster, to coin halfpence for Ireland. This patent was granted without any consultation with the Irish Parliament. Indignation boiled over in Ireland; Swift's famous *Drapier's letters* appeared in 1724, condemning the patent and asserting also that England had no right to make laws for Ireland. So fierce was the opposition in Ireland to the patent that it had to be withdrawn in 1725. The constitutional furore of the 1720s coincided with a decade of economic difficulties. It was only natural that, in a period of indignation about the constitutional issue, the English legislation binding Ireland should be blamed for the country's economic problems. The act of 1699 in particular came to be singled out as a factor responsible for them. Writers such as Swift asserted that the act had destroyed the Irish woollen industry, led to the migration of a huge number of weavers, and ushered in a long period of economic poverishment. Thus, if their assertions were taken at their face value, the act of 1699 was behind the economic problems of the day. In fact, in making such assertions they were of course powerfully influenced by the political significance which the act had acquired in the constitutional controversy of the 1720s. Assertions about the sweeping economic results that flowed from the woollen act were formulated for the first time in the 1720s. At the time of the passing of the act, there was no apprehension that its economic results would be disastrous. Even when economic difficulties set in in 1701-2 and subsequent years, the act of 1699 seemed to contemporaries to be one of six or more causes of depression : it was in no sense regarded at the time as the unique or foremost cause of the depression of the first decade of the eighteenth century.

The view that English legislation was responsible for Irish economic problems was widely asserted in the 1720s. Not all writers shared this view fully, but even writers who did not, gave a great deal of attention in their writings to the act of 1699 and accepted the case which had been advanced for its harmful economic results. The best-informed opinion of the age was, of course, aware that economic problems and their solution did not lie in a few legislative measures. But it is true to say that among the Irish gentry at large and in the eyes of Irish public opinion generally, a rather nebulous view was commonly accepted from the 1720s which held English legislation to have been directed against Irish economic interests and to have seriously prejudiced them. The point was often made incidentally in Irish writing in subsequent decades. At length, when in the late 1770s the political ferment in Ireland stirred up by the example of the American colonies coincided with acute economic depression, the case that English legislation had over the years deliberately and effectively depressed Irish trade was put forward more uncompromisingly than ever. Historians a century or more later took their assessment of English legislation affecting Irish economic interests from the writings and opinions voiced in the late 1770s.

English policy was not, however, inimical in intent towards Ireland. It was guided, of course, by the belief that Irish economic interests should be regulated in a way which would do no harm to England. But this was a very general principle and was often very limited in practical expression. It was only in tariff policy in both islands and in the Navigation Laws that it was consistently followed. English tariffs, especially on manufactured goods, were often prohibitive, and hence excluded Irish as well as foreign goods. On the other hand, Irish tariffs were relatively low, or where they were prohibitive a preferential duty was accorded to goods from England. Too much attention should not be given to this aspect, however. Transport costs were high in the eighteenth century; in every part of Europe a high degree of self-sufficiency even in industrial goods was common in the early decades of the century, and in consequence trade in manufactured goods was rather limited. The Navigation Acts reflected the belief that England was under no obligation to share its colonial wealth equally with Ireland.

These aspects apart, however, there was no intention to restrain Irish foreign trade or the country's economic development. It is true that Irish wool could be shipped only to England, but this was seen as a counterpart of the prohibition on English wool producers themselves of shipping off wool. Moreover, the Navigation Acts, where their basic principle was not affected, conceded advantages to Ireland. Thus, Irish shipping and seamen were treated as English, and could engage in the English coasting trade and in the direct trade between England and the colonies. The Navigation Act of 1663 admitted the direct shipment of provisions, horses and servants from Ireland to the colonies; in 1705 the direct shipment of linen was also authorised. The act of 1663 had been intended to prohibit the direct importation of goods enumerated in the act from the colonies to Ireland. It was legally ineffective, and the prohibition was made operative only in 1671 in an act which itself lapsed in 1680 and was not renewed until 1685. In 1696 the import even of unenumerated colonial products to Ireland was prohibited. In 1731 this prohibition was replaced by a less comprehensive one which admitted the importation of non-enumerated goods. Two of these non-enumerated goods proved to be of rapidly growing importance in subsequent years – flax-seed for the linen industry and rum. In addition, American flour was sometimes imported in quantity in years of harvest failure. These goods proved the basis of a substantial import trade from the colonies. Thus, the limitations on Irish foreign trade implicit in the Navigation Acts were themselves subject to substantial qualification. The acts did not prevent the growth of a significant volume of trade in both directions between Ireland and the colonies. The major goods provided by the colonies – tobacco and sugar – had, however, to be imported from Britain. This did not in fact greatly raise the price of the products to the consumer in Ireland, if at all – Irish consumption in these products grew impressively during the century – but it probably adversely affected the interests of some of the merchant community. If Ireland had been permitted to import colonial produce directly and re-export it, Cork would probably have taken from Glasgow some of the thriving entrepot trade which that city enjoyed, importing tobacco and then re-exporting it to Europe. However, the advantages of this facility would not have proved considerable outside tobacco, most of whose consumption in Europe was supplied by British colonies. Little sugar was re-exported from England itself for instance, because sugar from the French islands was so much cheaper and flooded the European markets. The Navigation Acts were a grievance to the Irish merchant rather than to the consumer, and even for the merchant the benefits that their repeal would have conferred rested in some respects more in the appearances than in the reality of the situation. After repeal of the restrictions in 1780, Ireland remained debarred from re-exporting colonial goods. Nominally a handicap, this was of little consequence in practice. The only colonial product exported in huge quantities from Britain had been tobacco, and the flourishing re-export trade was a factor in Glasgow's rapid growth. Direct shipment from the United States to Europe, however, became the established method of trade in the 1780s : Glasgow's entrepot trade decayed rapidly. The entrepot trade in tobacco proved in the nature of things transient. For Cork, the effects would have been more transient than for Glasgow, because unlike Glasgow there were no local sources of coal and iron in which trading profits might be invested and which would provide compensation for decaying colonial commerce.

In other regards, measures directed against Irish economic interests were few. Moreover, the establishment of these measures represented the triumph of vested interests rather than an expression of official policy. The outstanding illustrations of this are the Cattle Acts and the Woollen Act of 1699 itself. The prohibition by the English Parliament of the import of hops except from Britain in 1710, and of the exportation of glass from Ireland in 1746, were similar measures. Neither attracted much attention at the time. Nor had the measures any significant effect on the growth of the Irish brewing and glass industries, although at a later date the fact that both acts were measures by the English Parliament binding Ireland drew some suggestions to the effect that they had proved inimical to Irish economic interests. In fact, there was an Irish lobby in the English Parliament, consisting of landowners who owned estates in Ireland or of members who represented regions which benefited by imports from Ireland. Vested interests eager to restrict Anglo-Irish trade could not, therefore, always prevail. Measures which were passed had been subject to a spirited resistance in the English Parliament itself. Some were rejected, as for instance a proposal in 1711 to impose a high duty on woollen yarn imported from Ireland. There was thus no general system of restricting Irish foreign trade, and the major restrictions placed on Irish foreign trade – the Cattle Acts in the 1660s, the Woollen Act in 1699 – were passed against the wishes of the governments of the day.

In the eighteenth-century assessment of legislation and policy the act of 1699 seemed especially effective in distorting Irish economic development. But, in fact, the level of economic activity remained high until 1701. Exports fell, however, from a peak level in 1698. They had been £996,305 in 1698; they were only £814,746 in 1700, and £670,412 in 1701. But this was only in part the consequence of the Woollen Act. The termination of the export trade in woollens accounted for only a half of the decline in the value of exports between 1698 and 1700; and 30 per cent of the decline between 1698 and 1701. More important was the fact that rapidly rising prices within Ireland were beginning to offset the competitive advantages which the rate of exchange had given Ireland and that butter prices which had been remarkably high in 1698 and 1699 fell sharply in 1700. Imports in the three years 1699-1701 were above the level of 1698 – the excess varying between 20 and 40 per cent. A high level of activity and rising internal prices ensured this. The continuing high level of economic activity was also reflected in the revenue yield. Excluding temporary or additional taxation,* the revenue yield increased from £331, 597 in 1698 to £360,209 in 1699, £385,400 in 1700 and £396,860 in 1701. Decline came only in 1702 when the yield fell to £337,033. In the following year it was down to £309,406.

Thus, economic recession came only in 1702, three years after the act of 1699. When it did come, there were, as we shall see, well-defined reasons to account for it. Nor did the woollen industry itself decline disastrously as later writers suggested. There was apparently some migration of weavers in the years following the act : probably some of the English artisans whose going to Ireland had so alarmed the merchants of Bristol and Exeter in the mid-1690s returned. Numerically, however, the numbers involved were small. Later, however, in the 1720s when sweeping generalisations were made about the effects of the act of 1699 on the Irish industry it was claimed that thousands had migrated. By the late 1770s it was asserted that the number who had migrated had been 30,000. In fact, the industry did not decline disastrously after the act of 1699. Over the first half of the eighteenth century as a whole its output is likely to have risen. The industry had a large home market in 1698. Imports of cloth had fallen sharply in preceding decades. As a proportion of imports from England, cloth had fallen from 14 per cent in 1665 to 1.7 per cent in 1698. Imports fell further in the first decade of the eighteenth century. By 1709 they were almost halved. The industry did of course experience acute difficulties in the first decade of the century; the sharp decline in domestic income from 1702 reduced demand for manufactured goods generally. The recession which the woollen industry experienced was shared with other branches of industry and did not flow specifically from the Woollen Act. Resolutions of the House of Commons in 1703, 1705

---

* With the exception of an additional excise duty included with the hereditary inland excise from 1695 to 1709/10, and for which separate figures are not available before 1705. In comparisons in the text with later years, the estimated amount of this additional excise is deducted.

and 1707 expressed concern at the situation and urged the consumption of Irish manufactures. The sharp reduction in imports must have helped the Irish industry. Imports recovered from the middle of the 1710s. But the increase was not sharp enough to make serious inroads into the Irish market, and imports fell sharply again at the end of the 1720s. Woollens rose to 3.9 per cent of total imports from England in 1718 and 5.3 per cent in 1728; they had fallen to 2.5 per cent of total imports from Britain in 1738. Thus the Irish industry withstood English competition remarkably well in the first forty years of the century. Output must have fallen in the first decade as part of the general recession in the economy. Not only did output recover, however, but it is likely, having regard to the marginal significance of imports even at their peak, that the rise in the domestic market in the long run more than made up the loss of export outlets. It is likely that the output of the industry in 1740 exceeded the output of 1698. The small size of imports and the fact that their rise in the 1720s had been temporary suggests that the home industry effectively commanded the market.

Even if the prohibition of exports had not been introduced in 1699 it seems likely that the development of the Irish woollen industry would have been tied to the home market. Later commentators did, of course, claim that the act had deprived Ireland of access to extensive markets. But this overlooks the exceptional and temporary advantage which Ireland enjoyed in the exchanges and which is the underlying factor in the rapid growth of cloth exports from Ireland in the 1690s. Significantly, Irish frieze – the only cloth lightly taxed in England – was exported in rapidly rising quantities to England up to 1701 when exports were valued at a sizeable £28,995. In 1701 the Irish currency was revalued, and in the following years exports declined abruptly. There was little evasion of the act. Some woollens did go abroad illegally – in the 1730s especially assertions were made that one type of woollen cloth, camblets, was smuggled to Portugal from Cork. But the quantities were small. Contemporaries, anxious to plead the case that the act of 1699 was made self-defeating by smuggling, tended to exaggerate the traffic. Interestingly, the export of small quantities of drapery and frieze is recorded in the official statistics to various foreign destinations rather consistently from 1723 to 1731. Under the act of 1699 this was prohibited, and may suggest some defiant disregard by authority itself of the terms of the act. The belief that extensive markets overseas had been denied to Ireland by the act overlooks the development of the industry within several major markets in the eighteenth century and the widespread resort in European countries to prohibitive measures or tariffs against textile imports. Irish frieze had been already virtually excluded from France before 1698 by duties; in 1701 an absolute prohibition was placed on the import of woollens from Britain and Ireland. There are a few cases on record of cloth smuggled from Ireland being seized by French port officials. The virtual closing of many markets to international trade made the competition on the remaining markets such as Iberia all the more acute. Even English exports did not rise dramatically in the eighteenth century. Including the captive colonial market, they somewhat more than doubled. The expansion in exports to Spain and Portugal was balanced by a decline in exports to other destinations in Europe in the first half of the century; exports to Portugal itself slumped in the 1760s. It is hard to see how the Irish woollen industry could have increased its exports significantly in the eighteenth century, or how the industry could have acquired a potential for transforming the Irish economy.

The act of 1699 emerges as irrelevant in the main to the central problems of the first decade of the eighteenth century. The downturn in prices in Ireland began in June 1701. The downturn in Irish prices preceded by almost a year the general decline throughout Europe. The reason lies in the revaluation of the Irish currency, long expected but not effected until June 1701. The high nominal value of coins in Ireland contributed to rising prices. In the short term, it was welcome to many especially by apparently cheapening Irish exports to foreigners. But rising prices affected different categories of income-earner unequally and obviously could not be allowed to go on indefinitely. A tenant who had leased a farm in the early 1690s did well: his money rent was low, and the prices of the commodities he sold much higher than either he or his landlord had anticipated. On the other hand, a tenant who rented a farm in the late 1690s paid a high rent, and his landlord received from him a much higher rent than he did from a tenant who had leased his farm in the early or mid-1690s. The guinea, which passed for 21s 6d in England, passed for 26s in Ireland. This was reflected in the exchange charged on bills of exchange. In April and May 1701, for instance, a bill for £100 sterling exchanged for Irish £122½ to £125. When the guinea was reduced in June to

23s, the rate fell from £122½ to £110½. Thus the foreign merchant purchasing goods in Ireland found immediately that the proceeds of £100 sterling remitted to Ireland fell from Irish £122½ to Irish £110½. This meant that the cost of Irish commodities rose sharply to the foreign importer and that he reduced his purchases. A reduction in buying by foreign merchants contracted sales on Irish markets, and the net result was that the altered valuation of money was quickly reflected in a general fall in prices. The fall in prices would help to make Irish goods competitive again on foreign markets. European war, however, broke out in 1702. With markets cut off, the downward spiral in commodity prices steepened. Wool prices were halved, and the prices of other agricultural staples fell nearly as much. The value of exports fell heavily. In consequence, incomes fell sharply. Tenants who had rented lands at high rates in the late 1690s suffered especially. Declining incomes, and for many such as the unfortunate farmers who had rented land in the late 1690s a heavier incidence of fixed charges, reduced consumption substantially. As a result, imports fell even more sharply than exports. Government revenue remained low throughout the decade as well. After recovering in 1708, it slumped in the following years, falling in the years ended 25 march 1710 and 1711 to a level not much above the depressed levels of 1703 and 1704.

The only redeeming feature of the decade was that domestic harvests were relatively good. The years 1708 and 1709 were years of dearth and even famine throughout Europe. Even the English authorities contemplated imports of grain from Ireland in early 1710. In the year ended 25 March 1710 grain exports from Ireland virtually dried up; this suggests dearth in Ireland; and the small size of imports in a year in which want was general in Europe must have aggravated the situation in Ireland. But famine does not appear to have accompanied want. The hearth money tax returns – a tax on each hearth or fireplace – continued upwards from 1708 to 1711 which would not have been the case if the mortality and migration associated with famine had been experienced extensively. But the economic effects of poor harvests were reflected in a credit squeeze, or scarcity of cash ' ye like of has not been since ye warrs ' in January 1710. Bumper harvests followed in 1711-14. They coincided with bad harvests elsewhere. The harvest failed in south-west France in 1712; in 1714 Irish grain was drawn in large quantities into the French market. Good harvest conditions had speeded some degree of recovery even before peace in 1713 permitted the normal resumption of foreign trade. The early years of peace were boom years. Exports of grain, already large at 101,589 quarters in 1711/2 and 59,016 quarters in 1712/3, soared to 138,216 quarters in 1713/4 and 109,122 quarters in 1714/5. At the same time, a cattle murrain on the continent, coinciding with the peace, had decimated cattle stocks, and boosted the demand for and prices of Irish beef and cattle. Exports soared to £1,422,227 in the year ended 25 March 1714 and £1,529,766 in the following year. However, these were exceptionally favourable years. Exports of grain fell sharply in subsequent years. Prices of beef and butter slumped. Animal disease in Ireland, after the bad spring of 1717, helped to restore prices somewhat, but hardly made for prosperity. Thus, after the short-lived upsurge of prices between 1712 and 1715, the underlying weakness of the agricultural situation reasserted itself. Prices of grain, beef, butter and wool fell. By 1720 the poverty of the countryside was again painfully evident. In March 1720 an agent in Carrick-on-Shannon advised his landlord of rents 'remaining due in ye poor ten.ts hands for want of marketts to convert the cows into money.' Yet the 'hereditary' revenue had probably recovered the 1701 level in 1715/16, and rose by a further 11 per cent by 1719/20. But the underlying weakness of the economy is seen in the fact that the level of 1719/20 was exceeded in only three of the next 15 years.*

Agricultural prices rose significantly in the second half of the 1720s. However, this did not improve social conditions. The second half of the 1720s was a decade of repeated harvest failure. Harvest failure, in fact, proved one of the reasons of higher agricultural prices because in the intervening years of good harvests all agricultural prices tended to be low. Rents tended to rise in the 1720s. Much land had been leased on 21- or 31-year leases at low rents in the early or mid-1690s. Some of these leases had fallen in in 1717 and 1718, and the rents rose. Others fell in during the 1720s and the rents were increased. Petty had estimated the total rental in 1687 at £1.2 million. Estimates in the 1720s put the rental at £1.6 to £2 million. The increase in the 1710s and 1720s in rents was

---

* Hereditary revenue. The additional revenue derived from new or variable duties is not taken into account as it would falsify comparisons. The lack of buoyancy is still more striking if it is borne in mind that the hearth money tax was returned net of costs prior to 1706.

therefore a substantial one, but not unduly so in so far as the original rents had been low and so had been the rents charged on land leased in the mid-1690s. The fact that agricultural prices, which had been so weak, rose in the 1720s seemed to provide an economic justification for the upward adjustment in rents as well. As leases fell in, landlords were eager to increase rents. Rising prices in the 1720s meant that the purchasing power of a fixed income was falling. This was particularly acutely felt by absentees because a significant worsening of the exchanges in many years in the 1720s meant that a given amount of money remitted from Dublin to London yielded less than had been customary once converted into sterling. Thus, everyone was dissatisfied in the 1720s: the landlord, resident or absentee, because he regarded himself as victim of a fixed income in a period of rising prices, the tenant because the rent increase was often a substantial one and because harvest failure made agriculture a difficult business in many years. From the landlord's point of view, it was fortunate that so many leases were due for renewal in the 1720s: it held out prospects of increasing his income in circumstances when its purchasing power would otherwise have fallen.

A rise in rents entailed an increase in the sums remitted to absentee landlords. The proportion of rents remitted to absentees has often been exaggerated; absentee rents probably accounted for about one-fourth to one-sixth of the total rent roll. But even at this reduced proportion, it was a very substantial amount, and rose as rents increased generally. Rents remitted to absentees had been estimated at £100,000 in 1698; in the 1720s the amount was probably in excess of £300,000, although in years of economic difficulty the amount actually remitted could decline sharply: the failure of tenants or delays in paying rents were bound to reduce remittances. By the end of the 1720s contemporaries were alarmed about the growth in remittances to absentees and about the consequences. It was feared that in the effort to pay absentee rents the whole supply of money in the country would be exported.

The rise in rents did pose a problem for the tenant and, in so far as rents were remitted to England, for the economy as a whole. The problem in paying rents – or in remitting them to absentees – did not lie simply in the amount, but in the fact that through intermittent harvest failure the surplus in agriculture was frequently reduced. This meant that in a bad year the tenant's income was insufficient for him to be able to pay his rent with comfort to a landlord, resident or absentee. For the country at large, the consequences were that through a fall in exports of grain and a sharp rise in imports of grain the surplus in the country's commodity trade fell short of its fixed obligations abroad.

Harvest failure lies behind the internal and external difficulties of this decade. It created difficulties in foreign trade. It impoverished the countryman. Without it, the rise in rents would have been borne more readily. In fact, complaints about remittances to absentees became general only in the closing years of the decade when the country was struggling through a run of singularly bad harvests. The decade had started with a sharp decline in economic activity in 1720. This was due, however, to the impact on Ireland of the breaking of the speculative activity in France and England associated with the South Sea Company and the Mississippi Company respectively and the disruption caused in trade with southern Europe by the outbreak of plague in the south of France. Harvests were on the whole good, excepting that of 1722, notably in 1723 and 1724. The first serious harvest failure occurred in 1726. 17,508 quarters of wheat alone were imported in the year ended March 1727 and expenditure on imported grain and meal was above £100,000. Imports soared to the highest level of the decade. For the year ended 25 March 1727 there was a deficit in the balance of trade: the rates of exchange in late 1726 and the first half of the 1727 were the most adverse of the decade. The harvest was bad in 1727 also, and failed disastrously again in 1728, so disastrously that 1728-9 was a year of famine in many parts of the country, especially in the north. There was some surplus, however, in parts of the south: the coastwise traffic in grain to Dublin was substantial in the early months of 1729. Imports soared through the winter of 1728 and the summer of 1729. 86,086 quarters of wheat were imported in the season between the harvests of 1728 and 1729.* In the eighteen months to September 1729 imports of corn had cost £274,000. In the year ended 25 March 1729 the favourable balance of trade was relatively small. The following year, because of the huge imports in the spring and early summer

---

* i.e., in the years ended March 1729 and March 1730. As the bulk of imports was concentrated on the spring and summer months of 1729, the data for the two years may be accepted broadly as those of the year following the harvest failure of 1728.

of 1729, the balance was a very meagre one. It was the reduced balance of trade in these two years that made the remittances to absentees seem so frightening. Prior's *List of the absentees of Ireland,* a pamphlet which caught the imagination of contemporaries, appeared in 1729. Famine spread poverty. Despite the heavy expenditure on imports of grain, the fall in other imports compensated for the rise in grain imports. Hence, the value of imports was relatively low in the years ended 25 March 1729 and 1730. Swift's *Modest Proposal* with its striking account of Irish poverty appeared in the aftermath of the famine of 1728-9.

Some contemporaries like Swift thought that the reason for a shortage of grain was a decline in tillage. This was blamed on the landlords who, it was argued, discouraged tenants from growing grain and compelled them to raise livestock. The members of Parliament itself clearly were inclined to believe this line of reasoning, and in 1727, following the bad harvest of 1726, an act was passed intended to compel owners or occupiers of 100 acres or more to till at least five per cent of their land. In fact, because grain prices were often very low, there was justification for tenants and landlords alike in reducing the dependence of tenants on grain and diversifying production more. The trend should not be exaggerated. Swift, for instance, resented the refusal of many landed gentry to pay tithes on pasture land; his dislike of the Irish gentry led him to level harsh charges at them. The best-informed contemporaries seem to have taken a different view of the situation. Their concern in the late 1720s was revealed in their proposal that public granaries should be established. In these granaries, surplus grain after a bumper harvest could be stored to guard against failure in other years. Their view seems to have been confirmed by the course of subsequent events. The harvest in 1729 was a good one, that in 1730 a bumper one followed by disastrously low prices. Poverty in the rural community, caused by harvest failure, was prolonged by the low prices; in particular very low prices made it difficult for farmers to reduce the indebtedness of bad years. Rent arrears mounted ominously after the bumper harvest of 1730. The hereditary revenue itself, always a revealing index of economic conditions, fell sharply in the year ended 25 March 1731.

The 1720s were thus a difficult decade. Only in two years did the revenue exceed the level of 1720. Fortuitous circumstances – a run of bad harvests – help to explain the acute difficulties of the second half of the decade. But not completely. The fundamental underlying weakness was clearly in the country's foreign trade. The value of exports tended to be lower than in the second decade of the century. Not only that but the rise in exports since 1700 is not reassuring, once examined. Exports had risen from £814,746 in 1700 – taking a year when the volume was normal and prices not unduly inflated – to £1,043,052 in the year ended 25 March 1731. However, if the rise in the value of exports of linen cloth and yarn is deducted, exports had actually fallen between 1700 and 1730/1 from £814,746 to £789,037. As far as the agricultural staples were concerned, long-term price trends were unattractive; this in turn was reflected in little variation in the volume of output. The output of wool and butter actually declined; grain growing – the years in which good harvests in Ireland and failure elsewhere coincided apart – was already proving unremunerative, and even in the 1720s there was some modest movement out of grain cultivation. Cattle grazing increased only from the second decade, and much of the increase consisted of substituting cattle for sheep on existing grazing land. With a modest but definite growth in population, this suggests that there was little if any rise in per capita incomes. If, as was the case, rents rose significantly the likelihood of some decline in per capita incomes is all the more likely. Long-term stagnation in the revenue yield and the fact that between 1715 and 1730 imports tended to be stable seems to support this possibility. The adverse trend could be offset to the extent that rural inhabitants diversified into the production of industrial products such as yarn or cloth for the market. This was already happening in the north-east, where spinning and weaving linen had progressed significantly. By the end of the 1720s, the north-east, 40 years previously part of what was still the most backward region of the country, was already better off than the other parts of rural Ireland. Diversification into spinning and weaving even in the north, however, was still modest in the 1720s. In Ulster it was largely confined to counties Down, Armagh, Derry and Antrim. Elsewhere, the penetration of the textile industry into rural Ireland was still limited; the smallholder poor, in part because prices were low or employment limited, in part because other occupations did not supplement his meagre agricultural income.

The 1720s proved to be a decade of economic crisis. It was a significant decade on other counts as well. The constitutional question had been sharply debated in the course of the decade. The acute economic problems of the second half of the decade led to a spate of writing in 1728 and 1729 on economic issues. The evident plight of the people caused a discussion, in effect, on economic welfare. Significantly, the participants in this discussion were among the group of public-spirited gentlemen who in 1731 established the Dublin Society, intended to promote the economic and agricultural welfare of the country. Some saw the causes of the country's economic problems in English legislation and policy. This was not true of all the commentators of the decade, but even those who took a politically detached view of the situation accepted and gave prominence in their own writings to the results attributed by contemporaries to the Woollen Act of 1699. From this time forward the belief that English policy had harmed Irish economic interests was widely accepted by public opinion. In the following decade, Berkeley's *Querist* as also some other of the writings of the 1730s were inspired by the belief that self-help could improve economic conditions and that difficulties should not be attributed to purely external circumstances. The colonial nationalism of the 1720s and the interest in economic welfare went hand in hand. Parliament itself was strongly influenced by the opinion of the period. It passed its Tillage Act in 1727. It was concerned too with the dependence on imported coal. ' The Irish are national in every-thing ', lamented Sir James Lowther, the owner of the Whitehaven collieries in Cumberland. It was, in fact, Parliament's interest in the coal trade that led it to take a further step (after the establish-ment of the Linen Board in 1711 the next major one) into the direct financing of economic development. Coal prices fluctuated widely, and high winter prices often seemed to leave the Dublin consumer, despite legislation intended to prevent abuses, at the mercy of the English shipper. In the winter of 1728/9, while the country was in the grip of famine, coal prices soared from a normal level of 15s a ton or even less to 33s in Dublin. Parliament, at its next session, was no longer prepared to rest content with the situation. In the spring of 1730 it passed an act appointing Com-missioners of Navigation in each of the four provinces. With the aid of the monies provided under the act, the execution of a canal from Newry to Lough Neagh was under way in 1731 in the belief that supplies from the coalfield in co. Tyrone would break a resented English monopoly.

3

Markets and Harvests
1730-1793

The 1720s proved a particularly difficult decade. It was, of course, complicated by three successive bad harvests in 1726-8, the poor harvest of 1728 bringing famine in its wake. But even in the first half of the decade, when harvests had been good, the outlook had proved difficult and prices had fallen. This situation existed in peacetime, unlike the first decade of the century when the prolonged economic difficulties could in part be attributed to wartime disruption of traditional markets. Apart from recovery from the low level to which they had fallen in 1720/1 when speculation had played havoc with the business world in England and in France, and quarantine regulations made necessary by plague had disrupted communication with the south of Europe, exports had remained static during the decade. Exports in the best year of the 1720s were exceeded by the figures for five years in the second decade of the century. The poor performance of exports was in part a consequence of falling prices. But only in part. Agricultural exports fell in volume during the 1720s. This in part reflects the contraction in exports of grain from the high level they had attained in the 1710s. Good harvests in the early 1720s were paralleled by good harvests elsewhere; exports virtually dried up during the bad harvests in the second half of the decade. Some rise in beef exports was offset by a decline in wool and butter. But for the expansion of the linen industry, the Irish economy would have experienced an alarming crisis in the 1720s. By the end of the 1720s linen for the first time accounted for over half Irish exports to England, or roughly a quarter of total exports to all parts.

In contrast to the 1720s exports rose sharply in the 1730s: from £1,043,050 in 1730/1 to £1,259,853 in 1739/40. The improvement was due solely to linen. If the increase in the value of linen is excluded, exports had actually fallen from £1,043,050 to £1,007,737. Linen exports had soared between 1730/1 and 1734/5 when their value had risen by 80 per cent. Prices had risen sharply at the same time, the Earl of Egmont noting in 1735 that 'our kingdome will infallibly loose its trade with England for coarse linnens unlesse we keep to ye old price and raise them not as we have done of late in so much as ye linen drapers are resolving to send again to Hamburg'. Exports of linen experienced a very sharp recession in 1737/8, though recovering in 1739/40 to the level of 1734/5. The expansion in the linen industry between 1730/1 and 1734/5 was, however, remarkable – except for that in the late 1780s and early 1790s the most rapid in the industry's history. Thanks to the expansion in these years, the value of exports rose sharply over the 1730s.

Agricultural exports continued to present an unreassuring picture: agricultural prices which had risen during the second half of the 1720s slumped badly again after the opening years of the decade. Some contemporaries suggested that the situation was made less gloomy by the existence of a huge clandestine or secret trade in smuggled wool. However, these arguments were claims put out or seized on by individuals whose motives and judgment were suspect, either the representatives of interests in the woollen industry in England anxious to secure Irish wool for their own industry, or contemporaries in Ireland who seized on the argument, claiming that the Woollen Act of 1699 had encouraged the Irish to send their wool to rival manufacturers on the continent and that the illegal traffic could be halted only by the removal of the prohibition on the export of woollen cloth from Ireland. Some of the contemporary estimates were very sanguine, claiming as much as four-fifths of the wool produced in the country to be smuggled to France. Even a moderate observer, Arthur Dobbs, suggested that smuggled wool might amount to 100,000 stone, or more than half the size of legal exports of wool and yarn to England at that time. In reality, as the records of the French ports show, little wool was landed there from Ireland in the 1720s. The quantities increased sharply only when wool prices broke dramatically in the mid-1730s: from an average of almost 9,000 stone for the four French ports of Nantes,

Bordeaux, La Rochelle and Le Havre in 1730-3 to one of 30,000 stone in 1736-9 for Nantes, Bordeaux and La Rochelle. The year 1736 was the only year in which smuggled imports really soared. Imports in Nantes, Bordeaux and La Rochelle amounted to some 45,000 stone. At Nantes, the main centre of import, cargoes landed had soared to 56 in 1736, as against 30 in 1737, 30 in 1738 and 37 in 1739. At 6s a stone, the value of the wool smuggled averaged only £9,000 between 1736 and 1739. The trade in smuggled wool was of modest significance in relation to total exports in these years and of negligible importance before or after 1736-9.

Yet low though agricultural prices generally were, one significant feature was the rise in prices of cattle and beef. The rise in beef prices in 1713 had been short-lived and the growth in the beef trade soon lost momentum. Prices of beef had subsequently remained low until 1725. But as early as July 1725 an Irish landlord's agent wrote : ' I hear that cattle sell well at the fairs, but is allways in expectation of a slaughter in which they have disappointed some years past, tho' by the acct. I have from Nantes it promised better than the last '. In 1724 beef had fetched only 5s 9d a cwt. By 1726 beef prices were in the range of 7s to 9s a cwt. They fell a little after 1731 but throughout the 1730s they continued at a level 20 to 40 per cent higher than they had been during the decade 1715-24. On the other hand, prices of butter and wool showed no long-term improvement, and in both cases the reversal from a temporary recovery in the late 1720s and early 1730s was quite sharp. Years of harvest failure apart, grain prices fell considerably as well. The evidence of a swing to beef production was very definite : exports of beef for the four years ended 25 March 1732 were 23 per cent above the level of the four years ended March 1720. This was doubly significant : beef was the only main agricultural export to grow through the 1720s and 1730s, and the 1720s marked the end of a 50-year period of stagnation in cattle production. This was important in itself, but rises in the prices of wool and butter in the course of the 1740s confirmed that the improvement in beef in the 1720s and 1730s was a prelude to a general long-term improvement in the prices of pastoral products. Beef was around 12s a cwt by 1750, 17s in 1765, 20s in 1774, 25s in 1792. Butter, which had been down to 20s or even lower in the late 1730s, never fell below 32s in the early 1750s. The price was around 40s in 1770 and 63s to 65s in the early 1790s. Prices were to soar much higher still during the long and almost uninterrupted period of war from 1793 to 1815.

The 1730s marked the beginning of a long period of rapid growth in Irish foreign trade. This was not altogether apparent to contemporaries. Even the very rapid growth of the linen trade from 1730/1 to 1734/5 did not appear very reassuring because it was followed by depression and linen exports did not again reach the level of 1734/5 until the end of the decade. In fact, however, the volume of linen exports grew rapidly in every subsequent decade, except the 1770s, linen accounting at the end of the century for about half the greatly swollen value of Irish exports. Exports of linen were less than 500,000 yards in 1698; in the 1790s they were above 40,000,000 yards. The Irish linen industry was perhaps the most remarkable instance in Europe of an export-based advance in the eighteenth century. England's major export, woollen cloth, increased only by 136 per cent between 1700 and 1796. The rise in cattle grazing was viewed with disquiet especially in the second half of the decade. But in fact the growth of beef exports was the first stage of a prolonged growth in Irish agricultural exports after decades when their volume had been virtually stagnant and prices low. In 1749/52 beef exports were 49 per cent above the level of 1717-20; in 1769/72 73 per cent. Butter exports in 1737/40 were only 15 per cent above the level of 1683-6; in 1765/8 they were 76 per cent above the level of 1737/40. Thus, virtual stagnation in beef and butter was replaced by an expansion in exports which was remarkably rapid in the middle decades of the century. In the 1780s grain began to re-emerge as a significant export, and grain along with butter soared in volume and price during the period of the Napoleonic wars.

The weak trend in exports in the first three decades of the century is evident from the table on the next page. What increase took place over the period as a whole was due solely to the growth in linen. From the 1730s onwards, the rise in exports was impressive right up to 1815. It was also broad based, accounted for not only by the continued growth of linen (excepting the 1770s) but by an upsurge first in provisions and then in grain as well. This expansion, moreover, occurred in a period in which most countries were to a large extent industrially and agriculturally more or less self-sufficient, and when protectionism – agricultural and industrial – was both general and becoming even more pronounced.

Exports and Imports of Ireland

Year ending 25 March	Exports	Imports
	£	£
1700*	814,746	792,473
1710	712,497	554,248
1720	1,038,382	891,678
1730	992,832	929,896
1740	1,259,853	849,678
1750	1,862,834	1,531,654
1760	2,139,388	1,647,592
1770	3,159,587	2,566,845
1780	3,012,179	2,127,579
1790	4,855,319	3,829,914
5 Jan 1801	3,714,779	5,584,599
5 Jan 1811	6,099,337	6,564,578
5 Jan 1816	7,076,123	6,106,878

* Year ending 25 December

In fact, the growth of Irish foreign trade was little stimulated by conditions on the continent of Europe. Its progress was tied up predominantly with the transatlantic traffic and with Britain. The European market for provisions actually contracted in the course of the eighteenth century. Irish beef landed in French ports was almost invariably intended for re-export: in France high duties had virtually excluded beef from the internal market since 1688. Butter exports fluctuated widely in the short run, as variations in weather, fodder supply and animal mortality often opened markets for a short time. But the growth of dairying in Europe reduced even these markets in the long run. The French, for instance, had been obliged repeatedly to reduce the duties imposed in 1687 and 1688 on butter. After 1737, however, reduction was no longer accorded to butter imported for the domestic market. Exports of Irish butter to France fell sharply in consequence, and by the 1780s exports to every continental destination except Spain and Portugal had fallen. Much of what butter continued to be shipped to Europe was, moreover, intended for the colonial market. Thus, Irish beef and butter to a large extent met a specialist need: the colonial market. This was especially true of beef. Once the supply of cattle had contracted after the Cattle Acts and beef prices had fallen to a lower level, beef prices were remarkably stable by comparison with butter prices. This was simply because Irish beef supplied a stable and predictable market into which European supplies scarcely entered, whereas the demand for Irish butter expanded or contracted in response to fluctuations in European dairying. The main source of demand for beef came from the slave populations of the West Indian plantations and from the victualling of ships engaged in colonial voyages. Some of the beef was first shipped to European ports : much of it was taken by vessels that called at Irish ports, especially Cork, on their outward voyage from Europe. This market was, at first, limited by the relatively slow rate of colonial expansion. The quickening demand for beef in the 1720s was due to the acceleration in plantation sugar output and population at that time. In fact, the expansion of the sugar plantations on the French colony of St Domingue (modern Haiti) was exclusively responsible for the improvement in relative prices of beef in the mid-twenties. Indeed, in the 1720s and 1730s exports of beef rose simply because the rise in exports of beef to France exceeded some decline in exports to other destinations. Between 1727 and 1741 French vessels outward bound for the Americas were accorded by French law the quite exceptional permission of calling to Irish ports to load beef directly for the colonies. Somewhat later, the demand from the English colonies also intensified, and in the 1760s and 1770s between two-thirds and three-quarters of the total export of Irish beef was taken by the English colonies and France combined. Colonial demand for butter, at first small, grew in step with the colonial trade generally. In France, for instance, the downward trend in the domestic market for Irish butter was offset to some extent by a greater demand for butter for the colonies. In 1722 butter imported for their needs and put into entrepot for re-export was freed from duty, and in the 1730s the French vessels putting into Cork on the outward voyage to the colonies loaded some butter as well as beef. Much, and perhaps most of the butter taken by Spain and Portugal, was intended for re-export to their colonial possessions. Some rise in colonial demand, coinciding with more short-lived upsurges in the Dutch and north European markets in the middle of the century, was responsible for the recovery in butter prices from the 1740s onwards.

In addition to the colonial demand, another source of demand was the victualling requirements of navies. Irish beef had for them the same appeal as it had for the planters and the owners of commercial vessels – a competitive price and through heavy salting, good keeping qualities. While the English Admiralty could not import Irish beef to England after the Cattle Acts, it victualled many of its ships in the ports of Cork and Kinsale. In the 1690s various merchants in Cork through purchasing beef for the navy were in a position to draw bills of exchange on the Navy Victualling Board in London. A consequence of war was an increase in business of this sort. Sir Robert Southwell, a co. Cork absentee landlord in London, for instance, ran an account with the Victualling Board : in effect, for cash received in London from them, he provided the Board with cash out of his rents in co. Cork, for the purchase of provisions for the navy. The naval demand for provisions grew heavily during the war from 1689 and in the wars of the eighteenth century. All these wars were, to a large extent, wars at sea, and the size of the English and French navies expanded enormously in the course of the eighteenth century. A consequence of this development was that beef prices no longer slumped disastrously in wartime as they did, for instance, during the war with Holland in 1672-4. Although beef prices were relatively low in 1696 and 1697, they had not in fact slumped sharply : they conformed more or less to their prewar level. In the war of the Spanish Succession (1702-13), the prices of beef, in contrast to those of wool and butter, fell only moderately. This development became even more evident in subsequent wars. The prospect of war itself was sufficient to cause beef prices to soar.

A consequence of this growing dependence on Irish beef was that beef came to be regarded as one of the prime strategic commodities of the age. In 1667, to relieve low prices in Ireland, the English Government had actually agreed to license Irish trade, including trade in beef, with enemy countries. In 1780, on the other hand, the official philosophy in London was that ' stopping these provisions is equal to the gaining of a battle at sea, and may go further towards giving his Majesty supremacy over his enemies '. While in many wars some official countenancing of trade with the enemy continued, this toleration never extended in the eighteenth century to provisions. Given the general dependence by European navies and their support ships on Irish beef in particular, the official policy was to take all steps possible to prevent provisions reaching actual or prospective enemies. As the prospect of war led to a general upsurge in demand for Irish provisions, the first step in the enforcement of the policy was the imposition of a general embargo. This was not intended to last. While imposed, it had the advantage of depriving the enemy of provisions and at the same time ensuring that enhanced foreign demand might not reduce supplies for the provision of the English navy. In February 1740, as the war with Spain looked like widening, the first general embargo in Irish history was imposed. It was quickly lifted, however, and by April was no longer in force. In October 1740 with French embroilment again in sight an embargo was placed on trade in provisions. Butter was soon freed from embargo, but while the embargo was relaxed for shipments of beef to other destinations in early 1741, trade in beef with France remained under embargo till April 1742. In February 1744, a general embargo was proclaimed and was on occasion re-imposed in the war that followed; general embargo was resorted to again in March 1756 and from time to time during the ensuing war. Again, in 1770 an embargo was placed on the shipment of provisions because of a deterioration in relations with Spain and France, although it was not implemented in practice as the crisis quickly passed. A problem in the administration of embargoes was, however, that once the embargo was relaxed or consignments dispatched by licence, provisions might reach enemies, actual or prospective, under cover of shipment to neutral or friendly countries. English policy on the embargoes and its enforcement at sea was on the whole successful in preventing the shipment of Irish provisions to France in wartime from the 1740s onwards. But it failed, and was known to the authorities to have failed dismally in preventing the shipment of Irish provisions to the French colonies in the West Indies. Dutch ships gave bond to land their provisions on the Dutch islands in the West Indies but by one evasive method or other the provisions were sold on the French islands. The prospect of French involvement in the war with the rebellious English colonies that began in 1775 thus seemed alarming. In the extensive naval campaigns likely in American and West Indian waters the French navy should, if previous experience was a precedent, have no difficulty in victualling. A general embargo was imposed in February 1776 on trade in provisions except to Britain and loyal colonies. In contrast to previous embargoes it was not, however, followed by early relaxation or by licensing. The reason was the fear of the French navy being victualled from supplies exported on the shipping of neutral countries.

There had been some resentment of the general embargoes. It had been alleged at the time of their imposition that their purpose was to benefit certain London merchants who had contracts for victualling the navy. In fact, this allegation need not necessarily have substance : the strategic aspect and the need to provision the English fleet would have seemed sufficient justification in the ministerial view in London. Embargoes were not popular with merchants : they held up the filling of contracts already accepted, and disrupted contact, even if only for a time, with established markets. In March 1744 the merchants of Cork petitioned the Lords Justices about the detrimental effects of the embargo especially at the beginning of the season for butter. The grievance was, however, relatively minor. The general embargoes were always quickly relaxed, evasion as far as shipment to the West Indies was concerned was extensive, and prices invariably rose very substantially.

The embargo of 1776 caused a furore in Ireland. This was in part because it was not followed by general relaxation as in the past. Much of the resentment was constitutional, however. Stirred by the example of the rebellious colonies, Irish public opinion and the opposition in the Irish Parliament regarded the embargoes as the exercise of the prerogative power of the English crown. It was claimed that the embargoes caused prices to fall and entailed loss for the Irish merchants. These claims were to a large extent unfounded. The English demand for provisions for the navy and for the military forces in the Americas was unprecedented. Prices soared in 1776 and 1777. But the embargoes did create serious problems for merchants. Beef supplied to the French colonies was the poorer cow beef. In previous wars, this beef had continued to be taken by Dutch ships trading to the West Indies. The fact that the embargo was not relaxed until 1779 meant that merchants found themselves with this beef on their hands and no market for it.

The provision trade in peacetime was tied to transatlantic markets. These markets were at their peak in the 1760s and 1770s. The trade in butter was a little less tied to the West Indian market than the trade in beef. But alternative sources of supply made both trades vulnerable. Exports of butter to Europe dropped very sharply in the 1780s because of the continued improvement of European dairying; beef exports in the same decade fell sharply because for the first time Northern American supplies of provisions were beginning to make serious inroads into what had been a virtual Irish monopoly. In fact, a serious crisis would have affected the Irish livestock and dairying industries in the 1780s if the English demand for beef and butter had not expanded at that time. At the end of the 1750s, the prices of cattle and provisions, more or less stable for almost a century, rose sharply. The English Parliament was petitioned from all over the country for the repeal of the Cattle Acts. The prohibition of cattle was suspended in 1758; that of beef and butter in 1759; suspension became repeal in 1776. This had far-reaching implications for Irish agriculture. By 1800 the former markets had almost all disappeared. Apart from some market for butter in Spain and Portugal, Irish livestock husbandry was now geared almost exclusively to the English market. A growing population in England created an expanding market for Irish dairying. Exports of live cattle to England did not rise very significantly after their re-admission to the British market in 1758. The Napoleonic wars, however, with the inflated demand they had generated for salt beef to victual navies and armies, masked the necessity of adjustment in beef production in Ireland. Even taking into account official purchases not entered in the trade statistics and the shipments of live cattle, beef and cattle were of declining significance in Irish foreign trade generally in the 1780s and early 1790s. After 1815 the livestock industry had, for its survival, to re-orientate itself. The shipment of live animals was to acquire gradually the importance that it has traditionally held in modern Irish foreign trade.

In the provision trade dependence on the England market came late in the eighteenth century. In the linen trade access to the English market had been the very condition of its expansion. The English Treasury was to pay to the Huguenot Louis Crommelin, in return for the efforts he was to undertake to expand the industry, interest on his own investment, a salary and the salaries of three assistants. The growth of the industry has sometimes in consequence been represented as part of a compact in the late 1690s between the two countries in which the linen industry was to be promoted and the woollen industry discouraged. The most effective step in favour of the linen industry, however, was the granting of permission in 1696 for Irish linen to enter England duty free. The linen industry was poorly developed in England; most of the linen worn came from Northern Europe. The competitive advantage of duty-free entry made it possible for imports from Ireland to expand more rapidly than those from Northern Europe; in the second half of the eighteenth century, Irish linen gradually drove foreign linen out of the English market altogether. Other factors do not appear as decisive as the advantage of duty-free entry to the English market in the growth of the industry. The role of the Huguenots has often been emphasised. In fact, their role was very much a subordinate one. The industry was already expanding before their arrival, and if any one religious group had an especially close and extensive association with the growth of the industry in the north in the late seventeenth century and early decades of the eighteenth century, it was the Quakers. However, the significance of the religious factor has been exaggerated. Much of the linen industry in Armagh was in predominantly Catholic districts. With a large Catholic population, the value of linen cloth marketed in the contiguous linen districts of counties Monaghan and Meath in 1770 amounted to £200,000, a level exceeded only in counties Down, Armagh, Antrim and Derry. Government assistance was, of course, relevant to the growth of the industry. The Linen Board was established in 1711 to regulate the industry, to subsidise various projects and to spread the knowledge of methods and techniques throughout the country. Its endeavours helped undoubtedly to spread flax-growing and better methods. Yet the industry was at first slow to develop outside the northern counties generally, and when it spread rapidly in the closing two decades of the century in other regions, it did so at a time when the prestige of the Linen Board was waning. The impression the Board's activities give is that it helped, but that the industry's success or diffusion was due to other factors. Vital too in the expansion of the industry was the provision of working capital. Industrial methods in the industry were simple in the early eighteenth century and did not require much capital. But the countrymen who wove the cloth did not have the capital to market it; and the drapers who purchased the linen on the local markets in the north had little capital themselves. In fact, they borrowed money, short-term, in Dublin on the security of cloth itself or of bills of exchange. What this means is in effect that Dublin financed the growth of the industry. Without this constant stream of working capital supplied by merchants in Dublin the industry could not have expanded at anything remotely compared with its rate of growth in the 70 years after 1700. When the Linen Board opened in 1728 a White Linen Hall for the sale of bleached cloth, it did so in Dublin in recognition of the vital place Dublin had already acquired in marketing the cloth and in financing the industry.

In the early decades of the century the growth of the industry was most evident in the counties of the north-east – Antrim, Armagh, Down and Derry. But as the industry grew, it spread also into other counties, Tyrone, Monaghan and Cavan in Ulster, and Louth, Meath, Westmeath and Longford in Leinster. Spinning spread even more rapidly than weaving; the weaving districts could not produce enough yarn for their weavers, and by the middle of the century growing quantities of yarn were being produced in the western counties of Ulster, in Connaught and in the northern half of Leinster which were purchased by jobbers and carried to the yarn markets in the main centres of the industry. But the fact that the demand for woven cloth continued to grow meant that the conversion of yarn into cloth locally could easily follow. This had already happened by 1740 in counties such as Monaghan, Louth, Longford and to a lesser extent Westmeath. In co. Longford, for instance, Isaac Butler in his tour of this region at that time, found a thriving linen industry in Ballymahon and Mostrim. Though spinning for the market was spreading rapidly through counties such as Roscommon, Sligo and Galway, there was as yet little weaving for the market. By 1750 Robert French, a co. Galway landlord, had established a bleach green at Monivea, according to a contemporary report which commented that ' the steps taken by Robert French Esq. to introduce the linen manufacture may in time have the desired effect.' In 1770 there were 1,000 looms in co. Galway, and the value of the cloth sent to markets in the county in 1770 amounted to £40,000. By this time a significant amount of cloth was also woven in co. Roscommon, and in King's county and Queen's county.

Figures for the sale of cloth at markets understate the production of cloth because a large proportion of the cloth made outside Ulster was not exposed at local markets at all but sold in Dublin on the account of local landlords or manufacturers who had organised its production. This points to differences of organisation within the industry. Everywhere the cloth was woven in the homes of the weavers. In many districts the weavers wove the cloth on their own account, and sold it on local markets. Drapers purchased the brown or unbleached cloth at these markets, arranged for its bleaching and finally disposed of the bleached cloth on the Dublin market. In other areas, especially where weaving was of recent origin, the cloth was often made on the account of a landlord or entrepreneur who was seeking to promote the industry. The landlord's or entrepreneur's investment was often a substantial one. Where cloth went to market, the draper had few overheads and the bleacher none outside the business of bleaching. The entrepreneur who organised production, however, had many overheads. Not only did he see to the marketing of the cloth, but he ran his own bleach green, and had provided looms for his tenants or built houses to attract highly skilled weavers from farther afield. A severe depression struck the linen industry in the early 1770s : it was the only decade in which the industry failed to expand. Profits were low, perhaps a third of the weavers were unemployed and enterprises with high overheads had to give up business altogether. The failure of these enterprises has often suggested to historians that the depression in the early 1770s marked the end of the linen industry outside the northern counties. In fact, it did not mark the end of the industry in the south. In the 1780s the linen industry recovered remarkably. Exports almost doubled between 1783/4 and 1791/2, or trebled if we take a very depressed year, 1780/1. The labour force in the traditional weaving districts was already fully employed. There were no increases in labour productivity – the flying shuttle which speeded up the output of the individual weaver was not adopted until the nineteenth century. The remarkable expansion of the industry in the 1780s was feasible only because the industry spread with greater vigour than ever in centres outside the traditional manufacturing areas. The contrast with the previous decade, however, was that the industry in the south was no longer centralised. The initiative for expansion came largely from the country people themselves. Not only is this a feature throwing further doubt on the proposition that religious factors may have influenced the evolution of the linen industry, but it also casts doubts on an associated factor, the widely held assumption that the land system had encouraged the industry in the north through allegedly greater security of tenure and discouraged it in the rest of the island.

The growth of the industry in the 1780s was especially pronounced in some of the poorer regions. In co. Kerry, for instance, the value of linen sales at markets had been only £400 in 1770; in 1800 output was valued at £56,000. More remarkable still was co. Mayo. Spinning was already widespread, in parts universal, in the 1770s. Weaving spread with rapidity in the 1780s. By the end of the decade the small farmer was as likely to pay his rent from the sale of cloth as from the sale of agricultural produce. The Mayo poet Riocard Bairéad had, for instance, satirised a bailiff in 1788 in terms suggesting that linen was as likely as agricultural produce to pay the rent:

> Ba soirbh ag tógáil an chíos é,
> Is ba bheag aige mí nó dhó
> Nó go ndíoltaí an bhó ar an aonach,
> Nó an giota bhí ins an tseol.*

A newspaper report in 1790 noted that linen had become 'the principal source of the wealth and independence of the county'. The occasion of this comment was the opening with the assistance of Lord Lucan of a linen hall in Castlebar. The rapid expansion of the industry was reflected in the approaches to the towns as well as in the countryside. The Mayo smuggler, George O' Malley, has left us with a description of a visit to Ballina around 1800:

> We arrived at Ballina after passing through a populous suburb called Bunree and Ardmuree. The primitive looking domiciles were a hive of manufacturing energy and industry. The number of large pots outside the doors gave me to understand that these localities were abodes of linnen and woollen weavers. The 'click, click' of the shuttle, the smack of the reel and the chuzz of the spinning wheel soon convinced us that occupiers of mud hovels could enjoy the comforts of a palace provided that manufacturing industry held there its kingly sway. We entered some of these snuggeries and we found them as clean as the cabin of a man-of-war ship.

The linen market was in progress when O'Malley reached the centre of the town. He was told by an employee of the Linen Board that 2,000 webs of cloth (48,000 yards) would be sold and out of their produce at least £2,000 would be laid out 'on life necessaries and the rest of the money would be expended on the purchase of yarn'.

The significance of the linen industry lies in the fact that it was not confined to Ulster but was far flung in the island, increasingly

* 'He was pleasant in collecting the rent; a month or two, until the cow was sold at the fair or the piece of cloth in the loom, was readily agreed to'.

so as the century went by. No less significant was the fact that the industry was socially widespread in the sense that spinning provided a valuable supplement to their income for many labouring families and that weaving was resorted to by many small farmers as well as by specialist weavers. Spinning occupied the women and children. Earnings per woman or child might only amount to 1d or 2d a head per day, but in a period when the wages of a day labourer were as low as 6d and employment itself was intermittent, these earnings made all the difference between poverty and security. Seventeenth-century commentators had already noted how much idle time poor families had on their hands, and had rightly seen in this underemployment one of the causes of extensive rural poverty. The expansion of the textile industries in the eighteenth century provided welcome opportunities of gainful occupation; rural families had on the whole less leisure than in the past; the income the added occupation gained made poverty less universal.

The linen industry was not alone in increasing the opportunities of gain for the rural poor. The woollen industry expanded in the course of the eighteenth century. It was a substantial industry. Petty had estimated in 1672 that three times as much wool was worked up into cloth within the country as was exported. Much of the industry's expansion took place in the towns, more particularly in the case of 'cloth' or old drapery made from short-staple wool, expensive and requiring greater skill, as opposed to the lighter cheaper worsted or new drapery made from long-staple wool or a mixture of the two. Dublin was the main centre of the old drapery and cloth woven down the country was also finished there. Other important centres of the industry, especially for worsted fabrics, were Carrick-on-Suir and many of the towns and villages in co. Cork. In fact, the urban location of much of the industry was one of the weaknesses of the Irish woollen industry. High living costs meant that the weavers had to be paid high wages, and combination among urban weavers added to the employers' costs. In contrast, weaving in the linen industry was based on the countryside and on the villages. The English woollen industry too was in the countryside. Its relatively low costs were one reason why it could undersell Irish woollens and why a crisis was in the making for the Irish woollen industry in the closing decades of the century. Another reason was that master-manufacturers made too many types of cloth and that in consequence their weavers and finishers did not have the same expertise as their English counterparts, or their cloth the same quality. There was, of course, a tradition of cloth-making in the countryside, and in parts this did develop into pro-duction for the market, notably in Clare, Limerick, Waterford, Wicklow and the midlands. The urban or semi-urban weavers were organised by master-manufacturers; the farmer-weavers, on the other hand, sold their output on local markets.

The expansion in the woollen industry created significant employ-ment in weaving. The total output of new drapery or worsted cloth in the 1770s was of the order of 9–12 million yards, or about one-third of the output of linen. The employment content of the worsted branch was both substantial and growing. Requiring less skill than old drapery, intermediaries, as the industry grew, put much of the yarn out to families in the countryside beyond the traditional weav-ing towns and villages. Imports, though they grew, did not affect the industry adversely. Imports at their peak with over 700,000 yards in 1776/7 and 1777/8, were modest in relation to output. The level of those two years was, moreover, not exceeded until 1799/1800. Exports, however, made possible by the repeal of the 1699 act in 1779 were not only smaller than in 1698, but fell off rapidly after 1785. Old drapery fared less well. Based on the towns, it was more vulnerable, affected by high costs, inflexible organisation and an inelastic labour force. It was already in difficulties in the 1770s. Imports of old drapery at 378,077 yards in 1777/8 accounted for a high proportion of consumption, and they grew alarmingly in the 1780s and 1790s, reaching 2,232,415 yards in 1799/1800. The number of woollen workers in Dublin and its vicinity, the main centre of the old draperies, fell from 9,000 in 1768 to 4,038 in 1800. A particularly important factor in the decline of old drapery was a shortage of short-staple wool – the demand for long-staple wool suitable for worsted had encouraged its production at the expense of short-stapled.

As much of the weaving was conducted in or near urban centres, the significance of the industry's expansion for rural families often lay in the increased demand for yarn. A weaver, often a specialist worker, quickly wove yarn into cloth; spinning on the other hand was a slow and tedious operation, and the output of three or four spinners was barely sufficient to keep one weaver fully occupied. The spinning of worsted yarn increased enormously in the middle of the century. A labour shortage was being experienced in England at that time : in 1739 the import duties on yarn from Ireland were repealed. The Irish wool supply had fallen sharply from its former peaks. From the late 1740s, however, much of the wool was converted into yarn for the English market. The demand for wool pushed up prices in Ireland, cheap labour in spinning still left Irish yarn competitive on the British market, and the high prices offered for wool by the Irish master-combers halted for two or three decades the decline in sheep grazing in Ireland. The combing of the wool and its spinning into yarn were widespread in the midlands, the Suir valley and counties Cork and Kerry. The master-combers bought the wool at the fairs, had it combed, and then distributed it to country people to spin. The thousands of spinners spread throughout co. Cork were, for instance, supplied with wool purchased at the great wool fairs at Ballinasloe which came into prominence in the 1750s. The big combers in the south relied on Ballinasloe for their requirements; their needs, reflected in the high prices offered at the fairs, led to a rise in wool sales at the fairs in the 1770s, despite a decline in wool output as a whole. By the 1780s, however, high prices for grain had greatly accelerated the ploughing up of some of the grazing lands. Half the wool spun into worsted in the 1770s was for export. The export trade in yarn had all but disappeared by the early 1790s. It is probable that employment in spinning had contracted by half by that time. The significance of wool spinning in the period of its rapid expansion in the 1750s and 1760s was that it had provided extra income in parts of Ireland where landless labourers were already relatively numerous and where the linen industry had made either little or uneven headway. The shrinking of this supplementary income helps to account for the evidence of social deterioration among the labouring classes in parts of Munster in the last two decades of the century. The loss of income could have affected as many as 10,000 to 20,000 families. Fitzgibbon had singled out Munster when he claimed in 1787 that ' the lower order of the people are in a state of oppression, abject poverty, sloth, dirt and misery not to be equalled in any other part of the world '.

The significant expansion of the textile industries in Ireland dates from the 1730s; the growth of the linen industry at that time caught the attention of observers outside Ulster, and provided the stimulus for investment in the industry beyond a narrow base in the north. It was not the only factor in economic recovery. No less important – especially for farmers – was the recovery in farm prices.

In the 1730s this appeared to be evident only in beef, whose prices
held well in the second half of the 'thirties although all other agricultural prices plunged downwards. To contemporaries the 'thirties
appeared a decade of crisis. Imports and revenue were stagnant,
suggesting that there was little if any improvement in living standards outside Ulster in the first half of the decade, or in any part of
the country in the second half. The linen industry was depressed
in the second half of the decade; the only agricultural product
which augured well was beef. But cattle farming was regarded as
anti-social. Some contemporaries thought that it displaced people,
and caused poverty. They also thought that it led to a decline in
tillage. Two bad harvests just before mid-decade appeared to give
substance to this conviction. Some of the contemporary writings of
this time convey a sense of gloom : the most relevant example is
perhaps Berkeley's *Querist* which, published in 1735, followed the
poorest harvests of the decade. The extent of the swing to pasturage
was exaggerated. It was in part the expression of a fear already
reflected in the 1720s in writings such as those of Swift or in the
measure taken by Parliament in 1727 when it tried to compel
larger occupiers to till at least five per cent of their acreage. The
claim was taken up again with vigour in the 1760s. At that time
Catholics were campaigning against the statutory limitation of leases
granted to Catholics to a term of 31 years. Leases of 31 years or less
were declared to be short ones, and the uncertainty thereby engendered to have driven Catholic tenants into grazing at the expense
of tillage. This claim has little or no substance; it is the old fear
employed in a new guise as an argument intended to influence
public opinion to relax the statutory restrictions on Catholics.

In fact, the reduction in tillage, to the extent that it took place,
was not disastrous. Grain prices had fallen to low levels, in the
1730s to extraordinarily low levels. The increase of cattle grazing
at the expense of wheat growing – the cereal in which the price fall
was sharpest – was a means of keeping rural poverty at bay at a
time when low prices impoverished farmers year after year. The reso-
lution of the Irish House of Commons in 1735 against the levying
of tithes on pasture has frequently been described as a potent factor
in accounting for the advance of pasturage. It was in fact nothing
of the kind, although the bitter controversy between churchmen and
gentry about tithes on pasturage – perhaps even more than the social
preoccupations of the time – riveted the attention of contemporaries

on cattle grazing. Later writers sometimes suggested that falling tillage prices were a consequence of English policy. In 1673 and 1689 bounties had been granted on corn exports from England when prices were low. This legislation had not, however, adversely affected the Irish farmer then or in the generation following. What did alter the situation was the development of mixed farming on the low-cost sandy soils of eastern England, in which sheep were folded on the wheat lands. The cheap sheep and wheat of eastern England explain the contraction in Irish wool exports in the eighteenth century and the replacement of a wheat surplus by an import deficit within a few years of the halycon prosperity of the Irish grain farmer in 1711-14.

There was no progressive worsening in cereal output. The country remained more than self-sufficient in its main food cereal, oats; it had a surplus of barley until the early 1740s; and, although the country had become a net importer of wheat, domestic production accounted for a high proportion of consumption even in a bad year. The level of imports of meal, flour and unground corn in the year 1729/30 was exceeded in only five years in the next 20 years – 1734/5, 1735/6, 1741/2, 1745/6 and 1746/7 – and only in two years – 1745/6 and 1746/7 – by a significant margin. The largest imports in the 1750s – 1754/5 – were only a half of the level of 1745/6. Imports in 1766/7 – the highest of the 1760s – had been exceeded in seven years of the preceding decade. Imports in 1770/1 were higher than in any year in the 1760s but had been exceeded in two years in the 1750s. Thereafter, the level of imports fell off sharply : even after the bad harvests of 1782 and 1783 they did not reach levels comparable to those in the past. In the intervals between bad years, domestic supplies often proved sufficient, imports even of wheat falling to very low levels. The famine of 1728/9 was followed by a bumper harvest in 1730. Following the famine of 1740/1, grain prices fell in the second half of 1742 and in 1743 to levels even below those of 1730. Good harvests occurred again at the end of the 1740s, the end of the 1750s and early 1760s, and after the early 1770s. What seems outstanding in the period is an abnormal degree of harvest failure in 1728, 1740, 1744 and the long run of bad harvests in the 1750s, the year 1756-7 being a year of near-famine. Famine in Ireland was caused not simply by the fact that the Irish harvest had failed but that harvests had failed elsewhere as well. In consequence, imports to Ireland, though they rose, did not rise sufficiently. England, for instance, which normally had a large net surplus for export, was a net importer of grain in 1728, 1729, 1757 and 1758, and in 1740 and 1741 had a net export which was among the most meagre of the first half of the century. A poor harvest in 1739, followed by an appalling winter, preceded a more complete failure of the harvest in 1740. The year 1740-1 was a year of famine, fever adding to its horror. Deaths may have been in the region of 200,000 to 400,000, and in the view of one commentator its incidence may have been heavier than that of the Great Famine of 1845/8. The significance of imports is shown in the failure of the harvest in 1744. The harvest had not failed in England, and grain poured into Ireland in the spring and summer of 1745. Charles O'Connor of Belanagare in co. Roscommon noted in his diary at the time that the failure seemed even more extensive than in 1740. Yet no famine occurred. Imports of meal, flour and unground grain soared to 351,112 quarters in the year ended 25 March 1746 compared with a mere 90,710 quarters in 1741/2. The significance of imports, concentrated in the spring and summer, is that they maintained much of the population after the inadequate domestic harvest and the potatoes had been consumed. The grain imported in the years ended March 1745 and 1746, most of it arriving in the spring and summer of 1745, would have sufficed to keep roughly one-seventh to one-quarter of the population alive for a half year.* In practice, of course, as people did not subsist exclusively on imports, they must have been distributed among an even greater proportion of the population. In the serious failure of 1756/7, £12,000 was disbursed out of official funds by the Lord Lieutenant, the Duke of Bedford, for the relief of the poor in different parts of Ireland: in June and July 1757 cargoes of grain were brought to Newry, Derry, Dublin, Waterford and Belfast. It was the near-famine of this year that led the Irish Parliament, at its next session, to institute with effect from 1758 a series of bounties on the transport of Irish grain, ground and unground, to Dublin. The idea was to stimulate grain growing in rural Ireland and to increase the domestic content of Dublin's consumption.

There can be little doubt that grain was important in the diet of the population at large. Grain was important in cultivation too,

* Excluding barley and malt, only part of which would have been used as a foodstuff, imports would have fed one-seventh of the population; including them, one-quarter.

especially among small farmers and in the eastern half of the
country generally. Louth and Meath in particular were grain-growing counties. Kildare was even more a tillage county, a petition to
Parliament in November 1765 stating, for instance, that 'the inhabitants of the said county are, for the most part, grain farmers
and poor'. Kilkenny grew grain extensively, little mills being dotted
along the banks of the rivers throughout the county. Even in the
mid-1750s, despite poor domestic harvests, Irish wheat accounted
for half the consumption of the city of Dublin. At the end of the
1760s the proportion of Irish wheat in market sales in Dublin had
risen to over two-thirds for the two years from 1st December 1769
to 1st December 1771. In the year 1 December 1769 – 1 December
1770, a year of serious shortage in Ireland, the proportion of
Irish was slightly less than half, in the following year, 90 per cent.

Grain was not only extensively cultivated; it was also immensely
important in the diet of the countryman and townsman. It is
necessary to stress this as it is often assumed that the diet of the
rural Irishman was largely or exclusively a potato diet. The potato
was, of course, widely cultivated, and figured in the diet prom-
inently. But it did not dominate the diet. Oaten bread was widely
consumed. Moreover, the significance of the potato as a foodstuff
in general consumption was seasonal. It was consumed in the winter
and spring. Thus, those above the poverty level consumed bread
and potatoes in the winter and spring, and the diet of the poor
themselves relied extensively on oatmeal from the spring onwards.
When grain prices were high in the autumn of 1765 a parliamentary committee of enquiry reported that 'potatoes are a principal
part of the food of the common people in many parts of this kingdom, and that the failure of these roots is one principal cause of the
present scarcity'. The committee also noted that the 'deficiency
of spring corn is another principal cause of the present scarcity'.
The contemporary definition of the poor was not an elastic one.
By the poor, contemporaries signified cottiers and labourers in the
countryside; unskilled labourers in the towns. Farmers and rural
craftsmen in the countryside and artisans and tradesmen in the
towns were regarded as being, by contemporary standards, above
the poverty line. To contemporaries poverty lay in economic
insecurity. As a contemporary official noted with reference to the
ability of cottiers to pay the hearth tax of 2s in 1792 : 'In years
of plenty and cheapness, with an industrious family and sobriety

this class may be able to pay the tax; but in case of the reverse, or any material misfortune, the tax might be distressing. Very many of this class are exempted from the tax under the present regulations'. Here is the rural social class which relied heavily on the potato : they could count neither on renting cheaply enough land to grow other crops as well as potatoes nor on their ability to supplement their diet with purchased foodstuffs. In the language of the day, a potato diet was associated with poverty. A petition from the high sheriff and gentlemen of Limerick to the House of Commons in 1768 described potatoes as 'the common food' of the poor; in October 1776 potatoes were described in Kilkenny as 'this chief food of the poor '. Even in Dublin potatoes were by 1774 'that great necessary of life ' for the poor. Poverty was associated with a general dependence on the potato. The real badge of poverty was continued dependence on the potato through the seasons. The line :

*Ba sógh leis prátaí is dríodar bláthaighe d'fhagháil mar bhiadh**

in Eoghan O'Súilleabháin's *Barántas do Dhomhnaill O Dálaigh* as a vehicle of ridicule reveals some of the social contempt which such a diet drew from contemporaries in the Irish-speaking countryside itself.

The grain harvest was immensely important in economic life. A bad harvest meant a scarcity of food and rising food prices. A good harvest did not always make the farmer happy – if the harvest was superabundant, for instance, prices fell dramatically – but the benefit of lower prices raised the real incomes of townspeople and rural labourers and artisans, and rising real incomes stimulated industry. A good harvest too, meant that exports of grain increased or imports fell; a bad harvest entailed a massive rise in imports. Fluctuations in economic activity from one season to another were to a large extent tied up with the outturn of the harvest. Roughly half the harvests were likely to be average or above; the other half below average. In consequence there was a certain regularity about the fluctuations in economic activity; a good harvest was followed by all the signs of general prosperity – buoyant revenue and rising output of industrial goods; a bad harvest on the other hand depressed economic activity, revenue and industrial output slackening for a year or two. Within each decade of the century, there

* ' He enjoyed potatoes and the dregs of buttermilk as a diet '.

were one or two prosperous years, one or two extremely bad years, the remaining years being characterised by an intermediate degree of prosperity or depression. The years of economic crisis were as a rule years when the harvest was bad. A particularly important factor in the depression that followed a bad harvest was the rise in imports. The rise in imports led to a reduced balance of trade or on a few occasions to a deficit. On all counts, credit restriction was inevitable. Merchants, faced with a falling demand for their wares, were less likely than usual to have surplus funds which they would lend short-term to others on the security of bills of exchange. Because imports rose relatively to exports, bills of exchange financed by earnings overseas were relatively scarce and were in effect rationed by a rise in the rate of exchange. Faced with these difficulties, many merchants went bankrupt. Many of their customers proving insolvent, the solvency of the banks often became suspect as well, the bankers in consequence experiencing a ' run ' by the holders of their notes, anxious to exchange them for cash.

The banking crises of the eighteenth century followed general difficulties in the economy. The banks have, of course, been represented as hopelessly reckless, and bank failures as endemic. In fact, however, bank failures followed the rhythm in economic activity closely, and few, if any, banks failed in years when business conditions were good and confidence general. The Irish banks, like banks in other countries, had been established by individuals with surplus economic resources. The great majority of banks were established by merchants, who could invest in banking some of the profits of their trade, or by land agents who, because they held the cash accounts of landlords, found that they had as a rule idle balances which could be used, in the short-term, for their own purposes. Bankers performed a two-fold role. First of all, they lent money on the security of bills of exchange which they purchased. Secondly, by selling and buying bills of exchange, they facilitated the transmission of money both within Ireland and between England and Ireland. A bill of exchange, where it was drawn on a party in another centre, constituted a claim to credit in that centre. Merchants could convert such credits into cash by selling them to a banker; if the merchant or an agent had no credit in a centre where he required one, he could purchase a bill of exchange from the banker. In this way, bankers handled much of the country's foreign exchange; through their correspondents in the countryside they also handled much of the inland movement of money within the country as well.

Dublin, and on a smaller scale Cork, were the only extensive centres of banking. The growth of banking had been particularly rapid in the 1720s. By the end of that decade the number of bankers in Dublin had risen to six. The number of banking houses reached its peak in the prosperous years at the outset of the 1750s, when eight operated in Dublin and some banking was or had been recently conducted in Waterford, Clonmel, Athlone, Belfast and Galway. The number of bankers was thus small. One reason for this was that many banking services were provided incidentally by merchants for other merchants and for private individuals. A bill of exchange could be purchased from a merchant as well as from a banker, and merchants were often eager to buy bills as well because they had constant need of money in other towns. Some merchants provided these services extensively and hence were for all practical purpose bankers. A banker usually issued promissory notes payable to bearer. But so did many merchants in the city of Cork, a circumstance which made it particularly difficult to distinguish between banker and merchant in that city. An Act of Parliament in 1756, following the failure of three merchant banks in Dublin and two in Galway in 1754-5, had prohibited bankers from engaging in foreign trade as merchants. However, the act did not prohibit merchants from engaging in the issue of notes payable to bearer provided that they did not describe themselves as bankers. The bank failures in 1759 – three banks in Dublin* – made financial houses and public alike wary of notes payable to bearer. From 1759 to 1793 there were only four or five private banks in Dublin. Cork, Limerick, Waterford and Belfast were the only other towns in which new banking businesses were opened within the same period. But without issuing notes payable to bearer there were many merchants with whom private individuals lodged money and who performed the vital banking functions of providing short-term credit and remitting money around which the whole economic life of the country revolved.

The most serious financial failures, involving bankruptcies of merchants and runs on the banks, came as a rule in the wake of bad harvests. The rise in imports of grain following the bad harvest of

* The Bank of Malone, Clements and Gore failed in 1759, not in 1758 as stated in the standard accounts.

1726 and the highest adverse rates of exchange experienced in the 1720s were behind the crisis which culminated in the major banking failure of the 1720s in Dublin in 1727. The huge grain imports after the disastrous harvest of 1744 were reflected in a prolonged restriction of credit in the course of 1745. Weakened by this, the banks were subject to a severe run during the Jacobite scare in October 1745. No bank failed, but one had temporarily to close its doors. The sharp rise in grain imports in 1752 and 1753 led to the most serious crisis yet experienced. Dillons' bank in Dublin failed early in 1754. The crisis deepened even further by the spring of the following year: two banks failed in Dublin in March 1755, and two in Galway. Following bad harvests, another major crisis was experienced in 1770-1 with the bankruptcy of many merchants and one Dublin bank temporarily closing its doors. Not all failures were due exclusively to harvest failure. But, whatever the reason, tight credit or widespread failure among merchants or bankers occurred in years when the balance of trade had contracted sharply and credit was in consequence severely curtailed. The only exception to the association between a deteriorating balance and a financial crisis was the tight credit situation of the first half of 1767, in part the result of slower cash returns in linen, leading to the collapse of many business houses. For even in this case the influence of a poor harvest is not irrelevant. Grain imports were exceptionally high in the year ended 25 March 1758 and the inland movement of grain abnormally low in the year ended 25 March 1767.* Poor linen sales could also adversely affect the country's exports, and hence reduce the favourable balance. The bad years in the linen trade often preceded or followed years of poor harvests: a credit system struggling to overcome one crisis was faced with a fresh one. Two years of harvest failure at the turn of the decade were followed by a fall in sales of linen in 1772/3 and 1773/4: in this lie the origins of the credit crisis of 1772-3 in which the house of Colebrooke went out of business in Dublin. In 1782/3 linen sales fell sharply; prices had also proved disappointing on the livestock fairs in the preceding autumn of 1781. This was the beginning of the long credit squeeze of 1782-4. Bad harvests in 1782 and 1783 made the situation more serious, and a major credit crisis affected the country's business life in 1784.

---

* There was also a remarkably harsh spring in 1766 with snow for weeks on the ground.

The credit crises of 1759-60 and 1777-8 seem to have been due exclusively to bad linen sales. Sales fell in 1758/9 and 1759/60. An acute crisis developed in the autumn of 1759 with bank failures in Cork and Dublin and widespread bankruptcy among business houses. The severe credit crisis of 1777-8 was caused by a sharp slump in linen sales. The war with America did not have a direct adverse effect on Ireland. But it caused a depression in England, and the English depression was reflected by the autumn of 1777 in slow sales and poor prices for Irish linen. The fall in exports in 1778/9 was made all the sharper by a poor flax season in 1777 which reduced the raw material of the industry. Reduced output, low prices and negligible profits made 1778 a disastrous year for the linen industry. Adverse rates of exchange from the autumn of 1777 heralded the beginning of an acute credit crisis. Unemployment was widespread in the towns. In the countryside the linen weavers were underemployed. Reduced incomes were reflected in a decline in the consumption of dutiable commodities; from the end of 1777 government revenue slumped; the government had to borrow from the banks. Credit became very tight. In April 1778 the banking house of Finlay had temporarily to close its doors, and three other houses failed entirely. Bankruptcies among merchants were widespread. The reduction in credit made it difficult for buyers to purchase cattle and wool at the fairs. Prices fell at the fairs, and many cattle and much wool remained unsold. Manufacturers laid off workers. Unemployment deepened. It was made all the more serious by the fact that emigration which had often relieved distress in the linen manufacturing districts of the north in time of economic dislocation was temporarily halted by the war with the rebellious colonies. A sense of economic crisis was pervasive. It was the second critical situation within a decade. For the first time in the century the output of linen had stagnated over a decade taken as a whole. The difficult economic situation of the early 1770s was reflected in a fall in rents during the decade. In 1778 arrears began to mount as well.

This precarious situation coincided with the political unrest associated with the Volunteer Movement. The combined political and economic unrest was responsible for the widespread formation of non-importation agreements from the early months of 1779, intended to cut the import bill and to create employment for Irish workers thrown into idleness by the recession. Irish public opinion, and in Parliament the opposition as well, had from the start shown a sympathy for the cause of the American colonies. Resentment began to build up against English policy since 1776. At first it revolved around the embargoes. But the non-importation agreements in 1779 directed resentment more sharply towards economic matters. The British Parliament had already granted a concession in 1778, permitting Irish exports, with the exception of woollens, to the colonies. The non-importation agreements and the Volunteer Movement caused a ferment in 1779. The display of the Volunteers on King William's birthday on 4 November was militant; government support within the Commons was also defecting and the Lord Lieutenant no longer able to count on a majority for the executive's measures. Faced with this situation, the English government had to concede the Irish demand for ' free trade '. By the end of 1779 the acts prohibiting the export of woollens and glass from Ireland were repealed; early in 1780 the prohibition on the importation of foreign hops was repealed, and Ireland was permitted to import all goods directly from the colonies. The concessions came at a time when economic conditions were recovering. There was an inflow of money in 1779. Significantly, the non-importation agreements did not spread in the northern half of the country, and the reason may have been the rapid recovery of the linen trade in 1779.

4

Land and Industry
1730-1793

Economic life was marked by fluctuation, good years giving way to bad and difficult years being followed in turn by better. Irish agriculture was closely allied to market conditions. In looking at the condition of the countryside at any point of time, it is necessary to know whether conditions in that year were below or above average. In fact, rural conditions were far from being chronically depressed in the way often suggested by historians. Moreover, rural diet was not confined to the potato. The countryside, and the social classes dwelling in it, represented a complex pattern. Its complexity is overlooked in the concept of a hidden Ireland which is often applied to the rural Ireland of the eighteenth century. Eighteenth-century poetry from Munster displays at first sight an obsession with the rents paid to the landlords. In fact, the resentment is that of the former proprietors or of a class identified with them. The rents paid to landlords, and the leases which expressed them, were resented because they were symbols of the great changes in land-ownership, which had occurred in the second half of the seventeenth century. The poetry reflected the nostalgia of the Gaelic upper class for its old position, and expressed the hope of restoration. To lesser countrymen, a lease, far from appearing oppressive, represented a degree of comfort and security. The Ulster poet, Peadar O Doirnín, free from the aristocratic nostalgia which underlies the Munster poetry of the eighteenth century, actually wrote:

Níl aon duine bocht i muinín cúpla mart
Nach dtabharfaidh mé bearach is féar dó,
Nó go gcruinneochaidh siad stoc is maoin mhor ar cnoc
Is go bhfaighidh siad téarma is léagsaí.*

Leases to Catholics were confined to a term of 31 years under the
penal laws. In fact, such leases were quite long. Contemporaries
did not always recognise this. In the 1720s and 1730s, when contemporary writers were anxious to encourage investment at a time
when the returns on investment in agriculture were low and the
country in their view underpopulated, much longer leases were
advocated as a means of improvement. Later in the century, however, opinion was generally of the opinion that long leases had
proved harmful and had acted as a disincentive to investment. In
the late seventeenth century and again in the early eighteenth
century, many landlords had granted long leases when long-term
prospects had seemed poor. The beneficiaries of long leases, however, often took little interest in the management of their lands
and sublet the land on shorter leases to undertenants. They were
secure in the tenure of their land on a long lease set at a low rent,
while they were able to take advantage of the subsequent rise in
rents in their subletting policies. Thus, long leases, regarded in the
1720s and 1730s as a sign of improvement, were frowned on later
by the advocates of improvement and landlords alike. Improvers
frowned on them because they admitted of substantial incomes
without any direct effort or investment. Landlords disapproved of
them for the same reason, as many landlords were, in fact, improvers. They also had their own selfish reasons, as a large estate set
out in long leases precluded a rise in landlords' incomes, though
costs generally were rising after the 1730s. Under the penal laws
the rent of land let to a Catholic was to be not less than two-thirds
of the annual value of the property leased. In fact, this was unen-
forcible. Otherwise the substantial investment by Catholics in
livestock in grazing and dairying districts could not have taken
place. The proviso could have been readily enforced only against a
middleman, because his head rent and the income from sub-rents
were readily identifiable. But in practice it seems that, though its
enforcement against middlemen may have been contemplated on

---

* 'There is no poor person in charge of a couple of cattle to whom I will not
give a heifer and grass until they acquire stock and great wealth on a hill
and they obtain tenure and a lease '.

occasion, the proviso proved a dead letter. The restriction on long leases was not of great consequence to the ordinary occupier. It mainly affected well-to-do Catholics who would have done still better from sub-letting their lands if they had been able to take long leases at a time when rents were low. Long leases were not in themselves an unmixed blessing. Their benefit to their holder depended on the rent at which they were taken and whether good prospects held out. In the economic difficulties of the first decade of the eighteenth century or of the 1770s, the very rigidity of the lease created difficulties, for instance, for tenants who had rented lands at high rents around 1700 or in the 1760s and then had to experience the low prices of the first decade of the eighteenth century or the economic difficulties of the 1770s respectively. On the other hand, when prices rose, as they did throughout the greater part of the second half of the century, the rigidity of a lease was very much to the tenant's benefit. Rent was fixed for 31 years or more : the prices realised by farm products rose almost year after year. It was this circumstance, and not a clearly defined tenant right, which explains why a tenant selling his interest in the remaining years of a lease could realise a substantial cash sum from the incoming occupier. In 1778, the restriction on leases taken by Catholics was removed. Its removal did not prove of great significance because it came at a time when a policy of granting shorter leases to Catholic and Protestant tenants alike was being adopted.

The granting of shorter leases helped to undermine the middlemen. Landlords were eager to eliminate the middlemen, and in some instances were able to do so extensively. The middlemen eliminated, the landlord granted leases directly to the occupying tenants. The extent of the middleman system has often been exaggerated. But its undermining was a long-drawn-out policy because the middlemen often held very long leases, in many instances leases which were in effect perpetuities. Middlemen were to be found in many parts of the country, but in most districts they were not universal. The system was entrenched in the poorer parts of the south-west. Middlemen were not always drones. Many of them farmed directly an extensive acreage in addition to subletting land. Moreover, they served a useful function in the dairying districts in providing capital for the developments of dairying. In Waterford, Cork and Kerry, they rented cattle as well as land to small dairy farmers in return for an annual payment, in cash or part in kind per cow. The middlemen obnoxious to improvers because of their hard-drinking, idle ways were those of the dairying districts of Cork and Kerry. It is, in fact, their way of life which is eulogised in the Munster poetry of the eighteenth century.

Agriculture was dominated by the farmers holding leases from a landlord or from a middleman. In grazing districts individual farms were often large. In grain-growing areas farms were small. Small though the farms were, and badly housed though the farmers often were, they had some capital. The possession of a stock of capital, however small, marked farmer off sharply from labourer and cottier. Arthur Young, the English agricultural expert who toured Ireland in the late 1770s, thought their capital deficient by English standards. Each farmer, however, owned some livestock, draught animals, farm implements, ploughs and carts. The contrast was regional as well as social. North co. Meath was, for instance, a grain-growing region of small farms. The poet, Uilliam O Maoil Chiaráin, living in Machaire Cluain in Monaghan at the time, wistfully recalled the more prosperous farming life in the region of north Meath where he had formerly lived with its haggards full of corn, patterns at which the country people gathered and meat for sale on stalls at markets ('*an fheoil 'na spólaibh ins na stallaibh dhá dhíol*').* By contrast Monaghan and south Armagh seemed very poor indeed. The potato was already prominent in the diet there; the smallholders migrated as seasonal labourers at least as far back as the mid-century to co. Meath in the haycutting and harvesting seasons. As late as 1759 the countryside south of Newry presented a primitive picture: ' The cabins one sees on the sides of the hills are the most miserable huts I ever saw, built with sods and turf, no chimney, the door made of a hurdle, the smoke goes all out of the door, the cocks and hens, pigs, goats and if perchance they have a cow, inhabit the same dwelling.' Such families could make little out of agriculture. Hence the importance of migration to many of them : after saving the rich harvest of co. Meath they returned to save their own meagre one. For such families the spread of the textile industry was of immense importance. In fact, the spread of the textile industries transformed such regions in the course of the century. Mayo, for instance, a poor county in agricultural terms, experienced a dramatic improvement in the closing

* ' Shoulders of meat being sold on stalls '.

decades of the century. What it entailed is shown in George O'Malley's description of the market in Ballina:

> In a street which shot straight as an arrow south from the cross, the meat market was held. Each side of the street was lined with a row of tables and stalls from end to end. There was a large quantity of animal food for sale and from the thronged state of the market I concluded that Ballina was a place of unusual prosperity. . . . We returned to the Cross and saw a long line of tables running westward with piles of felt hats for sale. Opposite in another long line, the brogue markets had their standings arranged. Hatters and brogue makers were exchanging their value for money fast.

In regions producing cattle or grain for the market, farms were not subdivided readily. Farmers were reluctant to break up a farm; marriage itself did not necessarily take place at an early age; and a bride had to have a substantial dowry. A century later on the eve of the Great Famine the restraints on subdivision showed in the contrasts in farm size between Leinster, most of Munster and east Connaught and the rest of the country and within the same county between one district and another. Farmers subdivided land extensively only where agricultural output for the market was limited. This was the case in much of Ulster where linen rather than agricultural produce paid the rent, and landlord and tenant alike did not frown on subdivision. Unchecked subdivision operated only in such regions and on inferior or upland soil where commercialised agriculture did not exist, or on land freshly colonised from the waste. The fact that land was often held in partnership between countrymen under the rundale system facilitated subdivision. A whole group of peasants took a lease in partnership. Sons and relatives easily acquired a stake in the land and as population grew the landlord had less and less knowledge of the actual occupiers.

The cottier afforded a sharp contrast with the tenant farmer. The latter knew real want only in the worst years of the century; the former lived permanently at the subsistence line. The cottier who rented land for a nominal rent from a farmer and discharged his rent in labour reckoned by the day to the farmer enjoyed some degree of security. The cottier who was not able to obtain land from a prospective employer was in a more vulnerable situation. He paid an inflated cash rent for a plot and had to seek employment where it was available. Cash incomes often fell short of the rent. Unless there was supplementary income from spinning life was very precarious. It was only in the late eighteenth century that the pig became commonplace in the holdings of cottiers. The sale of a pig constituted a useful cash income; like the family the pig was fed from potatoes. Unlike the farmers, cottiers as a class fared badly in the period of rising prices. Their rents rose while their nominal or cash wages changed little. Significantly, relatively fewer cottiers possessed a cow in the late eighteenth century than previously; for the poorest families the necessity to buy milk from local farmers was an added drain on their scant income.

Farmers, and likewise smallholders who were able to supplement their farming incomes from textile activity, fared well in the eighteenth century. They had some cash to spend, local markets flourished in consequence, they had their own definite ideas of conventional comfort, and the dowries which they accumulated for daughters show that they could save a little. The dairy farmers who rented a herd of cattle from a middleman stood to gain from the rise in prices where the rent to the middleman was paid in cash. But in much of Cork and Kerry, the rent continued to be paid in kind; the middleman rather than the dairyman gained from the rise in butter prices, and the latter made only a bare living. The most acute evidence of poverty in eighteenth-century Ireland came from the dairying districts of the south; the dairymen fared badly; lower still in the social scale and in even greater poverty were the cottiers sometimes employed as cow herds and often eking out a bare living on a potato patch.

The landlords by no means played an inactive role in the economic life of the countryside. Their leasing policy changed significantly in the second half of the eighteenth century: this in itself enhanced their function in rural life as, where very long leases or perpetuities had been granted, the landlord had sacrificed both income and control. Taking a more active interest in their estates, landlords often invested substantial sums of capital. The improving landlord was quite common in the second half of the century. Leases were renewed on favourable terms for tenants who undertook to build or to drain or ditch. Landlords were often ground landlords of towns, and the remarkable amount of building taking place in the second half of the century would not have been feasible if they did not grant building leases on favourable terms. Landlords also invested in estate villages, in market houses, and on occasion in houses or cottages on tenants' farms. They often sought to encourage industry by attracting skilled weavers, building houses for them and providing bleach greens. They encouraged the building of roads and canals as well, and much capital from the landed classes was sunk in the turnpike roads and in the canals.

Absentee landlords have been given too much significance in the story of rural Ireland. Between the 1720s and 1770s the rent roll of Irish landlords perhaps trebled. Rents to absentees doubled. As a proportion of the total, absentee rents fell from a fourth or a sixth in the 1720s to an eighth in the 1770s. In any event, a large proportion of landed incomes was spent outside the estate. As far as a rural district itself was concerned, it was immaterial whether some of the landlord's time and income was spent in Dublin or London. A nominally resident landlord was not necessarily that much more beneficial economically than an absentee. Absentees were, however, as a class unpopular : the size of the remittances was large enough to disrupt the foreign exchange market in a year when export income fell, and the idea that absentees should be taxed was politically popular. Absentees, however, did not always fail to take an interest in their estates. Many of the larger estates were very well managed by professional agents : the absentee kept himself informed of their management by an exchange of correspondence week by week with the agent, and the improvement of the estate and the welfare of the tenants were discussed in detail.

It is, of course, widely held that landlord and tenant had little in common. Alienation of tenant from the land system is held to have been complete, and the countryside after 1760 to have existed in a state of suppressed land war. This is far from the truth. The unrest which made itself felt from the 1760s often had very specific causes. The Oakboys in the north in the 1760s had been occasioned by resentment caused by the county cess or rate for road building : the Steelboys in the 1770s by steep renewal fines on Lord Donegal's estate, and Whiteboys in the south by enclosure of commons around 1760. A demand for tenant-right by name does not occur in the agrarian grievances at all. Nor do the two main features which made up the nineteenth-century concept of tenant-right crop up – compensation for improvements and security of tenure – in a direct form. In fact, the concept of compensation for improvements did not arise, as it was considered that a tenant was amply compensated for his efforts over the long period characteristic of eighteenth-century leases. The issue of security of tenure did arise indirectly. The general practice was that, where a lease fell in, the occupying tenant had a right to renewal subject to paying the new rent. This did not normally create difficulties, but in a bad year, if the new rent was contested by a local farmer and the farm given to an outsider over his head, the traditional idea of relative security of tenure became a live issue, and was on occasion reflected in violence against the incoming tenant or the agent. The only continuous resentment running through the agrarian unrest in all the provinces over the decades was opposition to the payment of tithes to the Established Church. This obligation was obnoxious to both Catholics and Presbyterians who had to maintain their own churches in addition to paying tithes to the Established Church. Resentment of the tithes was shared by all rural classes, large farmers as well as small, and often by members of the Established Church as well as by others. Cork, Tipperary and Kilkenny were the counties in which manifestations of Whiteboy unrest were most serious. In the course of the 1790s the organisation of the Whiteboys – or Defenders as they were often called at this stage – had become more elaborate and had spread into further counties. On occasions they gathered together in hundreds, and sometimes raided gentlemen's houses for arms. The improved and spreading organisation of the Defenders did not, however, derive in the main from agrarian motives. Clashes between Catholics and Protestants in the northern counties from the 1780s had spread religious fears – the very name Defender suggests a defensive intent wider than the narrow and local aims of Whiteboys or Right Boys – and a growing sectarian consciousness was a novel, and in the rapidly deteriorating political and religious situation in the 1790s, effective organising bond.

Ireland was a predominantly rural country. In 1725 roughly one-twelfth of the population lived in the eight largest towns; today the proportion is about a third. Most of the towns were small. Ross, a town of the second rank, had only 300 houses in the 1680s. Ennis, a less active town, had a mere 120 houses at that time. A total of 787 houses was sufficient to make Lisburn the tenth largest town in 1725. In 1798, on the other hand, there were 23 borough towns (i.e. towns returning members of Parliament) alone with a larger number of houses than Lisburn had in 1725, and there were in all

58 borough towns with 300 houses or more, that is with a likely population in excess of 1,800. Two cities stood out from the remainder because of their size : Dublin and Cork. Throughout the century, Dublin was far and away the largest town in the island. Significantly, its population was already growing rapidly in the second and third decades of the century while the national population grew slowly : the number of houses in Dublin rose from 9,505 in 1718 to 11,466 in 1725. The reason for this was that changes in economic organisation enhancing its importance were reflected in its population. The proportion of the revenue from exports and imports collected in Dublin rose from 40 per cent in the second half of the seventeenth century to over 50 per cent in the eighteenth century. The city also handled most of the island's foreign banking requirements, excepting those of Cork. Dublin merchants provided the working capital of the linen industry in the northern half of the county; this sufficed to ensure that for the greater part of the century the bulk of linen was exported through Dublin. The capital's importance was also reflected in inland transport. The first stage coaches radiated from Dublin. In the early 1730s coaches ran to Drogheda, Kinnegad and Kilkenny; soon coaches served Athlone and Newry, and for a very short time Belfast itself. At the end of the century, Dublin had a population not much below 200,000.

Cork, with a population in the late eighteenth century of 70,000 to 80,000 (plus some 20,000 in adjacent rural districts) was the only town which could remotely bear comparison with Dublin. Limerick, alone of other towns, had more than 20,000. Cork had an extensive trade in yarn, butter and beef. Apart from Dublin, it was the only extensive banking centre in the country. It was easily the most cosmopolitan port in Ireland. Much of Dublin's trade was with Britain. Cork, on the other hand, supplied provisions to every country in Europe, and ships bearing the flags of most European maritime nations also loaded provisions there for their colonies. Cork was, in fact, one of the major ports of the entire Atlantic economy in this period. The city was at the peak of its commercial prosperity at this time : its population around 1810 was probably not exceeded until well into the twentieth century.

In 1725 eight of the ten major towns were ports. Kilkenny, the only large inland town, ranked next in importance to Dublin, Cork and Limerick, a circumstance reflected in the existence from an early date of a stage-coach route from the city to Dublin. Of the 23 major towns or cities in 1798 six were inland towns: in order of importance Kilkenny, Clonmel, Bandon, Cashel, Lisburn, Armagh. Of these towns, Kilkenny was, however, the only one which bore comparison with the ports in wealth as more than half the houses paid the hearth tax whereas in the other five the exempt houses greatly exceeded the better-off houses. Existing towns grew significantly in the second half of the century. Many insignificant villages also grew rapidly in this period, expanding around a market for livestock, produce or cloth. Examples are Mullingar and Ballinasloe growing up around fairs; Maryboro', and Mountmellick around the cloth industry. Many towns, large and small, had a substantial core of modern buildings, although only Kilkenny and Dungannon had over a half of the houses paying the hearth tax. Towns such as Bandon, Portarlington, Athlone, Ennis, Mallow, Carlow or smaller towns such as Middleton, Trim, Ballyshannon, Enniscorthy, Roscommon or Belturbet presented a picture of sturdy prosperity with a third of the houses paying the tax. Although towns were neither more numerous nor larger in the north, towns with an active linen market presented a prosperous impression from Dungannon and Armagh to Strabane, Monaghan, Enniskillen and Cavan. Commerce rather than the manufacture of cloth itself brought prosperity to them. Towns with a large number of resident manufacturers like Coleraine, Antrim or Drogheda or the town of Longford had a high proportion of exempt houses, weavers and spinners accumulating in the cabin districts. Towns without exception had a much higher proportion of exempt houses than the countryside. In other words, extensive poverty was more an urban than a rural problem. In towns such as Kells in co. Meath, Cashel and Fethard in co. Tipperary, Callan, co. Kilkenny, or Dungarvan, co. Waterford, it seems unlikely that by-employments were sufficient to alleviate the extensive poverty suggested by the acute disproportion between taxed and exempt houses.

The towns could not have grown except in the context of expanding trade. Trade itself could not have increased unless transport facilities improved. All the larger towns were deeply involved in trade, a fact highlighted by most of the major towns being seaports. Seaports were connected with the interior by road or waterway and improved transport facilities and internal markets grew up as part of an internal network of communications serving the ports. Villages and small towns flourished around markets: one of the first objectives of an improving landlord was to establish markets and fairs and often to erect a market-house. Apart from the major ports and inland towns, the number of subsidiary centres grew very rapidly in the second half of the century. In 1798 there were no less than 80 towns or villages of borough status alone of 150 or more houses, i.e. with a population in excess of about 900. If unincorporated towns were included, there would be many more. Their growth or progress was in proportion to their marketing function in terms of agricultural produce or yarn and cloth produced in the surrounding district.

There was a striking increase in the volume of inland trade from the 1740s. One obvious flow was in wool. Raw wool moved from the west to the south and east. This traffic accounted for the wool fairs of Ballinasloe and Mullingar which channelled the wool to the combing and spinning districts in Leinster and Munster. From these districts, the yarn found its way to the ports of Dublin, Waterford and Cork. The road from the south midlands to Dublin bore the name of Wool Pack Road. Linen accounted for another main traffic flow – yarn from the west to the north and east, and cloth, from the north especially, to Dublin. Cattle and butter moved to the main ports from a wide hinterland. In effect, each of the four main southern ports, Cork, Limerick, Waterford and Dublin, purchased the beef and butter produced in a very substantial region. The cattle fairs loomed large in the economic life of the Irish midlands. Cattle, butter, wool and worsted yarn, linen and linen yarn constituted the major items in inland trade. The output of wool grew in the early 1730s; of yarn in the 1740s; that of linen and linen yarn continuously from the 1720s; cattle increased in the 1720s and 1730s, and butter from a decade later.

The 1730s and 1740s were a period of rapid road building. Many of the roads built between the 1730s and the 1750s were turnpike trusts, that is, they were built and maintained by a group of trustees who had put up the original capital, or borrowed further capital, and paid interest out of the income from tolls on traffic on the roads. The wave of building coincided with the upturn in inland traffic. From Coleraine and Belfast the turnpike roads were built in a southerly direction to carry linen to Dublin. From Dublin itself the roads were built to the west reaching as far as Roscommon, and to the south and south-west serving Cork and Limerick. A fairly dense network of roads covered the region from Dublin to the Shannon and south to Limerick and Cork. Within this region took place the most intensive agricultural exchanges in the country. This traffic was supplemented by the huge and growing land-borne traffic in linen from the north to Dublin.

Turnpikes trusts, while useful, had limitations. The toll income was often insufficient to bear the expenses of maintaining the roads. The utility of a turnpike trust as a financing agency for some of the existing roads and even more for the less economically-active regions farther afield was limited. Most of the road-building from the 1760s onwards was financed by other means. The Grand Jury in each county had always had the authority to build roads. Its powers were made more useful by the authority granted it by statutes in 1759 and 1765 to levy a county rate to support road building. Under the 1765 statute the Grand Jury took the decision; the cess or levy was paid by the barony within which the road works were undertaken. The great bulk of road building after the 1760s was financed by the Grand Juries. It made possible the execution of road construction without relating it directly to the income that the traffic might generate, necessarily a limiting consideration in much of rural Ireland.

The only major region in which no turnpike trusts were undertaken between the 1730s and 1760s was the hinterland of Waterford. The reason for this was that the three sister rivers – Barrow, Nore and Suir – served much of the region effectively. Some coal from the Castlecomer coalfield was already carried to Dublin by land carriage. Improvements in the Barrow navigation in the 1750s and later, made it possible to transport the coal from Leighlinbridge down the Barrow to New Ross; thence it was carried by coastal craft to ports around the island. As a smokeless fuel it was sought after in the brewing and malting industries. Canal navigation had been in mind as far back as 1715 when a statute envisaged the construction of a network of canals. Since 1730, the proceeds of certain duties were earmarked for canal building by Parliament. The only substantial work executed, however, was the Newry Canal completed between 1731 and 1742. In 1751 the spending of these funds was entrusted to a national body corporate called The Corporation for Promoting and Carrying on an Inland Navigation in Ireland. This body commenced the construction of the Grand Canal in 1756, and undertook navigation works on the Shannon,

Boyne and Barrow. At first it executed the works itself. From 1772, however, it was empowered to make grants to private companies of undertakers who undertook the administration of existing or new canal projects. Some of the subsequent work was undertaken by commissioners appointed after 1787 for individual rivers. From the 1770s an increasing amount of private money supplemented state funds in financing canal building either in the form of shares in companies such as the Grand Canal Company formed in 1772 and the Royal Canal Company of 1789 or by way of local investment in the bodies of commissioners charged after 1787 with executing navigation works on individual rivers.

Canals and improved rivers were especially valuable in carrying bulky goods such as grain and coal. Much of the huge traffic in grain was carried by road, but where water-transport or coastwise transport was available, it was more economic. The quantities of Irish coal carried by canal were small. In fact, the canal system, once established, helped to distribute imported coal into the interior. As early as 1798, 3,646 tons of the 4,780 tons of goods carried on the Boyne Navigation consisted of coal. But Irish-produced coal had been a powerful incentive to canal-building. The first canal, the Newry Canal, had been built to carry coal from the Lough Neagh region to Newry for shipment to Dublin; the Barrow Navigation, including the line of canal from the Grand Canal to Athy on the Barrow, had been influenced by the existence of the Leinster coalfield, and the Grand Canal Company itself became proprietor of a colliery on the Leinster coalfield in the early nineteenth century. The exaggerated prospects held out initially for the Royal Canal Company were in no small measure a consequence of the over-sanguine view taken in the late 1780s of the mineral wealth of the Arigna region in the north Shannon. The bulk traffic, especially in minerals, fell far below expectations on the Irish canals. Traffic in agricultural goods was insufficient to make the canals immensely remunerative, but where the traffic in grain and flour was large, as in the Barrow valley, and where railway competition was not direct, the canals offered a return on investment right into the twentieth century.

Traffic on the roads was light. This was partly because the traffic was agricultural, hence decentralised and even seasonal. But it was also light because industry itself was decentralised through its domestic organisation. The density or otherwise of the local road network reflected the degree of development of the district. Not all industry was rural, however. The towns had an extensive industrial base. Food-processing industries – distilling, brewing and sugar refining – were especially evident in the towns. A reason for the concentration of many of these industries in the ports was the importation of many of the raw materials – the raw sugar for the refineries, and some of the malt and most of the hops for the breweries. In consequence, all the refineries were in the ports, and with the exception of Kilkenny the main brewing centres were port towns as well. Dependence on coal, imported from Britain or carried coastwise, was another reason for the concentration not only of the food-processing industries but of other industries such as glass-making and iron-working in the ports.

Factory industry itself was often outside the towns. In fact, other things being equal, there was a preference for the countryside because water-power was the main source of power for industry. The most important food-processing industry of all, the milling of bread-grains, was mainly established along the course of rural rivers and streams. Thus, water-power attracted industry to the streams outside the towns or far beyond. Where abundant water-power was readily available, water-mills of all kinds congregated in the hinterland of the towns. The most outstanding concentrations of such activity were the linen-bleaching works in the hinterland of Belfast, and – a still more varied group of industrial activities – the mills which congregated together in the hinterlands of Dublin and Cork. Along the Dodder, Camac and Poddle and, from Islandbridge upstream, on the Liffey, ironworks, grain mills, textile-finishing plant and paper mills stood. Around Cork, similar enterprises accumulated on the tributaries of the Lee, especially on the Shorney at Beechmount and Blarney, and in the valley of the Glanmire.

The Industrial Revolution affected Ireland strongly in the eighteenth century. Historians generally agree that the Revolution not only embraced industry but transport, banking and economic organisation as well. In this wider sense, with many changes in transport, banking and economic organisation, Ireland experienced the ' industrial revolution ' very extensively. But it also experienced the revolution significantly within industry and technology themselves. The first steam engine appeared in Ireland in 1740 – 28 years after the introduction of the first practical working engine by

Newcomen in 1712 – on the Leinster coalfield. Engines were either erected or proposed for the Tyrone and Lough Allen coalfields in the 1780s. The first engine in the Belfast region was erected in 1790 at Lisburn. In Dublin, one merchant alone, Henry Jackson, had three engines at work in 1798 : one in a foundry in Church Street ' the first ever erected in Dublin ', another on the quays for rolling and slitting iron, and the third in Phoenix Street for grinding wheat.

The revolution in technology was not confined to the introduction of the steam engine; it also involved the application of water-power to new uses, or on a larger scale than in the past. In the seventeenth century woollen cloth had been finished by hand as well as by water-driven finishing machinery. In the early eighteenth century the beetling of linen cloth was still conducted manually. As the century went by, water-driven mills to finish woollens – tuck mills – appeared in all the centres of the industry. In co. Clare alone there were 15 such mills in 1808. In the second half of the century water-driven mills were erected in the linen districts : 'scutch mills' to scutch or prepare the fibres for spinning, and ' beetling mills ' to finish the cloth. In tuck mill, scutch mill and beetling mill alike, the machinery was driven by a water-wheel. Most of the industrial firms were on a small scale in countryside and in town. Not only were the breweries and distilleries small, but many of them were simply artisan firms making a limited quantity with simple equipment for a small clientele. It required a large number of such breweries or distilleries to serve the market.

Large-scale firms using more elaborate equipment began to appear in England in mid-century. Significant economies of scale made it possible for them to undersell small-scale enterprises. Large breweries, glass-works and flour mills in the English port towns had low costs of transport in shipping to Ireland. Competition from them created difficulties for Irish firms. By the 1770s the breweries and glass-houses in Irish ports were in difficulties. The rise in grain imports in mid-century was characterised by an altogether disproportionate rise in imports of flour suggesting that high milling costs as well as poor harvests were behind the situation.

Industry could be saved only by operating on a larger scale. This, in fact, happened in grain milling, brewing and glass-making in the course of the 1770s and 1780s. The larger scale of the breweries is reflected in the fact that in Dublin, which paid about half the total excise on beer, there were only 30 breweries in the 1770s and 47 in 1790. In the country at large, there were in all 291 factory-type firms and 646 retail brewers in 1790. There was not a single retail brewer left in Dublin, Limerick and Waterford, a sole one in Cork, and only two in Kilkenny, the main centres of the industry. In other districts, however, the factory-type breweries were few and small, and much or all the beer was supplied by retailing brewers, in effect publicans who made their own supply. A general change to a larger scale of production was at this time evident only in industries affected by competition such as glass or sugar, which, based solely on the ports, were especially vulnerable. In fact, facing English competition from its establishment, the sugar-refining industry was on a relatively large scale from the start. In 1766 there were 40 sugar-houses in the kingdom, in 1780 22 in Dublin alone. The industry was highly capitalised – an average of about £10,000 per house, and a sugar refiner – Edward Byrne – was reputed to be the richest merchant in Dublin in the later eighteenth century. In brewing, on the other hand, the change of scale came quickly only in the major centres: in the small or remote markets in other districts change came much more slowly. In distilling there were few factory-type premises outside Dublin, Waterford and New Ross. In malting, which supplied the raw material of both the breweries and distilleries, the scale of operation was particularly small. In 1785 there were 2,216 malt houses in the island: in Wexford, the main single centre, there were 195 minute malt houses.

The industrial revolution in flour milling is especially significant because it began relatively early – in the 1760s – and because flour mills provided a pattern of industrial buildings which was imitated in the early cotton-spinning mills in the late 1770s and 1780s in Ireland. They also provided an early example of new business methods in which the manufacturer made himself active in the marketing of his product. Early grain mills were small, one or one and a half storeys high with a single pair of stones grinding. The new mills were much larger: a large water-wheel was capable of working several pairs of grinding stones simultaneously. They were also much higher, rising to three or even five or six storeys. Within these buildings lifting gear, driven by the water-wheel, raised the unmilled grain to the top storeys. The first of the new mills were those at Naul, co. Meath, and Abbeyvale, outside Kilkenny city where a three-storey structure was set to work by William Colles in 1762. The greatest of the early mills was at Slane, begun in 1763 and completed in 1767. In all, it represented an investment of about £20,000. The long, slender building, some 148 feet by about 28, five storeys high, was the first major industrial building in Ireland. According to Arthur Young in 1776 it was ' a very large handsome edifice, such as no mill I have seen in England can be compared with '. From 1770 to 1814 large mills were erected all over the country. Even small mills were often re-built in imitation of the new style with three storeys and hoists.

Business methods were changing rapidly. The small mills ground grain for their customers for a commission. In fact in some of the small town mills, as in Galway, before its first modern mill, ' each baker had a large chest in the mill that ground for them, with a lock and key, in which he usually kept as much wheat as he judged would be sufficient until the next market day. As he wanted it, it was ground in the mill.' The large mills, on the other hand, purchased the grain for cash from the farmers, then stored it, kiln-dried it and eventually sold the flour, often in distant markets. These flour millers represented a new pattern of economic organisation in which large-scale producers undertook the marketing of their products. The same trend was evident in the bleaching branch of the linen industry. The early bleachers were small-scale business-men who bleached for local drapers. The big bleaching firms, emerging in the second half of the eighteenth century, bypassed the local draper to deal directly with Dublin merchants, and in time forsook the Dublin market entirely to ship their linen to England on their own account. In consequence, by 1825 the industry was increasingly dominated by a small group of bleachers. Their marketing role made the linen halls old-fashioned and obsolete. At the production end, the weavers had ceased to be independent craftsmen, and had become dependent on work put out to them by the bleachers.

The flour mills, especially the great mill at Slane, became the model for the first factories to spin yarn by water-power. The new method of spinning cotton by water-driven spinning frames, intro-duced in England in the 1770s, was quickly exploited in Ireland. In Ireland, as in England, the cotton industry spread rapidly. It is not quite clear where the first mill to spin cotton yarn in Ireland was erected. The credit is usually given to Joy & Co in Belfast. But according to a petition from them to Parliament in 1783 all they claimed was 'the first Irish adventure in the most difficult branches'. On the other hand, Richard Talbot of Malahide claimed that his machinery was 'the first that ever was imported into this kingdom', and Richard Colello, who moved from Dalkey to Slane in or around 1781, referred to 'his having the first set of machinery ever made in this kingdom'. However, wherever the first venture had been established, what is certain is that within a few years, spinning works appeared at Belfast, Slane, Balbriggan, Malahide and Dublin, and in Cork at Glasheen and Blarney. The new mills were reminiscent of the flour mills. Smith's mill at Balbriggan was 100 feet by 34, five storeys tall; Deeves' mill at Blarney was 110 by 28 feet, five storeys tall. Shafts turned by water-wheel transmitted power to each floor; on each floor belts from the shafts drove the spinning frames. The cotton firms provided much employment; labour was required not only to tend the machines but also for the preliminary processing and for bleaching the woven product. The weaving of cloth from the spun yarn provided employment for hundreds in homes in the cotton-spinning districts.

There was no shortage of the capital necessary to finance development. Merchants' profits were often invested in industrial development of one kind or other. Landowners, too, invested in industry. This was especially true of many ventures in the linen industry in the southern half of Ireland. But they also invested in other activities. Jeffreys, landlord of Blarney, for instance, provided almost one-half of the capital cost – £18,859 – of the 13 mills plus workers' houses in the village. Two of the three partners in the great flour mill at Slane came from local landed families. Landowners provided much of the capital of turnpike trusts, canal companies and other large-scale ventures. There was also an inflow of capital from England, attracted both by belief in the economic potential of the island and by slightly higher interest rates. Some of this capital was long-term. Not only was there English investment in the Irish public funds, but there was some direct investment in individual industrial enterprises. The linen industry in particular affords many examples. There was also much short-term lending by English merchants. This was particularly true of the linen industry where importers advanced money on the security of the unsold cloth in their warehouses. Without these advances the linen industry would have suffered a shortage of working capital, especially during the great expansion in the 1780s.

The growth of trade is reflected in a striking increase in the supply of money in Ireland. On the basis of contemporary estimates the supply of cash increased three- to four-fold between the 1720s and the 1770s and trebled again by 1797. Within this period (1720-97) population increased by only 50 per cent. The rise in the money supply highlights the existence of a favourable balance of payments on capital account. It also suggests that internal commercial transactions must have multiplied. There was, as has already been suggested, no very striking expansion in banking after 1760. Wholesale transactions between different parts of the country were financed by bills of exchange. With the increase in banks not keeping pace with the rise in transactions, much of the discounting was conducted by private discount houses. The Bank of Ireland, granted its charter in 1783, in no way revolutionised Irish banking. The bank grew slowly in the first ten years of its existence. To a large extent, it simply rediscounted bills. Even then most of its notes went into circulation not by the bank's direct role in economic life but by its rediscounting bills which other financial houses in Dublin had discounted for their customers. Its role was subsidiary. The fact that it took bills made it easier for the other institutions in the Dublin market to discount extensively.

The state itself also contributed to economic development and its financing. An economic nationalism had been evident from the start in the Irish Parliament. The rebuff that the parliament received from the British Parliament in the form of the Woollen Act of 1699 made it the more disposed to promote Ireland's economic welfare in other and compensating directions. The Linen Board, established by Parliament in 1711 and financed by the proceeds of several duties on imports, was the most important early measure. The Parliament on several occasions proposed measures intended to promote tillage. Some of these efforts were blocked by the English Privy Council; others were a dead letter. To some extent the Parliament's interest in tillage was alarmist, the consequence of fears engendered in the years of harvest failure. It was also doomed to be ineffective because as a result of low prices farmers throughout Europe found grain-growing relatively unremunerative. Rising grain prices from the 1750s made it easier for measures to have an effect. Bounties on the inland carriage of grain and flour to the Dublin market in 1758 helped to promote tillage, and the export bounties granted in Foster's Corn Law of 1784 were effective because they were payable at price levels much higher than formerly. Abuses in the coal import trade were regulated repeatedly. Parliament was not prepared to rest content with regulation. It financed the building of the Newry Canal in the hope of creating an alternative source of supply for the Dublin market. Monies for later canal building were granted in part because of the belief that they would promote coal mining on the coalfields in the interior. Some public money was granted for colliery development itself, and also for the construction of a harbour at the Ballycastle colliery in co. Antrim.

In the second half of the century parliamentary grants were made more lavishly in support of public works and economic development. The failure of Parliament in 1751 and 1753 to assert successfully its claim to control of the disposal of any surplus of revenue over expenditure is frequently suggested as having encouraged Parliament to increase expenditure to ensure that there would be no surplus to dispose of. In fact, it is unlikely that such an intent can have been more than a single factor influencing the policy of the Irish Parliament. At least equally important was the desire of members to promote domestic economic development. As long as a deficit existed in the public accounts, the Commons was powerless to promote extensively by financial subventions what it regarded as desirable economic ends. A buoyant revenue from the end of the 1740s gave it the means of doing so. The growing amounts voted for assistance to industry, agriculture, mining, harbours and canals came from the enhanced ability of Parliament to indulge long-felt aspirations to encourage economic development by financial aid. Financial subventions from Parliament were not of themselves the decisive factor in the economic improvement evident in the 1750s and the 1760s. Low interest rates stimulated private investment in this period. Many of the applications for assistance from Parliament came from individuals who had already invested substantial sums of their own and other private money in their projects.

The policies pursued by Grattan's Parliament in the last two decades of the century were therefore nothing new. In fact, it is possible to argue that the industrial development of the period owed little to legislative measures or to the financial assistance of the legislature. The emergence of bigger firms with their consequent economies of scale was a factor in the growth of glass, milling and brewing in this period. The stimulus to expansion in the cotton industry was imitation of the technological developments that had just taken place in the industry in Britain. Their imitation was already under way before 1782 and cotton firms were being established rapidly in many locations in the ' eastern half of Ireland. During the depression in 1783 demands for tariff protection were widespread. They died away with subsequent recovery. The expansion of the cotton industry, however, was vigorously supported by Parliament. Grants were made to a number of firms, notably to the venture which Captain Robert Brooke had already set up at Prosperous in co. Kildare in 1780; bounties on home sales were instituted in 1783 and on exports in 1784, and in 1794 a fairly stiff tariff was imposed on imports, imports from Britain, contrary to practice, not being excepted.

In the closing decades of the century, Ireland's economic prospects seemed attractive. Prices of agricultural products rose sharply relatively to industrial prices. In industry itself, the technological features of the Industrial Revolution were being adopted in Ireland rapidly in the 1770s and 1780s. The expansion of the linen industry in the 1780s was remarkable; much of this expansion, too, taking place in regions such as Mayo seemed to suggest that the industry might well regenerate poor and backward regions. Ireland's industrial prospects seemed to be confirmed by the violence of the reaction among industrial interests in Britain to the Commercial Propositions brought forward by Pitt in 1785 for a commercial arrangement between the two islands. In essence, it was proposed to establish a free interchange of goods between the two countries. Duties, where levied, should be the same in one country as in the other. Where the existing duties differed, the higher duty was to be lowered to the level of the lower. In Britain, the manufacturing interest launched a campaign against the proposals, based on the argument that lower wages and taxation in Ireland would enable Irish manufacturers to flood the British market with cheap goods, and that they would result in a massive migration of British capital and artisans to new industrial centres in Ireland. These views were alarmist, but not wholly unrealistic. Ireland's industrial development had been rapid in recent years; an inflow of British capital and skilled labour had contributed to it. In many of the less mechanised activities such as weaving labour costs were the main manufacturing cost. It is true that Irish labour was often less skilful than British, or that it was wastefully managed. But it was precisely in this regard that fears seemed justified to some Englishmen. Mechanisation and more effective management might well make it possible for Ireland to capitalise the advantage it enjoyed in terms of the wage rates of unskilled labour. The Commercial Propositions, debated earnestly in both countries, did not come to anything, largely because the British Parliament added to them the requirement that the Irish Parliament was to enact immediately and without alteration British measures relating to navigation and colonial trade. To the members of the Irish Parliament, this meant in effect that one of the stipulations of an arrangement would be that Ireland should surrender a large part of her legislative independence. The majority in the Irish Commons for the altered propositions was so slender that the government abandoned the project.

The Union in 1800 in its economic clauses gave effect to what had proved abortive in 1785. The causes of the Union were primarily political. In fact, both the proponents and opponents of the Union gave evidence of an optimistic assessment of Irish economic prospects. William Pitt held out the prospect that free entry to the British market would encourage Irish industrial development and that the Union would be followed by an inflow of British capital. In effect, he was offering what British manufacturers had feared in 1785 might happen. Foster, the speaker of the Irish Commons, and one of the main opponents of Union, felt that the economic progress of recent decades justified the retention of the Irish Parliament. There was little opposition to the Union on economic grounds. When it was proposed, attitudes in favour of it or against it were determined by political rather than economic grounds. Dublin itself and the districts in the north strongly influenced by Orangeism were against Union. Much of the rest of the country favoured Union, and the representatives of Cork, second economic centre in the island, favoured it. After the Union the issue was treated with apathy. Writers such as Newenham, who drew a contrast with the policies of Grattan's Parliament and who saw in the decline in the trade balance a consequence of the change, were hardly widely representative of public opinion at the time.

Nevertheless, behind the façade of prosperity, weaknesses were

evident. First of all, the population had increased sharply in the
closing decades of the century. This growth continued in the early
decades of the following century. It was reflected in a disproportionate increase in the number of cottiers and labourers, and in a
sharper contrast between social classes. Second, the future of the
domestic textile industries, vital as a source of employment for the
growing proportion of the population not sharing in the country's
agricultural prosperity, was far from assured. While the decline of
domestic work in the cotton and linen branches lay in the future,
the woollen industry had already declined. The wool combing
districts had reached or even passed the peak of employment in or
even before the 1780s. Rising imports of woollens severely affected
the weaving branch in the 1780s and 1790s. Unemployment was,
for instance, rife in the Dublin Liberties in the 1790s. Significantly,
the concessions held out to Ireland in the Act of Union caused none
of the furore that the Commercial Propositions had occasioned only
15 years previously. As a rival Ireland was beginning to appear less
credible than a few years previously. The textile industries were
especially important for rural welfare. They were labour-intensive,
and the preparatory processes as well as spinning and weaving
provided abundant opportunity for the labourer or the smallholder
to supplement agricultural earnings. Most factory activities
employed little labour – a great flour mill like that at Slane
employed only 10 to 12 men. It was the textile industries alone,
therefore, that held out the prospect of widespread supplementary
employment. To understand the emerging character of pre-Famine
Ireland, one has to look both at the growth of population and at
the crisis which by 1815 was already affecting the domestic
industries.

5

Economic Structure and Rural Crisis
1793-1851

The war years between 1793 and 1815 were a period of boom. Between 1792 and 1815 the volume of exports rose by 40 per cent. The rise in prices was especially sharp. Exports, valued at current prices, rose by 120 per cent. The rise in prosperity was due more to the rise in prices than to the increase in volume. In fact, in the closing years of the eighteenth century and early years of the nineteenth the estimates of Irish overseas trade seemed to reveal a deficit in the balance of trade. This was because the static official valuations of commodities did not reflect the sharp rise in export prices. Valued at current or market prices in place of the archaic official valuations, exports were worth more and exceeded imports. Especially after the early years of the new century, the surplus rose sharply, reaching £4 million – four times the size of the late-eighteenth-century surplus – in 1808. Investment was at a high level during these years. The years from 1793 to 1815 were the culminating phase of a long wave of expansion going back to the 1740s. Investment had been heavy in the late eighteenth century. A crude measure of this is the fact that imports of capital goods such as timber and iron rose more rapidly than imports of consumer goods in the closing decades of the century. During the war years from 1793 to 1815, apart from a sharp recession in investment in 1797 and 1798, capital formation continued at a high level. In this period, the two great canals, the Royal and Grand, the most capital-intensive projects yet undertaken in Ireland, were completed. New factory investment was at a high level too. The building of flour mills reached a new peak, the largest mills in pre-

Famine Ireland being completed by 1814. Town growth was very rapid in this period, the major expansion of Irish towns and urban building being crowded into the years between 1790 and 1815.

The high level of economic activity was reflected in the expansion of banking. Payment of Bank of Ireland notes in specie was suspended in 1797; in practice this was taken to mean that private banks could honour their commitment to the holders of their notes by payment in Bank of Ireland notes rather than specie as well. The expansion in trade was therefore financed by an enormous expansion in bank circulations, and for the first time the great bulk of transactions in the south and west of the country came to be effected in notes rather than in cash. During the long period of high prices, bank failures were comparatively few. For the farmer, high grain and cattle prices made the war years a remarkably prosperous period. Farm prices rose more sharply than the general price level. Wartime demand and inflation was one reason. Another reason was that bad or poor harvests in the first decade of the nineteenth century kept prices at an artificially high level. In fact, poor crops of grain and potatoes in 1799 and 1800 resulted in near-famine conditions for the labouring classes. The farmer, however, fared well. Farm prices had risen sharply; rents rose more slowly, farmers holding leases gaining especially. Many farmers, in contrast to the labourers they employed, were able to save a rising portion of their income, a fact reflected in a substantial rise in the size of dowries among the farming community.

The boom was halted with the termination of hostilities in 1815. Prices fell sharply from their inflated level, and the trend was now downward. Despite a 10 per cent rise in the volume of exports between 1815 and 1820, their value fell. The volume of exports rose further in 1821; their value fell still further. A major economic crisis occurred in the spring of 1820, the most severe in two decades. It was in the main a consequence of falling prices, induced by falling markets in England where severe depression was experienced in 1819. Grain prices fell through 1819 and 1820: between 1818 and 1822 they were halved. Prices of beef and pork fell by about a third between 1819 and 1820. The abrupt character of the crisis in 1820 was contributed to by monetary deflation. Since 1797 the suspension of payment in gold had been followed by a sharp rise in the circulation of bank notes. The circulation of notes rose more sharply in Ireland than in England. To some extent, this was simply a consequence of the fact that agricultural prices rose more rapidly than other prices; the supply of money passively followed the rise in prices. To some extent also it represented an excessive creation of credit encouraged by the speculative and heady market conditions in many of the war years. When in 1819 the re-establishment of the convertibility of notes into gold was envisaged, some reduction in credit creation seemed prudent. The Bank of Ireland restricted credit in late 1819 and early 1820. Falling prices were already making merchants vulnerable; customers, suspecting the solvency of the banks, were eager to convert their claims against banks into cash and to seek payment not in local bank notes but in those of the Bank of Ireland. The bank carried out its policy of credit restriction by reducing its rediscount of bills for other banks. This meant that banks could not get the notes their customers wanted; and many failed. The banking crisis was to a large extent confined to Munster, where the wartime rise in prices and consequently in circulation had been sharpest, and where prices fell most sharply after 1815. Seven of the 14 banks in Munster and Kilkenny failed. A sole bank closed its doors in Dublin. From a peak of £1.3 to £1.5 million in 1813 the circulation of private bank notes in the south fell to £400,000 to £500,000 in 1823.

The banking crisis had little repercussion on the north, although the Dublin house which failed was one with close connections with the northern linen districts. Cash – gold rather than notes – had continued to form the mainstay of the circulation in the north. One reason was that landlords in the north had continued to insist on payment of rents in gold. Such an insistence could have proved successful only to the extent that it was economically feasible. Continued payment in gold in a period of rising prices was in fact practicable only because the rapid substitution of banknotes for gold in Munster economised the use of gold and made it available for the north. Continued payment in gold was also facilitated by the fact that in absolute volume of output the linen industry was stagnant throughout much of the period from 1800 to 1815. The immediate hinterland of Belfast, in which the cotton industry displaced linen rapidly in this period, did in fact develop some limited banking facilities in this period. With payment in gold so prevalent, banking was not likely to spread. In 1820 there were only four banks in the north, and these were relatively modest even as private banks went. Credit supplied by Dublin bankers and merchants was still important for the north; many of the bills received in payment of the north's exports continued to be discounted in Dublin, and the Dublin money market acted as a vehicle to transfer surplus guineas from the south to the north.

The war years with their attendant high prices had concealed many of the difficulties of the Irish economy. In fact, the prosperity of the period was caused more by rising prices than by rising volume of output. A rise of 40 per cent in the volume of exports between 1792 to 1815, a period exceeding two decades, signified in effect that the growth of the Irish economy, so rapid in the eighteenth century, was already slowing down. A rate as high or even higher had been achieved within shorter decennial periods in the eighteenth century. In particular, the market for salt beef and pork was contracting. By 1800 England had become the main market for Irish beef and salt pork. It had emerged as the main market because the colonial demand was being supplied to an increasing degree since the 1780s from North American sources. British demand itself grew rapidly only in wartime when Admiralty demand and the victualling requirements of land forces overseas were boosted. The regular predictable demand from the plantations was falling. Geared to a fluctuating demand for naval and military use, the beef market had become even during the war years noticeably more volatile and unpredictable. After 1815 exports of beef were only a quarter to a third of what they had been at their peacetime peak in the 1770s. Pork exports were halved by comparison with their wartime peak. They continued to decline subsequently. By the early 1840s exports of beef and pork to destinations outside the British Isles were only 1/35th of the corresponding exports at the end of the 1780s. Butter exports, except to Britain, fell sharply as well: from an average of 120,900 cwt for the years 1788/90 to an average of 16,388 cwt in 1842-4. Cork, geared more closely than any other Irish port to the transatlantic markets, suffered disproportionately from the decline in exports of beef, pork and butter outside the British Isles. Its altered economic fortunes are reflected, after decades of expansion, in demographic stagnation from 1821 onwards.

The high prices for grain were abnormal, due more to a fortuitous run of bad harvests in the early nineteenth century than to the war itself. Prices plummeted after the bumper harvest of 1814. The agricultural crisis of 1820 in the south of Ireland was to a large extent the consequence of the impact on an already weak market situation of the recession of 1819 in Britain. Deflation by the Bank of Ireland simply ensured that the crisis would run its full course, unmitigated. Commercial distress affected both farmers in the countryside and merchants in the towns. Famine occasionally directly affected the poor. Potato failure in 1817 and 1819 had already brought suffering, and famine affected the poor in the south in a widespread way in 1822. The early 1820s were the grimmest years for a long time. Low commodity prices and bank failures had disrupted the commercial life of the south, and impaired the living standards of the farming community. Famine in 1819 and more seriously in 1822 took its toll among the poor.

The Union of 1800 was in no way responsible for this situation. Some like Newenham claimed that the altered situation of the Union had turned a surplus in the country's trade into a deficit. But this was a conclusion drawn from the figures of the country's foreign trade valued at official prices rather than at market prices. Even at official values, the deficit was confined to the late 1790s and early 1800s when political disturbances and difficult economic conditions tended to hold exports down and to swell imports. In later years, both at official and at market prices, a large surplus existed. The fiscal arrangements of the Union did, however, lead to difficulties. Under the Union, each country was to retain and service a separate national debt, and Ireland was to contribute 2/17ths of the common expenditure of the United Kingdom. When the respective national debts of the two kingdoms reached a proportion of 2/17ths, the two exchequers were to be amalgamated. In 1800 a future of peace had been envisaged, and the British national debt, it was expected, would fall from its abnormally high level. In fact, however, the 15 years after the Union were years of almost uninterrupted war. The Irish contribution to the expenditure of the United Kingdom rose sharply. Revenue, despite tax increases, rose less sharply, and by the end of the war, the Irish exchequer was covering the deficiency in its 2/17ths share of the common expenditure of the United Kingdom by borrowings amounting to roughly half the size of its contribution. The debts created by these borrowings were added to the existing pre-Union debt of the Irish exchequer, raising the ratio of the Irish debt to the British national debt to that visualised in the Act of Union and leading to the abolition of the Irish exchequer with effect from

January 1817. Later in the nineteenth century, when the unpopularity of the Union was becoming much more evident, it was claimed that the fiscal arrangements under the Union had led to an outflow of money from Ireland on government account. This is not altogether true. There was an inflow of money on exchequer account in the 1820s, and the outflow in the 1830s rarely exceeded £500,000. Moreover, these figures do not include the substantial amounts remitted to Ireland to defray the large army establishment. Though the exchequers were amalgamated in 1817, Irish taxation was not brought into line with the higher British level until 1853. At that stage, the criticism may have some point; it does not, however, accurately describe the normal financial relationship between the two countries before 1853.

A very severe depression occurred again in 1825-6. Unlike the preceding crisis its effects on manufacturing industry were especially pronounced. Taking place after the Union duties (which had been continued in 1821) had been repealed in 1824, it could be construed as a consequence of their repeal and was so construed frequently in later times. Its effects were said to be especially evident where the woollen and cotton industries were concerned. In fact, however, repeal of the duties had not led immediately to contraction in the woollen and cotton industries. The woollen industry had already declined sharply in the late eighteenth century, although decline was slowed by the emergence of factory-type firms which by better methods made the industry more competitive and halted the decline in output and employment. Their success is reflected in the trend in imports. The rise in imports, very evident in the late 1790s, was halted, and despite a growing home population imports were no larger in the mid-1820s than in the late 1790s. In fact, imports in 1825 at 3,384,918 yards were somewhat below the total of 3,498,969 yards for 1799/1800.

The possibility that the Irish woollen industry, despite its poor performance in recent years, might still be made competitive seems to be reflected in the opposition offered in 1800 by the woollen industry, alone of industrial interests in England, to the commercial provisions of the Act of Union. Some of the disadvantages of the Irish industry had nothing to do with productive methods themselves. Irish wool production was increasingly geared in the eighteenth century to the requirements of the wool combers and the worsted branch of the industry. The poor quality of Irish yarn put the Irish manufacturers of cloth or old drapery at a disadvantage, and the better performance of the ' cloth ' branch of the industry in the early nineteenth century is associated with growing use of imported wool or yarn for quality goods. In fact, in the high-priced cloth, higher production costs mattered less than in the manufacture of the cheaper worsted goods. The decline in the cloth branch in Dublin and its vicinity between 1800 and 1822 was limited : while the number of manufacturers fell from 91 to 45, the number of workers fell only from 4,038 to 2,885. However, the panic of November 1825 in England hastened the decline of the industry. Unsold goods were disposed of at ruinous prices by the English manufacturers. The business of the Irish manufacturers was at a complete stand for many months; the smaller ones succumbed, and it was nearly two years before the large ones recovered from the shock. Imports rose sharply : from 3,384,918 yards in 1825 to 7,884,000 in 1835. By 1838 the Irish woollen textile industry, which in the late eighteenth century still supplied by far the greater part of Irish consumption, supplied only about 14 per cent of Irish needs. In the Dublin area output of cloth was more than halved between 1822 and 1838. In the south output was only one-eighth of its former extent; the trade in flannel produced by farmer-weavers in counties Wicklow and Wexford was virtually extinct. The worsted trade at Mountmellick and Abbeyleix fared better, but against the general background of decline in the industry – worsted or cloth – in the rest of the country. Even the Irish country-man, once clothed in home-produced frieze, was now dressed in imported fabric.

The cotton industry had expanded in many districts, nowhere more than in Belfast and its immediate hinterland where water-driven spinning mills were numerous and the weavers had trans-ferred from linen to cotton. The mills, too, succumbed in the depression. Outside Belfast, the industry disappeared in all but a few centres; in Belfast itself the spinning mills switched over to linen or went out of business. Weaving declined more slowly, in part because cheap imported yarn was also used. A few hundred weavers were still at work in and around Balbriggan in the late 1830s; a larger number in the Belfast region. The industry, how-ever, was now contracting rapidly, and cotton weavers' earnings in Belfast no longer compared favourably with linen weavers'.

The crises in 1819-20 and 1825-6 have sometimes been regarded as a consequence of monetary deflation in Ireland. Monetary deflation there had been in 1819. There may also have been some deflation between then and 1826 as the Bank of Ireland pursued a policy of stabilising the exchange between Ireland and England from 1822, and the decision to abolish finally the separate Irish exchange was taken in 1825. Stabilisation of the exchanges – which entailed smoothing out fluctuations in the exchanges – could only be achieved by making bills available at par, the par being Irish £108 6s 8d to English £100 as long as a separate currency existed, and £100 in Dublin for £100 in London when the Irish currency was abolished in 1826. The Bank of Ireland could make such a policy of stabilisation effective only by building up a large reserve in London on which it could draw bills, and this purpose may have led it to pursue a deflationary policy between 1822 and 1826 as a consequence of leaving in London funds which might otherwise have discounted bills of exchange. Principally, however, the severity of depression in Ireland in both periods simply reflected the gravity of the crisis in England, which experienced the two most severe recessions of the first quarter of the century. The short-term effect of recession on the Irish economy was inescapable. The short-term effects in the 1825-6 depression were especially noteworthy in industry. But only in textiles did the depression have a permanent adverse result. And the rapid decline in the cotton and woollen industries, moreover, reflected long-term weaknesses that were already becoming evident in both industries. It is doubtful whether the continuation of protection could have insulated the Irish industries from long-term decline. Outside Belfast the cotton industry had already lost ground rapidly before 1825. In England itself, the cotton industry gradually declined in Derbyshire, one of the cradles of the industrial revolution in cotton, and old-established centres of the woollen industry in Norwich and the south-west were unable to compete with the expanding Yorkshire industry. Specialisation, a large scale of production, and the external economies associated with the intense localisation of the woollen industry in Yorkshire and of cotton in Lancashire created a rapidly improving competitiveness against which protection could not prove an adequate answer.

The severity of the crises in 1819-20 and 1825-6 was due more to the impact on the Irish economy at large of sharp recession in England than to any other factor. Except in cotton and woollens, the

effect of recession was also temporary. This was especially so in the
case of the linen industry. The linen industry had in fact stagnated
in the first two decades of the century. The level of exports recorded
in 1795/6 was exceeded for the first time in 1817, when they
soared to 56 million yards. They slumped sharply subsequently in
line with the general recession in 1819-20. In 1825, however,
exports had recovered to 55 million yards. They grew very rapidly
in the early 1830s, reaching 70 million yards in 1835. The linen
industry was now beginning to concentrate in the north-east, its
growth after 1825 reflecting a very buoyant level of economic
activity in and around Belfast. The spinning of flax by power-
machinery was introduced into Belfast in the 1820s; the collapse
of many of the cotton-spinning firms facilitated the transfer of
capital from cotton business to linen. The first mills in spinning
used water-power. Steam-power was rapidly adopted and the big
linen mills appearing in the 1830s were, in the main, steam mills. In
1838 there were 15 linen mills in Belfast and its suburbs;
another four in neighbouring towns. Farther afield there were two
mills in Newry (that of the Nicholsons at Bessbrook was in fact the
first linen mill in Ireland, opened in 1813). In 1852, there were
28 mills in Belfast. The linen industry, therefore, from the mid-
1820s was characterised both by growth of output and by reloca-
tion and re-organisation.

In the south, too, the worst effects of crisis were temporary. Even
in the textile industry, more precarious there than in the north,
several large cotton mills remained in production. The cotton
industry survived in Balbriggan and Drogheda, and the large mill
established at Portlaw in co. Waterford in the 1820s continued
to flourish with a substantial export trade for many decades. The
fact that cotton spinning had taken root in counties Meath and
Louth may have facilitated the transition there as in the north to
factory spinning in linen. In the 1830s there was a flax-spinning
mill in Navan and several in Drogheda. The woollen industry was
severely affected by the 1825-6 crisis; some of the larger firms
survived, however. The Drummond Commission concluded:

> upon the whole, the woollen trade of Ireland, though much less
> than what it formerly was, is now in a sounder and healthier state
> than when existing under the paralysing influence of protecting
> duties. The manufacturers, though few in numbers, carry on their
> business with activity and intelligence; they have adopted every

new improvement in machinery, and they have generally an abundant supply of water and water power.

The crisis at this stage was confined to textiles. Outside textiles,
there is no evidence of serious industrial decline in the 1820s.

The crisis was more general in agriculture. All agricultural prices
fell very sharply after 1815, the prices of grain being particularly
low around 1820. Grain prices recovered in the second half of the
1820s, and after falling sharply at the end of the decade, they rose
again in the second half of the 1830s. Prices of livestock and livestock products also recovered very well in the second half of the
1830s. Despite the decline in beef and pork exports, the volume of
agricultural exports rose throughout the 1820s and 1830s. Exports
of livestock doubled between the 1820s and 1830s and doubled
again by the mid-1840s. Butter exports in the three years 1824-6
were 40 per cent above exports in 1808-10 and were apparently
even higher in the 1830s. The most remarkable expansion was
in exports of grain and flour. From less than a million quarters a
year in the first 18 years of the century, they doubled in the course
of the 1820s, and climbed to above three million quarters in 1837
and 1838 on the eve of the bad harvests of the late 'thirties and
early 'forties. A rise in volume of agricultural output associated with
a recovery in prices is hardly consistent with a picture of general
depression. A rise in output in part compensated for the fall in
prices in the bad years, and in other years the farming community
must in fact have fared well. The fact that depression in Munster,
hard hit in the early 1820s, was temporary is revealed also in the
recovery in note circulation in Munster. From the depression level
of £400,000 to £500,000 in 1823, it rose to £1,300,000 in 1838,
according to the estimate of the Drummond Commission. Allowing for the sharp fall in the price level, the real purchasing power
represented by that sum must have been larger than the circulation
of £1.3 to £1.5 million in the south in the height of Napoleonic
wartime prosperity. It is likely, however hard hit the farming
community was in the postwar depression, that they fared well,
especially in the 1830s. Of course, prosperity among farmers did
not necessarily denote a similar condition among the labourers. As
the Drummond Commission noted :

these signs of growing prosperity are, unhappily, not so discernible
in the condition of the labouring people, as in the amount of the

produce of their labour. The proportion of the latter reserved for
their use is too small to be consistent with a healthy state of society.
The pressure of a superabundant and excessive population . . . is
perpetually and powerfully acting to depress them.

The composition of the countryside was varied and complex. Sharp
contrasts existed, and generalisation often serves to conceal their
existence and universality. According to the 1831 census 100,000
farm occupiers employed hired labour. These occupiers would be
in general the more comfortable section of the farming community,
and would approximate to the occupiers of the 127,000 holdings
above 15 acres counted a decade later. In addition to the 100,000
farmers who employed labour, the 1831 census returned 564,000
occupiers who employed no labour, and 567,000 agricultural
labourers. A few years later, the Poor Law Commission, regarding
both these categories as being alike, lumped them together. In fact,
this procedure ignored the many contrasts among smallholders.
While the half million labourers were in many instances destitute
and had no secure stake in the land, many of the smallholders had
the security of a farm. They were therefore by no means totally
destitute. They had some surplus for the market and especially
where textiles had been prevalent often derived their income as
much or more from textiles. In such circumstances they had often
fared well, and even in the altered circumstances of the 1820s and
1830s they afforded a contrast with the labourers. Smallholders
like this did not as a rule hire wage labour or let conacre land to
a labourer. The Drummond Commission itself, though showing
signs of not appreciating to the full the relative weight of different
social categories in the countryside, recognised among the smallholders a superior category, holding from 8 to 12 or 15 acres, who
engaged ' as farm servants, young men from between 16 and 25
years of age, who reside in the family of their employer, and hire
themselves out at remarkably low wages, seldom exceeding £1 per
quarter, and, in numerous instances, scarcely more than half that
sum '. Of the 558,000 holdings between 1 and 15 acres in 1841,
almost half were above 5 acres, so that the number of smallholders
employing farm servants could have been quite substantial. In fact,
the 1831 census, in addition to its figure of 567,000 farm labourers,
returned a total of 98,742 male servants.

The 1841 census divided the population into four categories
according to their means. The division depended on substance,

also in rural areas on the size of holdings. The first category included property owners, also farmers of more than 50 acres. The second included artisans, and farmers with from 5 to 50 acres, the third category included labourers and smallholders up to 5 acres.*
For the rural districts of the country at large, the first two categories accounted for 30 per cent of the families. Seventy per cent of the rural population of Ireland as a whole therefore consisted of labourers, smallholders with less than five acres and the less prosperous artisans. However, what is more significant is the contrast between the two broad divisions in the different regions within the country. The first two categories combined ranged from as high as 40-42 per cent in a number of eastern counties to as low as 15 per cent in Mayo.

Three broad regions can be distinguished in Ireland. The first is a region embracing the eastern counties in Leinster and the Ulster counties with the exception of Donegal and Fermanagh. In some of these counties, the proportion in the first two `categories fell below 34 per cent. In Monaghan (30 per cent), Cavan (30 per cent) and Louth (32 per cent), however, the situation had rapidly deteriorated within the preceding 20 years through the decline of the linen industry. A generation earlier they would have presented a much more prosperous picture. The same consideration applies to co. Meath (32 per cent). In most counties contrasts existed between local regions. This was especially true of co. Meath, where a growing contrast existed in the pre-Famine decades between the prosperous smallholding regions supported by textiles in the north of the county and the region shared between larger farmers and a deteriorating proletariat in the countryside and in market towns such as Kells farther to the south. The second broad region embraced the more western counties of Leinster, Munster (apart from Clare and south-west Cork and much of peninsular Kerry), east Galway and parts of Roscommon, Leitrim and Sligo. In this region the proportion of the population in the first two categories ranged from 35 per cent in Limerick and 33 per cent in Tipperary to 28 per cent in co. Cork. This region was on the whole poorer than the first region. In particular, supplementary textile income was smaller or had declined more rapidly than in other parts of the country. This adversely affected the farming class; it still more adversely affected the labourers and smallholders with 5 acres or

* The fourth category 'means unspecified' was not of numerical significance.

less. In other words the contrast between farmer and other rural classes was sharper here than in the east and in the north. In the east and north, wage employment on tillage farms in the intensive tillage areas or supplementary income from spinning or weaving in the traditional textile districts made the lot of the labourer or smallholder less precarious. The third broad region embraced the districts along the west coast of the country. The existence of this region is reflected in the relatively low proportion of the families falling into the first two categories in counties Donegal, Sligo, Leitrim, Roscommon, Mayo, Galway, and Clare in none of which the proportion exceeded 23 per cent. The percentages in fact understate the contrasts within these counties. In all these counties, sharp contrasts existed between better-off and poorer districts. In a rough fashion, Roscommon and Leitrim were divided between a region of impoverished smallholders in the north or north-west and a mixed region of farmers and badly-off labourers in the south. The same pattern existed except with the geographical pattern fixed between a poor west and a prosperous east in counties Donegal, Sligo, Galway and Clare. Regions of impoverished smallholders existed also in peninsular Kerry and south-west Cork. The better-off areas in these counties formed part socially and economically of the intermediate national region centred on the south and midlands. The poorer districts formed an extensive and fairly continuous region along the western coast and its hinterland. It was most extensive in the case of co. Mayo which had some although not many pockets characterised by better conditions. In 1841 only 15 per cent of the families in co. Mayo came within the first two census categories. The Poor Law Commission in 1836 reported that Mayo was the most neglected county in Ireland.

In fact, it is impossible to state that the rural community as a whole was impoverished in pre-Famine Ireland. Farmers may well have suffered in the years of lowest prices. They were not, however, totally without resources even in the worst years. In the 1841 census, farms of 6-15 acres had, on average, two cattle; there were also almost as many horses as there were farms in this category. The average value of livestock on holdings of 6-15 acres was £22½. On farms of 16-30 acres the average was £46. Labouring families, on the other hand, possessed no livestock, apart from, perhaps, a pig. Farmers were not, moreover, crushed by the size of rents. Rents, despite the rise in prices, can hardly have doubled between

1778 and 1815 – they perhaps rose from about £6 million to £10-12 million. Thereafter, there is little evidence of a rise in rents, and in many instances their incidence fell either through abatements agreed between tenant and landlord or through a significant increase in arrears in the worst years. The increase in rents was, moreover, offset by a sharp increase in output which continued into the 1820s and 1830s. The rise in output was sharper in cereals than in livestock. Grazing, whose spread would have been to the advantage of many of the larger farmers, did not advance very rapidly. Consolidation of small farms into large farms made little progress in pre-Famine Ireland. Cattle exports had grown very slowly since the re-admission of Irish cattle into England at the end of the 1750s. The trade in livestock quickened in the 1820s and 1830s with the introduction of the steamship on the channel crossing. But many of the cattle were young stores rather than fat cattle, and a rise in the number of fat cattle shipped has to be seen in the context of a sharp decline since 1815 in the internal demand for fat cattle for the provisions trade. Only in the grazing districts of co. Meath does there seem to have been a move to consolidated grazing farming.

Prices recovered in the intervals between the troughs of very low prices around 1820 and 1830. The rise was especially noteworthy in the second half of the 1830s. In fact, agrarian unrest coincided to a marked degree with the troughs in prices, and was at its most bitter in the early 1820s and again around 1830. In between periods of very low prices it abated. Agrarian unrest was a complicated phenomenon. It was characteristic of particular areas, themselves as a rule relatively prosperous, and it was notably absent from the poorest regions. In the poor regions, subdivision of land provided access to a minute holding for every man. In other regions, there was a pronounced sense of property rights. The jealous sense of property rights showed itself in differences between farmer and farmer, and between farmers as a class and their labourers. Conflict could arise between farmers or with the landlord or his agent if a tenant's jealously guarded right to the holding he held appeared to be in question. Outsiders or the landlord's agent were normally expected to respect local property rights, and as a rule did so. The right of an occupying tenant to the renewal of his lease, subject to payment of the rent demanded, or – even if there was no lease – to the continuation of whatever agreement by which he held the holding, was universal. It was reported by the Commission on the Poor in Ireland in 1836 that ' throughout the greater part of Ireland there is a species of tenant right ' even for the tenant holding his land from year to year. When the agreement came up for renewal, there was normally no problem. Either tenant and landlord were in agreement on the rent for the renewal, or, if prices were rising, tenants were sanguine and accepted fairly readily a substantial increase in rent. But if a lease came up for renewal in a period of low prices, landlord and tenant might not come to agreement on the terms of a renewal, and failing agreement, the farm might be offered to an outsider who was prepared to pay a higher rent than the former occupier was prepared to accept. It was at this stage that tenant right and landlord's right came into conflict, and might culminate in violence directed against the agent or the incoming farmer who dared to transgress the traditional right of occupation which the former tenant considered he held. Conflicts between farmers in cases such as this were often intermingled with family feuds. Agrarian unrest was thus a complex thing, less universal and more intermittent than has often been suggested. In fact, the most universal and constant source of agrarian unrest had nothing to do with rents, and was concerned with the tithes for the Church of Ireland levied on farm produce. Tithes constituted an underlying source of unrest throughout the eighteenth century, resentment of them on occasion constituting a bond uniting rather than dividing landlord and tenant. Resentment was sharpest when prices were poor, and the agrarian unrest of the early 1830s revolved around the tithes question.

The landlord's economic position weakened in pre-Famine Ireland. The weakening in his economic role took place despite the fact that the landlord was more often in direct contact with the tenant than in the past. During the war years, the leases commonly offered to tenants shortened considerably. This was because landlords were anxious to share, by not granting long leases, in the general price rise as fully as possible. In the relatively uncertain years after 1815 tenants preferred short agreements as well, because they offered by their nature the prospect of adjustment downwards as well as upwards. Shorter leases were bad for the middlemen who had often intervened between the head landlord and the occupying tenant. The strength of the middlemen in the eighteenth century lay in the fact that they had taken their lands on long leases and reset the land on several occasions on shorter leases at rents which reflected the subsequent general upward trend in rents. Like all landlords, middlemen suffered by mounting arrears in the bad years after 1815 and given the general rise in rents before 1815 they could not hope to re-negotiate the renewal of their leases on advantageous terms. The middlemen's position had already been reduced in the age of landlord interest in estate management in the second half of the eighteenth century; their number was rapidly reduced in the decades after 1815. Almost paradoxically, the period in which the landlord's direct relationship with the occupiers of the estate increased significantly was marked by a decline in the landlord's direct involvement in economic improvement. Rent reductions and arrears often reduced rent rolls after 1815. Income was not rising, to an extent had become more precarious. Expenditure could not be reduced, partly because rising rent rolls especially during the Napoleonic period had accustomed landlords to a higher standard of living and ostentation, but partly because much of the income was committed to mortgage interest payments or to legally binding payments to widows and family members. The only way to maintain current income was to cut down on investment. After 1815 the volume of landlord investment in estate improvement, in local industrial activity and in transport infrastructure fell off sharply. The landlord's economic role was in effect curtailed. A paternal role socially as well as economically had been played by landlords and was accepted by the rural community in the eighteenth century. This social relationship was subject to increasing strains as a result of the sectarian issues raised by the foundation of the Orange Order in 1795 and the '98 rebellion, and the sectarian division was sometimes perpetuated and popularised by bitter electoral conflicts in the early nineteenth century between Liberal and 'Ascendancy' landlords. In 1800, many of the Ascendancy gentry had been bitterly opposed to the Union with Britain, but frightened by the democratic undertones of the Emancipation movement in the 1820s, landlords as a class became more conservative. By the time of the repeal movement in the 1840s, the division had therefore become political as well as religious. It still did not undermine the social prestige of the gentry; many of the more liberal MPs returned for Irish constituencies until late in the nineteenth century were themselves landed, and the two great popular figures of Irish political history in the nineteenth century –

O'Connell and Parnell – were both landlords. Moreover, recovery in investment in demesne farming and a renewed interest in estate management generally after mid-century seemed to show that the economic fortunes of the landed class were in a measure being restored.

The years of falling prices apart, the condition of rural Ireland in the pre-Famine decades has been painted too darkly, at any rate as far as the farming class was concerned. Their relatively secure and comfortable position is reflected in several aspects of contemporary life. The evidence of improved housing in pre-Famine Ireland, commented on at the time, was a reflection of their circumstances. So too is the existence of a substantial surplus of income spent on consumer goods and reflected in the large number of shops which already existed in Ireland as far back as 1831. The census of that year included a category described as 'shopkeeper: dealer in sundry necessary articles, such as are sold in a village shop'. Some 6,943 males upwards of 20 years of age were included in this category. The category effectively related to villages and small towns, as the 16 borough towns accounted for only 750 of the total. In the east, potatoes and meal were purchased frequently in the shops; soap, tobacco and candles, salt, and, increasingly, cloth, were purchased in shops even by the poor in most parts. Hucksters and pedlars supplemented the village shops; their number was in fact larger. Even in a poor county like Mayo, the number of hucksters, pedlars and shopkeepers was impressive. All this testifies to a substantial market among the better-off and to an extent even in the poorer regions. It is necessary to say to an extent because in a poor county like Mayo there was a substantial contrast between large towns like Castlebar and Ballina with their immediate hinterland and remote districts like Erris and Achill. The existence of a substantial market for shop products is shown, for instance, in the sales of tea, which was now beginning to enter into the regular consumption in the diets of all above the labourer or smallholder class. Tea imports doubled in the course of wartime prosperity and rose by a quarter between 1825 and 1835. Tobacco imports are difficult to interpret. The apparent decline after 1815 is in the main due to the sharp rise in tobacco smuggling, which became big business. However, allowing for the size of smuggling and a decline in it with the establishment of the coastguard in the early 1820s, it does seem unlikely that there was any per capita increase in tobacco consumption. Tobacco was a commodity with a mass market, and the apparent stagnation in per capita consumption may reflect the condition of the poorer classes in the community.

The pre-Famine crisis was concentrated on the labourers as a class and on the smallholding regions. It was among these classes that population grew rapidly. The labourers seemed to multiply in these decades in the country generally. In the counties where large regions of smallholders existed such as Galway, Clare, Mayo and Donegal, the population grew more rapidly than in the rest of the country. In these regions farming was organised more on a subsistence than a commercial basis. Smallholders divided their holdings, or moved to waste land which as it was colonised also became subdivided. Subdivided holdings of themselves did not entail poverty. The northern counties were as subdivided as the poor regions of the west. But incomes in the north depended more on textiles than on agricultural output. Subdivision, unsupplemented by domestic textile activity or accompanied by a decline in that activity, however, often entailed poverty for the rural classes. This was the situation in much of the west, where land, already relatively barren, was subdivided, or families moved to waste land and carved out poor holdings which yielded little beyond a crop of potatoes to keep body and soul alive. In such areas, were to be found cabins, primitive and poorly furnished, a diet consisting to a large extent of potatoes, and so little cash income that market purchases were minimal and shops or traders few. In the subdivided linen counties linen provided an income that raised the bulk of families above the bare subsistence level. In the poor districts of the north-west and west and in the peninsular regions in the south-west, on the other hand, whole districts barely subsisted or were reduced to that condition by the decay of textile industry.

In the richer farming lands of Leinster, Munster and east Connaught, which produced a substantial surplus of livestock and grain for the market, subdivision of farms was not prevalent. Landlords were against it; so were the tenants themselves. Marriages were entered into with deliberation, and not until the dowry was settled. Smallholders in the barren lands of the west, or landless labourers, may have married recklessly or at any rate at very early ages. The farmer typically married more slowly and at a later age. The growth in pre-Famine population was reflected in a disproportionate increase in the population of smallholders in the thinly populated but relatively barren lands along the west where an abundance of waste land and low living standards weakened incentives to caution. In other areas, labourers increased disproportionately to farming families.

In fact, the population increased sharply between the middle of the eighteenth century and 1841. Between 1735 and 1785, it rose from 3 million to 4 million or by 33 per cent; by 1841 it had risen to 8.2 million or by a further 105 per cent.

Early marriage has often been seen as the cause of this increase. It has been claimed that the spread of potato cultivation and diet facilitated subdivision, and that ease of subdivision promoted a move towards marriage at remarkably early ages by 1780. There is, however, no evidence of a universal trend towards earlier marriage, and definite evidence to suggest that among the farming community marriage was entered into cautiously and subdivision restricted. Around 1841 both the birth rate and the marriage rate seem to have been in line with other European countries. The potato diet itself spread relatively late, and a diet dominated by the potato emerged only among the labourers and among smallholders in the poorer or deteriorating regions. The farmers everywhere maintained a mixed diet; even in the decade preceding the Famine two-thirds of the huge amount of grain produced in the Irish countryside was consumed within the island. The rapid rise in population in Ireland in the century before the Famine is part of a Europe-wide phenomenon. It is doubtful if a trend towards earlier marriages than elsewhere either existed or was decisive. A likely factor in the rise in population is a fall in the death rate. Famines were fewer than in the past. The last general famine was that in 1740-1; thereafter no general shortage of grain sufficient to reduce the community to actual famine occurred. The partial famines caused by the potato failures in 1799-1800, 1816, 1817, 1822 or 1836 were confined to a single social class – the labouring population – or to the poorer regions of the country. A decline in grain shortages may have lessened mortality from the 1750s onwards. Excepting a few individual years, few had died from actual starvation, but undernourishment during the frequent ‘ dearths ’ characteristic of Irish – or European agriculture – up to the 1760s may have led to much higher mortality than in other years. If years of abnormal mortality were fewer after the 1750s, this of itself would have contributed to rising population. Epidemic diseases seemed, too, to have taken a lighter toll of lives from the middle of the century. Smallpox, of course, remained a virulent killer, especially of the young, but if, as is claimed, early innoculation was effective – and it was in fact quite widespread – it would also have contributed to reducing the level of mortality from the quite high levels often experienced previously.

Population growth had serious implications especially for districts where land was scarce and families were pushing out on to barren waste, or for labourers who had to rely on casual employment from farmers and on renting plots of land at inflated conacre rents. Where the textile industry flourished, the problem at regional or family level was not necessarily serious. But accelerated population growth added to the social problem if it took place at a time when domestic industry was precarious. And this in fact proved to be the position in much of rural Ireland in the first half of the nineteenth century. Weaving had been extensive in much of the countryside and, especially among the poorer classes, spinning was even more prevalent. Economic conditions in Mayo were, for instance, better in the early nineteenth century than later because the textile industry had diffused itself so rapidly in the county. In the 1821 census Mayo was one of only six counties, outside Ulster, in which a greater number of individuals were returned as being engaged in manufacture, trade or handicraft than in agriculture, and, in fact, if the returns were taken literally, Mayo would appear the most industrialised county, apart from Louth, of the six counties. Domestic textiles were, however, beginning to experience a crisis. This emerged earliest in wool, and earlier in spinning than in weaving. The fact that the woollen industry was located in the southern half of the country helps to explain why occupations outside agriculture appeared in the 1821 census to be fewer in Munster than in the other provinces and why acute poverty emerged at an early date among the labouring classes in Munster at large. The linen industry, too, declined at an earlier date in Munster than elsewhere. Bandon, for instance, had been a centre of the linen industry in the 1780s: decline in its linen industry was followed by decline in wool: in 1831 the town had only 375 weavers. According to evidence before the Poor Law Enquiry in 1836 some 4,000 to 5,000 weavers from Cork had gone to England since 1810. Cotton – spinning and weaving – had been undertaken in many regions, even as far afield as Mayo, but even before the major crisis of the mid-twenties was declining in the more peripheral locations.

The linen industry ceased to expand during the first two decades of the century; spinning – more than weaving – was affected because of the introduction of power-spinning in England. The recovery of momentum in the industry in the 1820s coincided with the spread of power-spinning in Ireland. Its introduction heralded the end of domestic linen spinning. Domestic spinning contracted rapidly in the traditional spinning districts in the 1830s, and yarn spun by the housewife had ceased by 1841 to be the great support it had been for poor families previously. As factory spinning concentrated in the north-east, weaving tended to centre on the north-east too. This tendency was accelerated by the decay of the cotton industry which led to the thousands of specialist weavers in the hinterland of Belfast moving back into linen. The farmer-weavers, farther afield, faced with a decline in the local output of yarn as well as with the competition of specialist weavers in the hinterland of Belfast, found themselves unable to compete at economic rates. The industry faded rapidly not only in counties far afield, but in counties such as Monaghan, Fermanagh, Cavan, Louth, Longford and north Meath which had long-established traditions in linen. Drogheda itself affords striking evidence of the changing situation. Drogheda in 1831 still employed 941 males alone above 20 years in the textile industry. The Poor Law Commission estimated in 1836 that weavers were one-third or one-quarter their former number, and between 1821 and 1841 the town's population stagnated. Yet Drogheda in fact had fared better than most areas because it was able to replace some of the declining domestic employment by factory textile work.

In the 1841 census one in five occupied persons was in textiles, and the prevalence textiles retained as a source of employment, especially for women, in the census returns of that year affords an illustration of the significance that they had enjoyed in supplementing rural incomes. The decline in textiles is a factor in explaining the deteriorating social conditions in many smallholding districts in the pre-Famine decades and among the labourers. In Mayo, for instance, contemporary opinion held that conditions had once been better. Lewis in 1837 wrote that ' in the districts about Westport and Newport the people were formerly in comfortable circumstances, uniting the occupations of farmer, weaver and fisherman, but for some years the change in their circumstances for the worse has been very great '. While the occupational statistics in the 1831 and 1841 censuses do not admit of direct comparison, Mayo is in fact one of the few counties for which the figures for shopkeepers could be construed as suggesting a significant decline. Cash incomes were probably smaller than previously, dependence on farm-grown food, especially the potato, greater, and consequently greater also the vulnerability of such families if the potato failed. The background to the Famine, through the crisis in domestic industry, is as much an industrial as an agrarian one.

The growth in population, accompanied by a decline in domestic industry, signified that Ireland was becoming more rural, more agricultural, than it had been. The fact that between 1815 and 1841, the towns as a whole failed to keep pace as they had in the past with rural population growth reinforced this pattern. Few of the major towns, apart from Dublin and Belfast, expanded between 1821 and 1841. Many medium and smaller centres stagnated in population, and some even declined. Maritime centres such as Kinsale and Cobh, tied up with naval requirements, are an obvious instance. Estate villages or estate towns, and textile centres outside the north, also stagnated. Not all towns stagnated. With a rapid increase in communications and with local wholesalers often replacing Dublin wholesalers in meeting regional requirements, some towns expanded their economic importance rather rapidly and this was often reflected in their population growth. Such prospects, however, tended to be monopolised by well-situated towns which waxed rich at the expense of less well-situated neighbours. Youghal, Middleton, Mallow, Kanturk and Tralee grew while ports such as Dingle, Cobh and Kinsale, estate towns such as Doneraile or Lismore, or industrial centres such as Bandon declined or stagnated. In the midlands Tullamore, Maryboro' and Mountmellick expanded while Mountrath, Portrarlington, Kilbeggan and Philipstown declined. Navan grew while Trim, Kells and Athboy stagnated. In Galway, Gort, Tuam and Ballinasloe – market centres – grew while Loughrea – a textile centre – declined. In Mayo, Ballina – a market town – grew, while Castlebar – centre of the linen trade – and Westport – a peripheral port – fared badly. As the main centre of import-export business, Dublin continued to expand – from 185,881 in 1821 to 232,726 in 1841 – even if its industries, especially its textile industries in the Liberties, were in

decay. The linen towns in counties Cavan, Monaghan and Longford had ceased to expand. On the other hand, Derry, Dungannon,
Coleraine and the linen market towns of Armagh, Down and
Antrim grew. Their growth was in most cases modest. They
remained essentially market towns. But something quite different
was presented by the growth of Belfast and some of its satellite
towns. Belfast had grown from 18,320 in 1791 to 37,277 in 1821 :
it doubled again to 75,308 by 1841. Newtownards and Bangor grew
rapidly in the same period. All three, with their spinning mills and
their urban cotton weavers, were the first industrial towns in Ireland. Belfast in 1838 already had 50 of the 150 steam engines in
Ireland.

The decisive importance of trade and communications can be
seen in the growth of Portadown. The continued concentration of
the linen industry in the eastern half of Ulster was bound to give
its function as a crossing-point of the Bann and a transhipment
centre to and from destinations on Lough Neagh an enhanced
significance. It had a mere 231 inhabitants in 1821; and 2505 in
1841. The railway from Belfast reached it in 1842 and within a
generation it had become the focal point of the railway network in
Ulster.

Canal building continued into the nineteenth century. In 1804
the Grand Canal was completed to the Shannon, branches to
Ballinasloe, Mountmellick and Kilbeggan were all opened by 1836.
The Royal Canal was completed in 1817. From 1800 a Board of
Directors of Inland Navigation was charged with promoting works
on navigations not transferred to separate bodies; after 1831 its
work was taken over by the Board of Works. The Shannon Navigation was perfected in the first half of the century; the Ulster Canal
between the Blackwater and the Erne was completed between 1825
and 1842, and the Ballinamore and Ballyconnell Canal from the
Erne to the Shannon was completed in 1860. The steamship helped
to revolutionise transport on the Shannon, especially on the lower
Shannon. On the lower Shannon, where three steamers plied in the
1830s, 23,851 passengers were conveyed in 1836. Road building
advanced rapidly in the early nineteenth century. Improvement was
reflected in two ways. First it showed in a greater number of coach
routes and, through improved surfaces, in much greater speeds. By
the 1830s coach speeds were twice what they had been a century
previously. These developments had significance for commodity

carriage as well, although it is more difficult to quantify. Secondly, roads were built in the more remote areas where previously they had been few, or as in Connemara and much of West Mayo even non-existent. Since 1822 parliamentary grants were available to help road building, and after 1831 the Board of Works, created in that year to take over from a variety of bodies the management or supervision of the state's interest in roads, canals and public works, itself undertook road works in remote areas. The consequence of improved communications is strikingly shown by the growth of Kilrush. Originally a poor and remote landlord and fishing town, its communications by land had been bad, and its trade on the Shannon small. Steam navigation on the Shannon estuary and the opening up of the hinterland behind it by road building between 1822 and 1841 revolutionised the town. It emerged as an active commercial town, dominating much of the estuary of the Shannon and a large hinterland in West Clare. Beside it Kilkee expanded as a watering and holiday resort. Communications were vital to the economic changes taking place in the early nineteenth century. Towns and merchants who gained by improved communications were eager to see them improve still further. The railway system, as it began to take shape from the 1830s, was a response to economic changes as much as a cause of change. Cheapened transport had a significance for industrial organisation too. Just as favoured towns expanded their commerce at the expense of other towns, individual industrial firms in these towns were likely to capture the markets of many smaller firms farther afield.

A large amount of industrial re-organisation took place in the first half of the century. Power spinning in cotton and from the 1820s in linen with its significant result in the growth of Belfast is the most striking but by no means the only instance. The results were most striking here because re-organisation entailed the transition of industry from a domestic and often rural setting to factory buildings usually sited in towns. But even where an activity had always been organised in a factory-type building and often in towns or villages, re-organisation was extensive. A most striking instance was in malting, which produced the raw material of both the brewing and distilling industries. In 1785 there had been no less than 2,216 malt houses scattered throughout the island. In 1835, there were only 388 producing twice the quantity. The number of distillers had fallen, even with an eightfold increase in output, from

815 in 1782 to 95 in 57 centres in 1835. The number of brewers had fallen too from 937 in 1790 to 247 in 1837, although output had risen by two-thirds. At the earlier date many of the country brewers had been mere artisan firms. They had all become factory-units by 1837, reorganisation helping the country brewers to hold their own against the Dublin brewers. Dublin had produced 45 per cent of the beer brewed in Ireland in 1790, and only 30 per cent in 1837. The distilling industry too was a highly competitive one in many of its locations. The three major distilling centres – Dublin, Cork and Belfast – accounted for only 40 per cent of national output in 1836.

Only in the textile industry was a general crisis experienced. Outside linen the textile crisis was a national one. Within linen itself, it was a social one because the north-east and factory spinning gained at the expense of the rural linen workers elsewhere. There was, however, no crisis outside textiles. Paper and glass works survived. Shipbuilding and ironworking had strong traditions in several centres. Between 1831 and 1841 the number of male shipwrights doubled, male glassworkers rose by 50 per cent, ironfounders by 25 per cent, ropeworkers by 20 per cent.* Nor was this activity in any way especially centred on Ulster. In shipbuilding, 40 per cent of the shipwrights were in Munster in 1841, reflecting the rapidly expanding shipbuilding industries of Cork and Waterford. The yards in both centres were the most enterprising in Ireland : the first paddle steamer made in Ireland was built in Cork in 1812, and the Cork and Waterford yards were the pioneers in the 1840s of iron shipbuilding in Ireland. Less than a third of the iron-founders were in the north. The ironworks in Dublin and Cork were very active. There were two manufacturers of steam engines in Dublin, four in Cork, and at least two in Belfast in the late 'thirties. The annual wage bill of one of the Dublin manufacturers, Robinson, was said to be £5,500. A famous firm which made loco-motives was still to open in Drogheda. In one regard, however, Belfast was beginning to emerge as a leader – in a miscellaneous category called 'machine makers' of whom 60 per cent were in Ulster in 1841. They probably made miscellaneous engineering goods, especially textile machinery. If one takes into account a large variety of other industrial occupations with significant num-

---

* Based on figures of males upwards of 20 years in 1831, and 15 years and upwards in 1841.

bers employed – tanners, soapmakers, papermakers, coachbuilders, pinmakers, cutlers, wiredrawers etc. – an impression of vigorous industrial activity remains. Some industrial products were made by domestic workers. The most typical were the nailmakers of whom there were 5,973 male adults in 1841 and who had increased by a third since 1831.

The volume of commercial transactions was rising; improved communications were also leading to changes in industrial and commercial organisation. This was bound in turn to influence the character and growth of banking. The Bank of Ireland had been founded by a statute of 1782 to increase the banking facilities in Ireland. It held the government account; and merchants and other banks often rediscounted with it the bills of exchange they received from their own customers. Its notes at first circulated in the main in Dublin, but even in Dublin its note issue in 1797 accounted for only half the notes in circulation. It grew more rapidly subsequently, facilitated by the rapid rise in government expenditure and borrowing during the Napoleonic wars. Its circulation remained confined. The bank failures in Munster in 1820, however, enlarged the market for its notes which accounted in the early 1820s for 75 per cent of the circulation in Ireland. The extension of the bank's influence, evident in the early 1820s, was halted by the establishment of joint-stock banks. When the Bank of Ireland had been granted its charter in 1783, any other bank with more than six partners was prohibited, which meant in effect a monopoly of joint-stock banking for the Bank of Ireland. This limitation was subsequently altered by a statute in 1821, following the failures in the south, which permitted the establishment of banks with more than six partners provided that they were outside a radius of 50 miles of Dublin. Some remaining technical difficulties regarding the establishment of such banks were removed in 1824 and 1825.

It is significant that the first initiative in establishing a joint-stock bank, culminating in the opening of the Northern Bank Company in 1825, came from the Belfast area, and that the capital subscribed for that venture and for the Belfast Banking Company (1827) came principally from local sources. The linen industry, which had stagnated for two decades, was now beginning to grow rapidly again, and expanded credit facilities were necessary. This accounts for the more immediate response to the possibilities opened by the act of 1821 in Belfast. The response in the south was distinctly more cautious. This was due in part to the difficult economic situation in the south during the 1820s. In fact, the first joint-stock banks which appeared in southern Ireland were to a large extent financed by English capital. The 1821 act had been construed as requiring every shareholder to be resident in Ireland. When this ambiguity was resolved by a statute in 1824, English capital was forthcoming to finance banking ventures in southern Ireland and interest in proposals for joint-stock banking quickened. The bulk of the capital for the Provincial Bank (1825) was subscribed in England, so was some of the capital for the Hibernian Bank (1825) and much of the capital of the National Bank, established in 1835, and of the Royal Bank established in 1836. The 1821 act had left banks free to establish themselves within the 50-mile radius of the Bank of Ireland, provided they did not issue notes. Two joint-stock banks chose this course – the Hibernian Bank (1825) and the Royal (1836). The other two banks, the Provincial Bank and the National Bank, extended a banking network through the underbanked west and south. The joint-stock banks introduced branch banking to Ireland. The Bank of Ireland itself opened branches, although the Provincial Bank had the most extensive network in 1845. In that year there were in all 172 branches of banks in 89 towns. Despite the opening of branches by the Bank of Ireland, banking in the provinces was largely dominated by the other banks. Bank of Ireland circulation increased by 40 per cent between 1820 and 1844, that of the other banks by 94 per cent. Taking into account its monopoly of government business and its dominant position in the Dublin area, it lost ground in the provinces and played a minority role in banking in rural Ireland. Its evolution contrasted with that of the Bank of England. The latter bank's notes were widely used throughout the length and breadth of England and Wales for decades; on the other hand, Bank of Ireland notes were a minority of provincial circulation except in the aftermath of the 1820 crisis, and with the continued growth of branch banking in the 1830s lost still further ground. This contrast accounts for the differences between the Bank Charter Act of 1844 and the Bankers (Ireland) Act 1845. The English act prohibited other banks from expanding their note issue beyond their existing level, and envisaged the Bank of England issue expanding at the expense of the circulation of other banks. The Irish Bankers Act, on the other hand, taking into account the minority circulation of Bank of

Ireland notes, in no way prohibited existing banks from expanding their issue, requiring only that their expansion should be backed by gold and silver in reserve.

This was not the only way in which the Bank of Ireland differed from the Bank of England. The Bank of England dominated the London money market, holding the reserves of the English banks and acting as lender of last resort. The reverse of this situation was happening in Ireland. In the eighteenth century Irish country bankers and merchants held balances in the hands of correspondents – bankers or other merchants – in Dublin, and these balances were enlarged, when necessary, by rediscounting with the Bank of Ireland bills of exchange sent up from the country. In this way Dublin provided a money market for the Irish economy, and the Bank of Ireland as the largest single institution in the market played a significant role in it. In practice, however, this relationship evolved differently in the early decades of the nineteenth century. Changing economic organisation and improved communications meant that wholesaling functions were being frequently transferred from Dublin intermediaries to intermediaries in the countryside. In export business merchants and bleachers shipped goods directly overseas on their own account, reducing their reliance on intermediaries in the Irish capital. In import business country wholesalers often chose to deal directly with merchants in Britain rather than rely on the services of Dublin intermediaries. The most striking change was the growing amount of direct exchanges between Belfast and England. The development was not, however, confined to the north. Everywhere, there was a growing amount of direct contact between intermediaries in the countryside and business interests in England, and Dublin wholesalers monopolised much less of the country's wholesale business than in the eighteenth century. This was true of external trade; it was true also of internal trade. For instance, much of the yarn from the west had been supplied to the north through the hands of Dublin intermediaries in the late eighteenth century; at a later date what remained of the trade in linen yarn often went direct from the west to the north. The fact that direct commercial links were so much more common than in the past meant that merchants and banks needed cash balances in England. In consequence of this changing trend, the Dublin money market which had financed Irish wholesale trade – including most of the linen trade at one time – was breaking up.

Irish overseas trade was being increasingly financed by balances held in London. Local banking began to revolve around the discounting of bills on English commercial centres rather than on Dublin. This development is reflected, for instance, in the decline of Dublin working capital in the linen industry in the early decades of the nineteenth century and in the growing disuse of the Dublin Linen Hall. Working capital supplied by Dublin was no longer behind the industry's growth in the north, and when the trade recovered in the mid-twenties, its expansion was necessarily accompanied by a rapid development of banking in the Belfast area. Less dramatically, the same development affected Dublin's relationship with every other Irish town or region. According to an appendix in the Drummond report of 1838 relating to Drogheda, for instance :

> formerly, the traders of the town had to make all their payments in Dublin : now a large portion of them must be made in Liverpool; and the principal number of them are made in the town, there being in it a branch establishment of the Bank of Ireland, and another of the National Bank . . ., in both of which bills are discounted, which formerly should have been presented for discount in Dublin.

In other words, goods were being ordered directly from English centres instead of by placing orders with Dublin intermediaries, and in consequence the bill on England was replacing the bill on Dublin in the financing of wholesale trade.

The bill of exchange had financed inland and foreign trade : it also constituted, as long as it was in use, a desirable short-term investment outlet for surplus funds. By the 1830s, however, the bill of exchange was beginning to disappear from trade between Ireland and England. Within Ireland, the cheque drawn on a current account was replacing the bill of exchange. In trade between England and Ireland, the banker's draft on his London correspondent replaced the bill of exchange. With the disappearance of this investment outlet, surplus or reserve funds of banks were invested increasingly in government securities. Each Irish bank had its own holdings of government securities. Irish banks in difficulties were not dependent on the Bank of Ireland for assistance. They could and did sell some of their own holdings of securities on the London market. In this way, the Irish payments and banking system of the eighteenth century built around a Dublin money market was absorbed by the economic and commercial changes into the London money market.

Many contemporaries advocated the extension of banking on the grounds that banking services would promote economic development and thus lessen the poverty which was painfully evident in a large section of the community. Others advocated drainage works in the belief that there would be a substantial economic return on capital invested in draining land. A certain amount of legislation was passed to facilitate drainage work, and the Board of Works was itself authorised to undertake such works or to make advances to help to finance drainage. In reality, neither banking nor drainage held out valid hopes of a solution to the problem. Ireland did not seriously suffer from a shortage of capital. There was, in fact, an abundance of capital, a fact reflected in the gradual purchase by Irish residents of the English interest in some of the Irish banks and in the first railways. More money was deposited in Irish banks than they could usefully lend, a situation reflected in the fact that if banks were to make a profit and sufficient possibilities of making advances did not present themselves, bankers could earn an adequate return only by investing a high proportion of their assets in government stocks.

Banking of itself, therefore, was not going to revolutionise the economy, as some had suggested. In fact, the real problem was one of finding remunerative investment outlets. In the eighteenth century, there had been a substantial inflow of capital into Ireland, which had helped to finance the rapid growth of the economy at that time. The economic changes of the early nineteenth century lessened the attractiveness of investment in Ireland. Notably in the textile industries, but to a lesser extent in other industries as well, changing organisation and enhanced English competitiveness was lessening the range of remunerative outlets. Lacking outlets in Ireland, Irish capital was beginning to flow to England. It is likely that in these decades the net inflow of former times was being replaced by a net outflow. The change was probably small at first, but the disappearance of a net inflow was significant none the less, reflecting a reversal in the prospects facing the Irish economy and in the rate of returns on capital invested in Ireland. Contemporary belief in the prospects of a large return on drainage works reflects the oversanguine prospects still entertained by contemporaries regarding returns on investment in Ireland. In the case of drainage contemporaries were also guilty of underestimating the intractability of the drainage problem on many of the bad lands and the magnitude of the capital costs involved.

Population growth added to the problems of underemployment and poverty. These problems were made especially critical by the rapid decline in domestic employment in the pre-Famine decades. As population grew and underemployment became more critical, diet deteriorated. The diet of the poor had become to a large extent a potato one, and even milk had become a luxury for many labouring families. Poor families had no savings or even assets which could be realised in an emergency. If the potato failed, they were faced with hunger, in many cases even with starvation. In the very poorest regions, the smallholdings regions along the western seaboard, there was no system of retailing food. In consequence, even if relief was provided in cash, there was the added problem that cash could not be readily converted into food locally. In these regions, too, the poorest were unfamiliar with the preparation of meal and bread, and even lacked the utensils. In these areas, as a potato diet had become established, occasional potato failures were followed by famine. The famine in the south-west in 1822 is an instance; that in Mayo in 1831 another, or in Donegal in 1836. In the rest of Ireland, the situation was less serious. The farming class was comfortable. Its diet was by no means confined to the potato, and although the potato was consumed, the families' cash resources made it possible to replace the potato in a season in which it failed. During the Famine years, farmers were able to add to the livestock numbers on their farms, a reminder that even with a reduction in their own consumption of the potato, their economic situation was not impaired. As for the labouring class, the fact that domestic industry had survived better in the north had spread some cash resources through the class, a fact reflected in the retention of oatmeal in their diet. In the east, the labouring class was less well-off than in the north. But accustomed to wage-paid employment and living in regions where retail trade was fairly well-organised, they were better able to survive hardship than the peasants in poor and remote lands. In Balrothery, co. Dublin, for instance, labourers were accustomed in the 1830s to buy potatoes and meal ' at little shops ', a pattern fairly common in the eastern half of the country. In terms of prosperity, rural Ireland could, it has already been pointed out, be divided into three broad regions : a prosperous east and north, a region embracing the midlands and south with a prosperous farming class and a poor labouring class, and a desperately poor region in a large area within the counties along the whole western and south-western seaboard. The incidence of the Great Famine reflected this pattern. There was little famine in the eastern counties or in the north. In the midlands and south the effects of famine were confined to the labouring population and were never general in the rural community. It was only in the poor regions of the west that the failure of the potato presented whole regions with the threat of starvation. The death rate did, of course, rise across the country. Fever followed famine, and because the desperately poor migrated from west to east, and from countryside to towns, it spread across the country. In the east and north, fever was the cause of death rather than starvation. Even in the midlands and south, where the death rate was higher, undernourishment exposed the labourer to fever more than to primary starvation.

Local famine had become no novelty in recent decades as the poor became more dependent on a largely potato diet and as their meagre cash incomes were contracted still further by the decline in domestic industry. But famine had been localised, and had rarely appeared in immediately successive years. The potato blight which destroyed the potato crop between 1845 and 1848 was a novel feature. It affected the crop in several years, and in the country at large. The blight had appeared late in the potato harvest of 1845; the early potatoes escaped, and it struck only in limited regions. The following year, the blight was general, the famine reaching its intensity in the summer of 1847 when people were awaiting the ripening of the new crop. Blight was absent in 1847, but because of a small supply of seed potatoes, the crop sown was a small one: famine diminished rather than disappeared. In 1848 the potato failed partially again. The Famine thus lasted in one part of the country or other from 1845 into 1849. Its effects were still evident when the census was taken in 1851 in the temporarily enlarged population of the towns in poor areas, in the swollen number of inmates of the workhouses, and in the large numbers still in receipt of outdoor relief in the poorer parts of the country, such as much of Mayo.

The failure in the autumn of 1845 had mainly affected poor regions where famine had been no novelty. Sir Robert Peel, the

British Prime Minister, in November 1845 purchased £100,000 worth of Indian corn, with a view to selling it cheaply so as to keep prices down. When the crop failed totally in the following year, this method was not repeated: the government has been criticised for not dispensing with laissez-faire principles and entering the market on a large scale. Instead, it chose to organise through the Board of Works relief works in the affected areas as a means of providing a cash income for the destitute. The government's attitude was in part doctrinaire, but it was also a fact that in much of the country affected after the failure in 1846 a retailing system existed, and government intervention could have harmed the fragile but extensive retail system that catered for food requirements in much of the country. Here the problem was not one of the absence of a food market, but of the lack of an income on the part of the poorer members of the local community. Relief works raised considerable administrative problems, and moreover they offered no solution to the problem of a family where no member was strong enough to accept employment. By March 1847 over 700,000 were employed on relief works. Given the extent of destitution, and the limitations of public works, they were abandoned, and replaced gradually by the provision and distribution of food through the Poor Law administration. By August 1847 the number being fed at the public soup kitchens or other public centres had risen to 3,000,000, i.e. roughly 40 per cent of the population. In many of the Poor Law regions of the west, up to 70 or 80 per cent of the population was in receipt of relief. In the east and north, the percentage was below 20 or even 10 per cent; in the midlands and south below 30 per cent. The Famine was less a national disaster than a social and regional one.

Between 1845 and 1851 the population fell by about two million; roughly one million had died during these years; another million emigrated. The Famine and famine fever should not be blamed exclusively for the abnormal mortality of the period. The cholera epidemic in 1849, first evident in Belfast, accounted for many deaths, and its ravages were most evident in some of the better-off regions of the country. The Famine is often regarded as responsible for the demographic decline of Ireland from mid-century. But even if famine had not intervened, a decline in population was inevitable. Emigration was already rising sharply in the decade before the famine. What the Famine did, however, was greatly to lessen the natural reluctance to emigrate and to accelerate the painful process of adjusting Ireland's population to its narrowing economic prospects.

6

The Emergence of Modern Ireland
1851-1921

The Famine, with its high rate of mortality and emigration, stands out from the middle decades of the nineteenth century. In consequence, it has been given a more decisive role in changes in Irish social and economic life than it merits. A rise in emigration and a falling population would have been inevitable even if the Great Famine had not occurred. The rapid rise in population in pre-Famine decades had been accompanied by a disproportionate increase in the numbers with no secure stake in the land; the decline in domestic industry deprived them of the prospect of an industrial income as well.

The population probably fell by about two millions between 1845 and 1851. Somewhat less than half the decline was accounted for by the abnormally high mortality of the Famine years. Mortality was heaviest in the poorer regions. Emigration on the other hand was more marked in the remainder of the country: contemporary observers noted that emigrants had as a rule some substance. Although emigration declined from a peak in the late 'forties and early 'fifties, it remained an outstanding feature of the Irish economic scene henceforth. In every decade right up to 1914 it exceeded the natural increase in population, i.e., the excess of births over deaths. A consequence was a continuing fall in population

Population and Emigration

	Population		Emigration
1851	6,552,385		
1861	5,798,967	1851-60	1,163,418

Population and Emigration

	Population		Emigration
1871	5,412,377	1861-70	849,836
1881	5,174,836	1871-80	623,933
1891	4,704,750	1881-90	770,706
1901	4,458,775	1891-1900	433,526
1911	4,390,219	1901-10	346,024

In the immediate post-Famine decades the population fell more sharply in the eastern and midland counties than in the poorer western ones. In the western part of the country, the rate of natural increase of population was more rapid than in the remainder of the country. On the other hand, though the western counties were poorer, emigration from them was no greater than from the more eastern counties. In fact, emigration was noticeably intermittent from the poorer regions. It rose sharply after bad seasons such as 1861, and whole families went at these times. In the east, on the other hand, emigrants more typically went as individuals and the current of emigration was much more steady than in the west. Given the high natural rate of increase and relatively low emigration in the west, population numbers increased in many districts there in the post-Famine decades. If the population in such districts did not again exceed the pre-Famine level of 1841, it was often only because the mortality had been so heavy in the second half of the 1840s. In many townlands, and even in some baronies as a whole, where mortality was low in the 1840s, the population by 1881 had exceeded the 1841 level. In Mayo, the poorest county, the population fell only by 4 per cent between 1861 and 1871, and, despite heavy emigration towards the end of the decade, rose marginally between 1871 and 1881. In such regions pre-Famine conditions survived. Marriage took place at an early date, and relatively few of the population remained celibate. The potato remained immensely important in the diet, in some districts the potato accounting for 50-60 per cent of the tilled acreage.

In the rest of the country the fall in population was much sharper. Emigration was as large as from the poorer counties; the rate of natural increase in population much less. The decline in population outside the poor western counties was concentrated on the labourers and cottiers. In fact, the cottier all but disappeared; the surviving cottiers became labourers depending on a money wage. Between 1845 and 1851 the number of holdings of an acre or less fell very sharply, the number above 1 acre and not exceeding 5 fell less sharply, and the number above 5 and not exceeding 15 acres less sharply still. The total number of holdings not exceeding 15 acres fell from 628,397 to 317,665.* On the other hand the Famine had scarcely affected the farmers at all. Farmers had, to start with, a varied diet; they also had cash resources which meant that the failure of the potato held no terrors for them. The number of farms above 15 acres actually rose between 1845 and 1851 from 276,618 to 290,401.* During these years farmers enlarged their holdings and increased the stocking of their land. A continued decline in the number of smallholdings ensured some continued enlargement of farm sizes in post-Famine Ireland. Right from 1845 – the eve of the Famine – up to 1910 there was a remarkable stability in the number of farms above 15 acres:

	1845	1851	1910
Holdings above 15 acres*	276,618	290,401	303,529
Holdings above 1 and not exceeding 15 acres*	493,083	279,937	216,236

This stability reflects the underlying strength of the farming community. The structure of the farming community already existed before the Famine; the Famine did not seriously affect it. Marriage ages were already relatively late among the farming community before the Famine. The apparent sharp rise in the age of marriage in post-Famine Ireland was in part a consequence of the fall in the number of labourers and cottiers among whom early marriage had always been characteristic. In the farming community families did not emigrate; emigration was confined as a rule to younger or more venturesome members of the family. Farming traditions were strong; the same family often occupied the same farm for generations, and the Famine did little to sap family traditions or settlement. Large-scale emigration, often in family units, was therefore confined to labourers and cottiers, and, after bad seasons, to the struggling smallholding families of the west coast and its hinterland.

* Figures for 1845 as adjusted in P.M.A. Bourke, ' The agricultural statistics of the 1841 census of Ireland: a critical review ', *Economic History Review*, vol. XVIII, No. 2, August 1965.

Farm output did not rise very sharply in post-Famine Ireland. Market output did, however, as the potato crop – a subsistence crop – fell from its pre-Famine acreage and the land was put to other uses. Livestock numbers continued to rise, and dairy cattle also rose. Moreover, the decline in arable land was itself limited. Between 1855 and 1864 the arable area (excluding flax) fell from 4,276,954 acres to 3,765,059 acres. Most of the decline was concentrated into a few years at the end of the 'fifties. In 1870, at 3,662,379 acres, the acreage had fallen very little further. Agricultural prices were high in the 1850s and 1860s, and, excepting the bad seasons of the early 1860s, these proved two prosperous decades for the farmer. The labour requirements of agriculture did not decline sharply therefore. On the other hand, the number of labourers had fallen steeply because of the Famine and subsequent heavy emigration. Farm labourers and servants fell from 1,320,239 in 1841 to 808,691 in 1861. The continuing demand for labour combined with the decline in the number of labourers was reflected in a significant increase in wages. From as low as 6d–8d in pre-Famine Ireland, they rose to 1s–1s 6d a day. This relative prosperity was reflected in a very modest decline in the number of labourers in the 1860s: the number stood at 749,541 in 1871. A fall in the tillage acreage in the early 1870s may be attributed to an aggravated labour shortage more than to any other factor. The decline was concentrated on the years 1872-4, the acreage (excluding flax) falling from 3,565,048 acres to 3,255,418. Thereafter, the acreage stabilised again until the end of the decade. The labour shortage seems the likely factor at the root of the contraction in the early 1870s. Between 1871 and 1881 the number of labourers fell to 473,070. The substitution of the scythe for the sickle – a reflection of a growing labour shortage – was to a large extent completed by the early 1870s, and in the 1870s interest in farm machinery and in its manufacture in Ireland quickened.

Rising rural prosperity was evident in post-Famine Ireland. The farmer gained; so too, to an extent, did the farm labourer. Apart from sharp depression at the outset of the 1860s, bank deposits, a sensitive barometer of agricultural incomes, rose rapidly. They doubled from £8 million in 1845 to £16 million in 1859. The only serious halt in their rise was in the early 1860s. Crop yields were bad in the years 1860, 1861 and 1862. The potato yield at 1.6 tons an acre in 1861 was the lowest since the Great Famine.

The wet season in 1861 destroyed the hay and ruined the turf and potatoes. In the west it was a season of hunger and hardship. Economic difficulties, even in the better-off farming community, were reflected in a decline in bank deposits to £13 million in 1863. They recovered to £17 million in 1865 and almost doubled to £33 million by 1876.

Living standards rose. Improvement was reflected in the rise in the number of shops and in the consumption of shop goods. Even in the poor regions, the entry of 'yellow' meal into the diet as a fairly regular supplement to the potato reflected a growing reliance on shops. Whiskey consumption fell off sharply, partly because of Father Mathew's temperance crusades in 1839 and later, partly because of the rise in whiskey taxation after 1853. On the other hand, per capita tobacco consumption rose to English standards around 1870, and per capita consumption of tea was not far off the English level by the end of the 1870s. For 150 years preceding 1845, per capita tobacco consumption had scarcely risen at all in Ireland. The fact that the consumption of such a conventional necessity rose after 1845 seems to suggest that the increase in money wages among the lower classes such as the agricultural wage earners reflected a real and very definite improvement in their still precarious circumstances.

Improved conditions were reflected in a decline in agrarian unrest. The rise in rents was moderate. It seems likely that rents did not exceed £12 million and that they were therefore not significantly higher than they had been at the end of the Napoleonic wars. Moreover, rent can only have absorbed 30 per cent of post-Famine net farm income of around £40 million. This would seem to contradict the view that the Famine by accelerating changes in ownership had resulted in a more mercenary landlordism. Many estates had been in difficulties in the 1840s: unpaid rents often reduced the landlord's income, and even if he received the income, encumbrances in the form of mortgage interest or payments to other members of the family often left very little income for the owner's use or for re-investment. The Famine, responsible for mounting rent arrears for landlords in the poorer regions and at the same time a sharp rise in Poor Rates, precipitated a crisis for many landlords. Under the Encumbered Estates Acts of 1848 and 1849 some quarter of the land acreage in Ireland was transferred in subsequent decades to new ownership. The view is often put forward that grasping middle-class merchants bought the land; but much of the land may in fact have been purchased by members of existing landed families.

Agricultural investment recovered in the 1850s. Even if rents did not rise very sharply, prompter payment in the prosperous 1860s and 1870s of itself greatly improved landlord finances. Landlord investment in farm buildings and drainage was often substantial in these decades. Tenant investment in dwellings and outhouses was often in evidence too. Tenants invested in an expansion of live-stock herds. The 1850s and 1860s were a period of prosperity in the dairying districts too. At one time much of the dairy farming in Munster had been conducted by dairymen who had rented cattle from a middleman; by the end of the nineteenth century the herds were farmer-managed. It seems likely that the re-organisation of the dairying industry with the large middleman herds being replaced by herds owned by small tenant farmers occurred between the 1850s and 1870s. The process of re-organisation is obscure but the fact of replacement of large herd owners letting cattle to impoverished dairymen by dairying tenants is undoubted.

Prosperity did not, of course, guarantee an end to agrarian conflict; in some respects it actually exacerbated unrest. It encour-aged the commercialisation of agriculture. The introduction of larger tenant farmers on estates traditionally occupied by pauperised smallholders, or the efforts by a landlord to replace smallholders by larger farmers, were bound to create conflicts of interest. For the struggling smallholder, his smallholding was his only hope of economic survival in the locality. For the landowner, on the other hand, the smallholder was a doubtful proposition. From the point of view of rent payments, the smallholder was often, unlike the larger farmer, heavily in arrears, a fact of which landlords were painfully aware in the early 1850s. From the point of view of rural improvement, the only hope of avoiding a recurrence of a tragedy like the Famine seemed to lie in a reduction in the number of small-holdings and in their replacement by larger farms which offered a more secure livelihood to the tenant himself and a more secure rent to the landlord. To the landlord, even if thoughtful and well meaning and perhaps especially if thoughtful and well meaning, smallholdings seemed to offer security to neither partner to the contract or bargain. Often, as it proved, it was a landlord, enlight-ened and progressive in intent, who fell foul of the interests of the small tenantry. The situation was most critical in the immediate post-Famine years, and landlords lived in an explosive situation in counties such as Monaghan. The situation was relieved partly by the gradual departure of many of the more insolvent tenants, partly by the high prices of the 1850s which helped to mend the fortunes of tenant and landlord alike. But sources of conflict often remained. In many counties agrarian conflict died down because landlords abandoned the efforts to replace smallholdings by larger farms and aquiesced in the situation. Evictions were not numerous, confined as they were to bad years or to landlords who persisted in the attempt to modernise impoverished smallholding regions. The Third Earl of Leitrim, landlord of 90,000 acres in four counties of the north-west, assassinated in 1878, is a tragic instance of the consequences of such ambitions. The Earl, on the evidence of his diaries, was obsessed by fear of a famine reoccurring; the rise in the number of holdings on his estates seemed to him to confirm his fears. From 1855 to 1869 the number of tenancies on the co. Leitrim estate rose from 736 to 776; on the co. Donegal estate from 1,572 to 1,664. His entire life was spent in the unceasing management of his estate, and his actions, though often arrogant or high-handed, were intended for what was by his own lights the welfare of his tenantry.

Rural prosperity was reflected in turn in the role of the towns. Their commercial importance was enhanced. As a result of better communications, the larger or better-situated towns became important wholesaling centres; large and small towns alike witnessed an expansion of their retail business. Town population as a whole did not fall in post-Famine Ireland, the apparent fall between 1851 and 1861 being due to the sharp decline in the number of indigent who were in institutions such as the workhouses in 1851. At that date, no less than 102,819 persons out of a town population of 1,218,676 were in such institutions.

Population of towns of 2,000 and upwards at date of census

1841	1,135,465	1881	1,189,592
1851	1,115,857*	1891	1,244,113
1861	1,140,368	1901	1,384,929
1871	1,201,344	1911	1,470,595

* excluding 102,819 persons in institutions

It is true, of course, that the population of Dublin with its suburbs, and of Belfast, rose sharply between 1851 and 1911. Even if the total increase of 364,000 in the combined population of Belfast and Dublin is excluded, town population at 1,106,595 in 1911 is only fractionally below the level of 1851. In Munster and Connaught alone did a sharp fall occur in town population in the immediate post-Famine decades.

Towns of 2,000 and upwards

	1841	1851	1861
Munster	386,941	343,263*	319,748
Connaught	80,224	69,588*	64,912

* excluding inmates of institutions.

In these regions, however, the reason for town decline lay in the large number of families which had crowded into them in pre-Famine decades and who depended for survival on a potato patch or on intermittent agricultural employment. In many Irish towns a disproportionately large share of their families – between a quarter and a third – had been engaged in agriculture. The sharp fall in many of the poorer towns in the immediate post-Famine decade reflected the decline in the number of such families. Ennis, in co. Clare, may be taken as a concrete illustration of this situation. Its population fell from 9,318 in 1841 to 8,623 in 1851 and to 7,175 in 1861. Around 1840 there were roughly 600 cabins on the approach roads to Ennis. According to the 1841 census, 496 of the town's 1,799 families were engaged in agriculture. In 1861 the number of families engaged in agriculture had fallen to 106. As a percentage of total families, those engaged in agriculture had fallen from 28 per cent to 7 per cent. Apart from a decline in many towns occasioned by a decline in the agriculturally occupied population of the cabin districts on the fringe of the town, town population remained remarkably stable. While comparatively few towns gained in population in post-Famine Ireland, changes in the occupational structure seem to reflect economic vitality. This was especially so for towns which lost little or no population after the Famine. For the poor the towns had always been a magnet; even in many towns in eastern Ireland the proportion of families nominally employed in agriculture was high before the Famine. In such circumstances a change in occupational structure, unaccompanied by population decline, seems to testify to the emergence of a considerable number of new employment opportunities.

The towns fared well as commercial centres. The volume of agricultural produce marketed rose; its value rose even more sharply. Per capita consumption standards also rose in post-Famine Ireland : in consequence retail grocery, drapery and hardware shops expanded in number and in the range of goods they carried. A remarkably large number of the leading retail shops in Irish towns in the 1890s seem to have originated in the 1840s and 1850s, testifying to decisive changes in commerce in those decades. Most of the country's imports continued to come through Dublin, Belfast or Cork, but wholesale merchants in the ports found themselves in competition with new wholesale firms in drapery, groceries, hardware, ironmongery and builders' goods in the large and medium-sized provincial towns. The rise of the provincial wholesalers was a response to the growth in depth of the retail sector where small retail businesses required more accessible wholesale points than the remote and lordly wholesalers of the major ports. Towns fared well as the indigent departed from the workhouses and commercial development created new employment outlets – as a rule unskilled and badly paid, but less precarious and less badly paid than the agricultural employment on which the urban poor depended before the Famine. Improved conditions were reflected in greater stability in town population. Ennis, for instance, which had fallen sharply in population between 1841 and 1861, declined little in the next twenty years. The population fell from 7,175 in 1861 to 6,503 in 1871 and 6,317 in 1881.

Changes in communications were an essential element of the changing fortunes of the towns. Roads and steamers had, for instance, accounted for the commercial role which Kilrush rather quickly acquired in the Shannon estuary and west Clare in the second quarter of the century. Railways achieved the same effect for many towns later in the century. The railway came early to Ireland. The first line, the six-mile-long Dublin-Kingstown line, was opened in 1834, only four years after the inauguration of the Liverpool-Manchester, which effectively launched England into the Railway Age. But after the Kingstown line, progress was at first slow in Ireland. In 1844 only two other lines were open to traffic, a 17¾-mile stretch of the Ulster Railway which had reached Portadown in 1842, and the 32 miles of the Dublin-Drogheda line

opened in 1844.* The boom in railway building in Ireland only
began in earnest in 1844-5 coinciding with the second and greater
wave of railway mania in England. Irish investors had been slow
to show an interest in the railway schemes so far promoted in
Ireland. English investment was essential to get the early schemes
off the ground, and railway building in Ireland got under way
rapidly in 1844-5 because the railway mania in England made it
easy to attract English investment capital into Irish schemes. In
1850 one half the private capital so far invested in Irish railways
had been subscribed by English investors. The railway mania or
speculation was past its peak by 1847, and some government
capital was essential to sustain the confidence of new investors.
Government loans were subsidiary in the financing of Irish railways. They accounted for only £1½ millions out of the total capital
investment of £12¼ millions up to 1852. But it was an important
element in attracting the cautious private investor after the speculative urge of 1844-5 had spent itself, and only three of the 19
Irish railways open in 1853 had been constructed without a government loan.

Railway construction was an impressive operation in itself. Of
the 1,000 miles open or under construction in 1853, 900 had been
built by native contractors, some two-thirds by William Dargan
alone. The mileage open in 1845 was only 65; in 1849 428 miles
were open and 183 were under construction. The line to Cork was
opened in 1849, and in the early 'fifties lines were in operation to
five major railheads : Belfast, Cork, Galway, Limerick and Waterford. Several striking engineering works were effected such as the
great tunnel through solid rock which brought the railway from
a temporary terminus outside the city to a new station in Glanmire
in Cork, and the lofty viaduct across the Boyne at Drogheda in
1855 which made possible direct through communication from
Dublin to Belfast. In subsequent years many other lines were built,
and spurs added to existing routes. The railways proved remunerative, partly because the companies avoided the poorer regions,
partly because construction costs – about half those in England –
admitted of a profit on routes where traffic was by English standards light. Between 1854 and 1866, the annual additions to the
railway network were little short of the rate of construction from
1845 to 1854. The network rose from 865 miles in 1854 to 1,909

* Not including the 1¾-mile line from Kingstown to Dalkey, opened in 1844.

miles in 1866. At this stage, with the bulk of the more remunerative routes completed and promoters uninterested in the more remote regions, railway construction fell to almost a third of its former rate. Only 461 miles were added to the network between 1866 and 1880.

The railways helped to further a commercial revolution that already showed signs of taking shape before their appearance. They brought goods cheaply to the retailer and without them wholesalers in provincial towns could scarcely have prospered at all. Their significance for retail and wholesale trade is obvious. But the railways had a significance for local industry as well. Goods from farther afield entailed stiffer competition faced by local industrial firms and crafts. The railway was bound therefore to reveal the existing weakness of small industrial firms, and once crafts elsewhere were converted to a factory basis, to quicken the decline of the surviving crafts in small Irish towns. The industrial base in the small town was therefore in danger. In pre-Famine Ireland this was often extensive : breweries, distilleries, ropeworks, tanneries were numerous, and paper mills and ironworks operated in many of the larger towns. Moreover, many goods were turned out by craftsmen, and every town and its immediate hinterland had even after the 1840s a host of craftsmen. The number of nailmakers, 6,276 in 1841, was 4,193 in 1861, and decline slowed sharply between 1861 and 1871. Blacksmiths – who not only shod horses but made a variety of articles and tools in iron – fell only by a quarter from 25,185 in 1841 to 18,679 in 1861, and fell moderately to 16,342 in 1871. Shoemakers, hatters, seamstresses and so on were numerous. The number of shoemakers, for instance, fell only from 55,728 in 1841 to 46,484 in 1861. Crafts therefore remained vigorous. In most cases they were exercised by isolated individuals, but on occasion outwork was organised by merchant intermediaries. In the early 1850s in Cork, the Arnotts had a thousand workers making silk ties, shirts etc.

Industrial decline in mid-century had so far been confined to a large extent to textiles. Apart from traditional centres such as Bandon and the Dublin Liberties, the decay in textiles was far more serious for the countryside than for the town. By and large the towns still presented a picture of industrial as well as commercial vigour. Few major town industries had as yet declined. The most outstanding example of decline was sugar refining. Importing its raw sugar from British ports, it proved vulnerable to competition from refineries in Britain. In 1769 the industry in Ireland had been reputed to support 4,000 families. In 1861 the census returned only 19 as being employed as sugar refiners. In 1870 a Dublin firm, employing 124 workers, was probably the sole refinery in Ireland. Glass making declined rapidly in mid-century. But it was a luxury or prestige industry giving comparatively little employment, and its virtual extinction in the early 1850s with the closing of Gatchells* in Waterford was not of great significance. Only 358 glass makers were returned in the 1841 census, and the decline in quality glass was to some extent compensated by the rise in employment in the manufacture of glass bottles.

The only industries in serious difficulties in the early 1850s were tanning and distilling. In both cases, moreover, the causes were exceptional. Irish tanning had been justly famous for the quality of its leather; in the south tanning was an extensive industry. Bandon at one time had 17 tanneries; Cork city 40. In Cork the number had fallen to 16 in 1853. In Bandon four tanneries still worked in 1875; a solitary one by 1892. The reasons for the failure of the tanning industry in Ireland were technological. New methods elsewhere could tan leather more quickly; the old method retained in Ireland produced a better-quality leather, but the longer time taken by the old process necessitated a much slower turnover and hence higher operational costs. Reluctance to change or conservatism – meritorious in so far as it sprang from the pride generated by the high quality of the old leather – was responsible for the difficulties of the industry. The failure of the distilleries was rather different. Father Mathew's temperance crusades had drastically reduced whiskey consumption at the end of the 1830s; the number of distilleries fell from 86 in 1840 to 51 in 1851. The raising of the duties depressed consumption after 1853. Distilleries all around the country closed their doors, and the number of distilleries was down to 22 in the mid-sixties.

Otherwise industry remained prosperous in the 1850s and 1860s. Even in tanning the numbers employed recovered temporarily between 1861 and 1871. In paper the picture was bright in 1850 with 37 mills in operation, and flourishing centres at Cork, Dublin, Limerick and Galway. Output continued to grow impressively:

* Letters in the Wright papers in the Friends' Historical Library, Dublin, suggest that the Gatchell interest in the business was wound up in 1835-6.

Output of paper in Ireland (lb)

1838	3,554,879	1852	7,373,012
1844	4,557,306	1860	9,314,985

Figures for output do not exist subsequently, but a continued rise in output may be inferred in a rise in employment between the 1861 and 1871 census, from 402 to 627. Grain milling flourished too, the number of millers actually rising between the 1841 and 1861 census from 4,309 to 4,417. Even with a definite fall in the 1860s the number of millers was 3,986 in 1871. Galway town had upwards of 50 mills. The industry was widespread throughout the country, and in some of the towns in the heart of grain-growing districts there were whole complexes of mills. The most outstanding complex was Clonmel, the largest milling centre in Ireland. The industry continued to export substantial quantities of grain, and even with a decline in grain production well-located mills, importing grain, preserved much of their export trade. The cotton textile industry showed some signs of recovery as well. The numbers employed in cotton factories rose from 2,734 in 1862 to 4,217 in 1868. Two large mills, one at Portlaw, the other at Drogheda, accounted for more than half the employment. In 1868 a new mill was opened in Cork. The mill at Portlaw with its waterwheels and steam engines producing 500 h.p. was an enormous one, the largest industrial employer of labour outside Belfast, part of a commercial empire run by the Quaker family of Malcomson. The Malcomsons of Portlaw were shipowners, ran a shipbuilding yard in Waterford, had business interests in textiles in Belfast, Manchester and Scotland, and held shares in a German coal mine.

Industrial crisis emerged only in the 1870s. Its early emergence was in part a consequence of the ending of the world-wide industrial boom in 1874. When the boom ended, British manufactures flooded the Irish market and prices fell. However, the antecedents of the Irish crisis preceded the termination of the boom. In cotton, for instance, employment was already falling: from 1,629 workers in Portlaw in 1868 to 1,445 in 1870, and in Drogheda from 820 to 683. The Malcomsons collapsed in 1874. In paper, a relatively small but flourishing industry at the outset of the decade, employment fell from 627 in 1871 to 507 in 1881. In ropemaking, soap-boiling and chandling, and tanning, decline accelerated between

1871 and 1881. In milling the numbers fell little at first sight: from 3,986 in 1871 to 3,834 in 1881, but there was a gathering storm at the end of the decade. The new roller mills put many of the old mills grinding flour by stone out of business. Mills in the port towns found it worth their while to modernise because they could rely on imported grain. The decline in the wheat acreage in Ireland, however, did not make it worth while for most of the flour mills in the interior to modernise. Individual mills did modernise, but the milling complexes in the interior, small such as Nenagh and Ballymahon, or huge like Clonmel, fell on lean days, and the scattered mills in tillage areas likewise closed one by one. Employment in milling was halved between 1881 and 1901. In one district in the south where there had been 27 flour mills in 1874, there were only three mills at work in 1902.

At the same time, the crafts were affected by novel competition. Blacksmiths fell steadily in number, although there was no long-term decline in the number of horses. The advent of factory-produced cheap iron goods reduced the blacksmith's importance. The consequences of factory goods were even more disastrous for the nailer. The number of nailers was almost halved in the 1870s, halved again in the 1880s, and halved yet again by 1901, only a few hundred surviving. The sewing machine had made possible the factory boot, and cheap boots from the factories reduced the number of bootmakers by over a third between 1871 and 1891, and by the same proportion again between 1891 and 1911.

Urban growth was virtually negative in the 1870s and 1880s. Town population fell in the 1870s, and, if Belfast is excluded, rose only marginally in the 1880s. This was a period of industrial crisis. Many industries folded up in towns such as Cork, Limerick and Galway. The decay of industrial crafts made the crisis all the more pervasive. The industrial crisis reflected external circumstances – cheap goods from English firms underemployed in the industrial slump in the second half of the 1870s, and a decline in rural purchasing power in Ireland in the agricultural crisis which spread across Ireland at the end of the decade. But the causes were more fundamental and were not transient. The traditional crafts were being overwhelmed by industrially produced goods; at the same time large factories undermined smaller, local firms. In brewing, for instance, some seven breweries closed within a radius of 20 miles of Tullamore in the last two decades of the century, and the total number of firms in the industry was reduced to 41 in 1901. This continuing trend reinforced the more transient causes of the industrial crisis of the late 1870s and of the 1880s. Industrial crisis was evident even in the north. The linen industry had boomed during the cotton famine in the early 1860s, and the expansion of the industry continued into the 1870s. The number of spindles in the industry reached their nineteenth-century peak in 1875, the total not being surpassed until early in the following century. The subsequent expansion of the industry in Belfast was deceptive. It reflected the substitution of the power loom for the handloom, a substitution which concentrated almost 60 per cent of the capacity of the weaving branch of the industry in Belfast. Concentration of weaving in Belfast reflected reorganisation more than a buoyant market. Factory employment in the industry grew only slowly after the 1870s, and money wages fell from 1873 to 1889.

It is hardly surprising that a sense of foreboding pervaded the Irish industrial scene in the early 1880s. A forthcoming annihilation of industrial activity in much of Ireland seemed imminent. Edward Blackburne published a book entitled *Causes of the decadence of the industries of Ireland: a retrospect*, in 1881. A quickened interest in industrial matters showed itself, accompanied by practical efforts to gain support for existing or surviving Irish industries. Hely Hutchinson's book, *The commercial restraints of Ireland*, which appeared in 1779, was reprinted in 1882, the reprint, according to the introduction being ' inspired by the effort for the revival of our native industries ' and intended ' to contribute somewhat to the all-important and patriotic impulse '. More practical steps were also taken. An industrial exhibition was held in Cork in 1882; one in Dublin in 1883. Dublin Corporation in 1883 appointed a committee to enquire into industrial development and efforts in Parliament resulted in the appointment of a select committee to enquire into the state of Irish industry in 1885.

The crisis in industry coincided with a grave one in agriculture. Up to and including the harvest of 1876, agriculture had been prosperous. Three bad harvests in the following seasons altered things. The output of the main agricultural crops, measured in fixed prices, fell, especially in the disastrous harvest of 1879 when output at £22.7 million compared with £36.5 million in 1876. Valued at market prices, output fell even more sharply because farmers, in contrast to the invariable experience after past bad seasons, found that declining yields were accompanied by falling prices. The reason was the advent of foreign competition created by the transoceanic steamship and the opening up of new agricultural lands overseas. In the second and third quarters of 1879 there was rain in two out of every three days on average. Crops, hay and turf were ruined. Poor and rich farmers alike had difficulty in meeting their rent obligations. Among the smallholders of the west the situation was disastrous. The potato yield at 1.3 tons to the acre, roughly a third of a normal yield, was lower than in 1861. The price of potatoes alone among food prices rose. The year 1879-80 was a year of near-starvation among the smallholders. In the Strokestown poor law union in co. Roscommon, some 60 per cent of the population were in receipt of outdoor relief in 1880. Relief measures such as the Mansion House Fund were organised to meet the situation in the western districts. The fact that none actually starved in 1880 is itself a sign of considerable change since the 1840s in regions such as Mayo. Yellow meal supplemented the potato in the diet; reliance on it denoted that cash dealings were more common, and shop credit helped to tide people over difficult periods. Part of the problem in counties such as Mayo was the decline in the modest cash incomes which had become general even among the smallest and most remote smallholders since the 1840s. The fall in prices of crops and livestock was one factor responsible; another was the fact that the wet seasons had reduced the amount of work available for migrant workers, and the migrants returned from England with little cash to tide the family over to the next season. Mayo was the county with the largest number of migrant workers; in the poorest part of Mayo, the Belmullet poor law union, a third of the population was in receipt of outdoor relief in 1880.

Unrest was general in 1879-80; the coincidence of unrest among smallholders and among the larger farmers provided the basis of a powerful political movement among tenants. The first steps in the foundation of the Land League may have been taken in the stricken county of Mayo and by a Mayoman, Michael Davitt, but the League swept the farming areas of the whole country. The Land League advised tenants to offer landlords what they regarded as a fair rent, and, if that was not accepted, to pay nothing. Landlords replied to this challenge with evictions; evictions in turn were resisted, and on occasion process-servers and bailiffs were attacked.

This was in effect economic war; if the landlord refused to accept the rent offered, the tenants had a new weapon against him – boycott. Agrarian unrest declined somewhat after the early 1880s, but it revived in the middle of the decade when farm prices fell further. The Land League now produced a new policy in 1886, the so-called Plan of Campaign. Advised by the League, tenants on estates where the rents were considered excessive were to lodge in the hands of trustees what was thought to be a reasonable rent; they were to offer this to the landlord not separately but in bulk; and if the money were refused they were to pay him nothing until he came to terms. Instead they were to use the money in support of any tenant who might be evicted. In 1886 and subsequent years the Plan was put into effect, at one stage or other, on about 116 estates. The landlords retaliated on some estates by wholesale clearances; the tenants resisted eviction with the help of neighbours and supporters. These evictions were great set-pieces in the economic war, attended by photographers and journalists. The difficulties at the beginning of the decade and the attendant unrest had already been responsible for one very significant bit of legislation in 1881 which gave tenants the right to apply to the courts for a reduction in rent. Where a reduction was sought, rents were reduced on average by 20 per cent. With the continued deterioration in prices, the reductions accorded in settlements made in 1888 had risen to 28 per cent. Although the reductions were not intended to be reviewed until the end of a 15-year period, an act in 1887 authorised the Land Commission to review reductions already sanctioned.

The 1880s were therefore a grim decade; industrial and agricultural difficulties were both acute; and emigration soared far above the level of the 1870s. Outside the north-east, town population as a whole stagnated or fell, in some individual instances falling sharply after a period of relative stability in the 1860s and 1870s. In such a difficult period, saving and investment were both likely to fall. Bank deposits, a sensitive barometer of prosperity in countryside and rural towns, fell from £33 million in 1876 to £28 million in 1881, and did not again reach the 1876 level until 1890.

Economic and social conditions began to improve again from around 1890. The relative improvement was most evident in the poor or congested districts of the west. In the past, emigration from these districts had been relatively light, and people continued to marry in the immediate post-Famine decades at early ages. A sign of emerging economic difficulties was foreshadowed in a rise in marriage ages in the 1870s. In the 1880s emigration from these regions rose sharply, and a definite pattern of later and fewer marriages took shape. Continued change has resulted in a conversion of a demographic pattern of earlier and more numerous marriages in the poorer regions than in the rest of the country into one in which marriage ages and celibacy are higher than the national average. The western fringe had changed little in the post-Famine decades. Diet had altered somewhat. Shops had become more numerous, and the purchase of yellow meal had created a habit of reliance on them. The rise in tea consumption in the poor regions also reflected the multiplication of shops. Tea had been little known in the 1860s, used only on Sundays and holidays. Its consumption rose rapidly in the subsequent two decades, the rise often denoting a peculiar pattern of retail purchases more than a commensurate rise in living standards in the west or north-west. The effects of retailing were not an unqualified blessing; because though poor and precarious his own position often was, the shopkeeper had a monopoly of the channels of trade in the more remote areas. The countryman relied on him for the sale of farm produce as well as for household purchases. The rates for farm produce tended to be depressed and the charge for retail goods inflated, and especially where purchases were on credit the usurious element in the retail price was large. In the smallholding regions of the south-west, on the other hand, where markets were well developed and the smallholder in the habit of selling his own produce on markets, the shopkeeper did not enjoy the same monopoly position, and the retail shop structure did not reveal quite the same pattern as it did in the west and north-west where the poorer customer paid disproportionately high charges for both retail services and credit.

The underlying social and economic structure was very precarious in the more remote regions of the west, south-west and north-west. Even if rent had not to be paid, the holdings were too small to generate an adequate income for survival. This explains the importance which domestic employment such as knitting, sewing or shirtmaking enjoyed in parts of Donegal, or the vital significance of migratory labour in many parts of Donegal or in the poorer parts of Mayo, Roscommon and Sligo. On the 90,000-acre Dillon estate on the borders of Roscommon and Mayo, for instance, half the workers migrated annually. Migratory earnings underpinned the precarious income of many smallholders, but dependence on migration added to the problems of local agriculture. From Tobercurry in co. Sligo, it was, for instance, reported in 1880 that ' the tillage has to be carried on during a great part of the year by feeble old men, women, boys and girls owing to the absence of most of the young men in England and Scotland where they go to seek employment '. Through repeated subdivision, a tenants' holding often consisted of scattered strips through a whole townland; a single field of one acre might be divided between 12 different occupiers. There was no regular crop rotation; animal breeds were extremely bad. The Congested Districts Board was established in 1891 to deal with the very special problems of the areas defined as congested in parts of all five counties of Connaught, and in parts of Kerry, Cork, Clare and Donegal. There were in all a half a million inhabitants in these areas. It was empowered to purchase land and distribute it among the tenants. It also had authority to undertake improvements such as consolidating scattered strips into compact holdings, erecting better farm buildings, introducing better animal breeds into local agriculture. Between 1891 and its dissolution in 1923, the Board spent some £9 million on the purchase and distribution of land; a further £2 million on improvements. It also sought to diversify local employment by the improvement of fisheries, provision of boats and establishment of home industries.

Change for the better became evident in the 1890s. It was partly a consequence of higher prices generally, partly a consequence of higher earnings by migratory workers in England and .Scotland, partly a result of the quickened emigration from the region. Not altogether insignificant was the increase in the quantity and price of eggs, an important source of pin money for the rural housewife. Cash incomes rose appreciably, a fact reflected in the replacement of credit dealings by cash dealings. Deposits in post office savings banks in counties Donegal, Sligo, Roscommon, Mayo, Leitrim, Galway and Kerry rose from a quarter of a million pounds in 1881 to £2¼ million in 1912. Diet improved as well; housing was much better, the older hovels often being converted into outhouses for farm animals; the manure heap removed from the front door. Roads had been bad or indifferent, public transport services almost non-existent in large areas. These regions were totally unattractive to the promotors of railways, railway building only reaching them when it was in effect subsidised under the Tramway Acts of 1883-96.

Under the act of 1883 the Grand Jury was authorised to guarantee the interest on railway capital by a baronial guarantee or contingent liability on the barony, and the Treasury was empowered to pay a subsidy in respect of part of the expenditure incurred by a barony under the terms of the act. The act of 1889 authorised the state to make loans or grants towards railways in such regions; and under the act some £2 million was provided in grants. In all about 605 miles of light railway was constructed under the legislation of 1883-96. The economic importance of the railways was considerable; they cheapened access to the ports and markets. Their psychological importance was also large, as the operation of a railway timetable brought a dimension of punctuality into the lives of the people : as the line reached along the north coast of co. Donegal, alarm clocks began to appear in the homes of people for whom before this the clock had little meaning or relevance. The railways did not solve the economic problems of these regions. The volume of produce generated in the regions remained too small to raise living standards to acceptable levels or even to make the railways profitable. The Congested Districts Board had to face the same problem. As an administrative step, the Board anticipated the work of Gaeltarra Eireann in the encouragement of local industry or the efforts of national governments in many countries in modern times to foster regional development. Its work, especially in agriculture, along with the building of the railways did contribute somewhat to improving living conditions. But their achievement was limited even in this direction. Heavier emigration and the earnings that emigrants, temporary or permanent, sent back were more important; and modernisation itself, by creating a greater awareness of outside areas and facilitating contact with higher living standards elsewhere, probably did more to reinforce the rise in emigration than to stem it.

The improvement in rural living conditions in the rest of the county was impressive. The recovery in farm prices in the 1890s was partly responsible. The land legislation had helped; rents had been reduced by 20 per cent under the act of 1881, and when these rents came up for revision fifteen years later, they were reduced by a further 20 per cent. By this time the idea of facilitating the tenant to purchase his holding was in the process of implementation. English liberals such as John Stuart Mill had many years before advocated peasant proprietorship for Irish conditions; when the

Church of Ireland was disestablished in 1869, its former tenants were facilitated in purchasing their holdings. Though they proved of little practical importance, the terms of the Land Act of 1870 had provided loans to facilitate land purchase by tenants. Loans were again provided under the act of 1881, and, more importantly, under the 1885 act – the so-called Ashbourne Act. Such early land legislation had envisaged funds simply for financing transactions agreed individually between the landlord and tenant. The Land Act of 1903, the Wyndham Act, which enormously increased the funds available for land purchase, marked a further stage in the development of land purchase by envisaging the negotiation of entire estates. The next stage was the introduction in legislation in 1907 and 1909 of the principle of compulsory sale. Transactions arranged before 1903 affected only a small number of tenants. The Wyndham Act began the process of land purchase on a large scale; by 1917 almost two-thirds of the tenants had acquired their holdings. When the Irish Free State was established the remaining tenanted land was vested in the Land Commission for transfer to the tenants. Tenants had to repay to the state the loans for purchase of their holdings by way of annuity. The annuity was lower than the statutory rent. Rents, statutorily reduced, or the annuity which for a tenant purchasing his holding replaced rent, helped to make the farmer more solvent but the benefits of either would have been quickly cancelled out if prices had not in fact continued to recover. The undoubted prosperity is reflected in the rise in the price of land in the first decade of the century. It may also be seen in the increase in bank deposits. They rose from £33 million in 1890 to £40 million in 1900, £51 million in 1908 and £60 million in 1913. The rise reached its peak in the great inflation just after the first world war. Deposits soared to £186 million. Holdings of English government stock on which interest was payable at the Bank of Ireland also rose from £44 million in 1915 to £102 million in 1921.

Of the major farming areas, the dairying districts probably improved on balance the least. Irish butter experienced more acute competition on the British market through the appearance of its Danish rival. Heavily salted, often dirty, and relatively unstandardised, the product of the Irish dairy industry was in no condition to meet a challenge. To hold a substantial share of its traditional market, re-organisation was necessary. Creameries – in effect miniature factories to separate the cream from the skim milk and to convert the butterfat into butter – on the Danish pattern offered the prospect of producing a more hygienic and standardised product. Many of the early creameries were established by merchants. But advocates of cooperation such as Fr Finlay and Horace Plunkett by their exhortations were responsible for the rapid development of cooperative ventures in the dairying districts. In 1893 there were only 30 cooperative creameries; in 1902 there were no less than 236 dairy societies. The advocates of cooperation had envisaged a widespread development of cooperative banks and cooperative societies for the purchase of raw materials and sale of agricultural produce. But in fact, with some exceptions, the cooperative movement proved successful only in the dairying districts, and apart from the cooperative creameries the bulk of cooperative ventures in selling or buying were themselves offshoots of creamery societies. To provide wholesale facilities for the cooperative movement, the Irish Agricultural Wholesale Society was established. The dairying industry was static in the two decades before 1914; the rise in dairy prices less sharp than that of other farm produce. The creameries – cooperative as well as proprietary – helped Irish dairy farmers to improve the quality of their product, but cheap new competition from Denmark and New Zealand inevitably moderated the rise in prices on the British market and was reflected in a declining Irish share of the market. The dependence of the grazing districts on the dairying regions for calves probably saved the dairy farmers from a lean time. The dairy herds – and hence the supply of calves – were not expanding; on the other hand the graziers' demand for calves was growing. Compared with 1820, the number of replacement animals needed to maintain the export trade had risen tenfold by the early 1900s, the annual output of calves scarcely at all. The growing disparity was bound to be reflected in an improved relative price for calves. Around 1820, calves fetched a low price; they represented a very modest return for the dairy farmer, often fetching, in all probability, little more than the value of a calf hide. At the prices prevailing around 1910, it seems likely that the sale of calves could have accounted for as much as one-third of the cash income of a dairy farmer selling milk to a creamery or factory. In consequence the rearing on surplus milk – or on skim milk returned from the creameries – of young calves, loomed larger in dairy farm income than in the past. In the introductory account in Dan Breen's *My fight for Irish freedom,* the chief complaint of farmers in Donohill, in Tipperary was that no ' back-milk ' was given to the suppliers of milk delivered to the new Cleeve's factory.

Even the lot of the agricultural labourer eased in these decades. By 1912 his wages were about double what they were sixty years previously, and though still below the British level, they had risen in recent decades more rapidly. Emigration was very heavy among the labouring population, and an acute shortage of labour was already evident in the busy seasons in the more prosperous counties. Legislation since the 1880s to rehouse the labourers under the auspices of the Poor Law Boards of Guardians and after 1898 the county councils was also beginning to take effect, and in replacing the hovels by neat cottages left the labourer more independent of his master or employer and better housed than his English counterpart.

Shops had become much more numerous in the second half of the century. Little shops had multiplied in the countryside, sometimes in or beside the post office whose role was itself a pointer to changing times. At the end of the century, the increased purchasing power of the rural community and – scarcely less important – its enhanced mobility was reflected in marked prosperity in the larger shops in the towns whose rural hinterland widened rapidly in these years. Hilliards of Killarney, for instance, sent some 10,000 copies of their price list to the names on the electoral lists within a radius of 30 miles of Killarney up to 1915. Small luxuries and gadgets began to appear in rural homes; the bicycle became commonplace. Emigration was at a low level, the rate in the first decade being the lowest since Famine times.

The prosperity of the period was reflected also in industry. There were even signs, well before 1914, of a recovery in industry in the small towns or at any rate of some diversification in the industrial base in them which had become very narrow. It was, however, in export industry that prosperity was most evident in the two decades before 1914. Industrial output was quite substantial. Industrial output had, however, shown powerful signs of concentration in large-scale units and especially so in export-dependent industry. The effects of the export boom were thus narrow in their diffusion – diffused among a comparatively small number of firms more especially in the north. The rise of large-scale industrial firms was an outstanding feature of industry at this time. So decisive were the

advantages of large-scale industry that even in a declining industry
like milling where the number employed was halved between 1881
and 1901, large-scale firms emerging in the ports were able to with-
stand competition from imported flour. The largest individual mills
were in Limerick and Dublin. The Russells' mills at Newtownpery
in Limerick had 19 sets of rollers for wheat, and 15 pairs of stones
for maize; the Clonliffe mill, at Jones Róad in Dublin, taken over
by the baking firm of Johnston, Mooney and O'Brien in the 1880s,
had a capacity of 13,000 sacks of flour a week. The port mills had
an advantage over inland mills where exports were concerned; the
Belfast mills in particular continued to have a sizeable export
market in maize meal. A dramatic instance of re-organisation was
the brewing industry where the number of firms had fallen from
247 in 1837 to 41 in 1901 and to 24 in 1920. The Dublin brewers
– and the single firm of Guinness was increasingly dominant among
them – produced about three-quarters of the total output, and
accounted for 96 per cent of exports at the outset of the twentieth
century. In the woollen industry, typically characterised by small
firms, the firm of Martin Mahony at Blarney was outstanding.
It integrated all the processes in a single firm – unusual even in the
English woollen industry at this time – employed 750 workers in
the early 1890s, and had a far-flung export trade. Another instance
of a large firm is Tait's factory in Limerick which was able to
compete successfully for large contracts for military garments. The
making of a single garment was subdivided into 36 different operations. At its peak, the firm employed over 1,400 although through
subsequent decline the number was down to 1,000 in the early
1890s.

Large firms were as a rule export-oriented. In fact, the industries which had contracted had to a large extent depended on the
domestic market. It was only by the development of export markets
that industrial firms could reach a scale of production which would
make their costs competitive, and hence enable them to survive on
the home market against foreign competition. The most striking
instance of how exports could alter the fortunes of an industry is
afforded by distilling. A contracting home market had reduced the
number of firms by closures and bankruptcies to 22 in the 1860s.
The industry recovered dramatically from the 1860s. Exports
doubled between the 1860s and 1870s, doubled again by the 1890s
and yet again by the first decade of the twentieth century. Output

rose from 5½ million gallons in 1865 to over 12 million gallons; exports, rising from a million gallons in the 1860s to 8½ million gallons in 1907, came to account for about two-thirds of output. By 1907 the industry accounted for a quarter of the United Kingdom output; allowing for the higher per capita consumption of whiskey in Scotland, it seems that the Irish industry exported a higher proportion of output than the Scottish distilleries. Exports were dominated by a handful of large firms. As far as pot-still whiskey was concerned, the bulk of the exports came from a single Dundalk distillery producing a million gallons a year in the early 1890s and the Dublin distilleries: the advantages of large-scale production were reflected in the amalgamation of three of the Dublin distilleries in 1889. The doubling of exports in the last decade of the century is associated with the expansion of blended whiskey. Pot-still whiskey was made exclusively from barley or malt; blended whiskey was made from other cereals, in particular cheap maize, and the distilled spirit was then blended with barley or malt whiskey. This branch of the distilling industry centred on Belfast which was already the chief centre of maize imports. Four large distilleries were in operation there in the late nineteenth century. In 1907 5.4 million gallons out of a total of 8.5 million were exported from Belfast.

The proportion of total industrial output exported was remarkably high. The gross value of industrial output in 1907 was £67 million. The value of manufactured exports was £20.9 million. If processed foods and drinks are added – a further £13.5 million – the total for all manufactures comes to £34.4 million, or half of total industrial output itself. This is a remarkably high proportion, well in excess of the corresponding total for Britain or any major country. Outstanding among the export-based industries were linen, shipbuilding, distilling and brewing. In each case a high proportion of output was exported – the bulk of output in linen and shipbuilding, well over half in whiskey and about a fifth in brewing – and the product had an international reputation of the first order.

Linen was the major industry, whether measured in terms of output, exports or above all employment. The growth of output was, however, comparatively slow. Output was probably of the order of 110 million yards of cloth in 1835; it had increased only to 230 million yards in 1907. This represented little more than a doubling. The expansion of the industry was therefore not very dramatic either compared with the expansion of other industries in the nineteenth century or with its own expansion previously. If the industry's development appeared dramatic in the nineteenth century, it was only because re-organisation led to its localisation around Belfast. Belfast was already the main centre of spinning by mid-century, by the twentieth century it accounted for almost two-thirds of the weaving capacity as well. The world export market for linen was not, in fact, expansive. It had reached its peak in the cotton famine of the 1860s when exports from the United Kingdom had soared to 255 million yards in 1866. In 1878 they amounted only to 160.3 million yards; in 1899 to 174 million yards. Given a contraction in the world export market, exports from Ireland were able to rise only because of the decline in the industry in the rest of the United Kingdom. The picture the rise in linen exports represents is that of capturing a larger share of a declining market. Linen came in the nineteenth century to be something of a luxury product; cotton had taken its place for many purposes. The market in the United Kingdom had declined heavily: in the early nineteenth century almost all the output of the industry was consumed within these islands; by the end of the century only a quarter of output. As a luxury its exports were also heavily dependent on a single market, that of the United States, which took some 70 per cent of exports. Once analysed behind the façade of this spectacular process of centralisation around Belfast, the industry does not represent a reassuring picture of prosperity. Net output per worker was lower than in any other branch of the textile industry; three-quarters of the workers were women; one-quarter of all workers in the industry were under 18. Of itself linen could not have made Belfast prosperous, and if the city had remained dependent on linen its expansion would have ceased by the end of the century. In fact, Belfast's growth slowed down sharply in the 1870s, and the dramatic growth of the city between 1891 and 1911 – when its population rose by half – is closely related to the spectacular success of the city's shipyards. The decisive upturn in Belfast's fortunes in shipbuilding dates from the 1850s, but the largest tonnage launched in any year in the 1860s and 1870s did not exceed 17,140 tons. It was only in the second half of the 'eighties that the industry really blossomed. Tonnage launched totalled 103,466 in 1891, and reached 256,547 in 1914. The entire output came from two giant yards, that of Harland and Wolff, founded in the 1850s, and the yard established by Workman, Clark and Company in 1879. The reputation and commercial success of the Belfast yards depended on passenger liners. Specialisation helped to offset the higher costs, apart from labour, which shipbuilders encountered in Belfast. As liners were more labour-intensive than other vessels, the lower cost of unskilled – although not of skilled labour – may also have helped to give Belfast a competitive edge.

Shipbuilding was vital to Belfast's prosperity. Otherwise Belfast would probably have fared much the same as Londonderry. Derry grew rapidly in the second half of the century, but on a more precarious base than Belfast. The major factor in its expansion was shirtmaking. From five factories in the 1850s, the number had increased to 38 in 1902. Some 18,000 operatives were employed in the factories in the city, at wages averaging 9s a week. Another 80,000 workers were engaged in their own homes in sewing shirts cut out in the factories, distributed to them for sewing, and then finished and packed in the Derry factories. Shirtmaking depended on low-wage female employment in the urban factories and on the readiness of rural women in a relatively poor hinterland in counties Derry, Tyrone and Donegal to accept badly-paid domestic work. In the countryside, the industry was supported by agriculture, and in Derry, except for a small number of skilled workers, the wages the industry paid would not support a family. Derry did not provide much skilled employment for men, although the enhanced importance of the city in the second half of the century as wholesaling and transit centre for the Foyle valley and co. Donegal generated a substantial volume of casual and unskilled employment. The rapid growth of the city – it doubled its population between 1851 and 1901 – is therefore deceptive, drawing attention away at first glance from the fact that the most regular and extensive employment in the town was for female labour. Derry was, despite its rapid growth, a poor city, and the origins of its twentieth-century economic problems can be detected in the fragile character of its nineteenth-century prosperity.

About a third of the net output of agriculture and industry combined was contributed by industry. By comparison with the rest of the world, this made Ireland at first glance a relatively highly industrialised country. The bulk of net output rested, however, on a narrow base. Some eighty per cent of total net output in industry was accounted for by three categories alone : linen spinning and weaving; brewing, distilling and aerated waters; and shipbuilding and engineering. Moreover, the narrow regional spread of major industry was striking. Apart from processed foods and drink, in which the greater part of exports came from the south, £19.1 million of the total non-food manufactures of £20.9 were in categories predominantly produced in the Belfast region.

Value of exports of manufactured goods 1907 (£ million)

Yarn, rope, thread	2.7
Piece goods, apparel, drapery	13.1
Machinery, implements, motors, ships	3.3
	19.1

However, one of the most striking aspects of Belfast's industrial dominance is not its expectedly high proportion of output in textiles and engineering generally but its disproportionately large share, emerging in the late nineteenth century, in many of the industries in the food and beverage category, more particularly where exports are concerned. In 1907, for instance, Belfast accounted for 5.3 million lb of Ireland's sizeable exports of manufactured tobacco of 5.7 million lb; in whiskey Belfast accounted for 60 per cent of exports in the same year. In aerated waters, Belfast was the main exporter; Belfast imported one-third of the maize imports, and was the only milling centre with significant exports in 1907. In ham, Belfast had a very creditable position also. It is not easy to account for this situation. It is possible that capital was more readily available in Belfast, but on the other hand there is no evidence of a shortage of capital elsewhere in Ireland or that industrial promotions failed simply because capital was not forthcoming. Possibly business enterprise was more plentiful in Belfast. This is likely but hardly decisive because the reorganisation of wholesaling and retail trade in the south belies the argument that commercial initiative was lacking there. The problem seems to reduce itself, so far as business enterprise is concerned, to finding out why the business enterprise was directed into channels other than manufacturing industry. The most likely explanation may simply lie in the external economies in foreign trade generated by Belfast's growth. Belfast from mid-century was the largest port in Ireland, and with the eclipse of Cork's provision trade was the only one with extensive direct contact with markets outside the United Kingdom. Even where goods were transhipped in Liverpool, the orders for them had been canvassed directly from Belfast, and the financing, insuring and handling of the consignments was arranged through local intermediaries. The slow growth of the linen industry was compensated by the rapid substitution in the nineteenth century of markets outside the United Kingdom for the traditional market for linen in Britain. Commercial contacts with the American market facilitated the import of tobacco and maize and thus indirectly accounted for the rise of tobacco manufacture, maize milling and blended whiskey in Belfast. On the other hand, isolated firms in small towns in the rest of Ireland had no direct foreign contact; local facilities for the specialist needs of financing, insuring and handling export consignments did not exist; and the arrangement of such services for small or irregular consignments proved expensive. Only firms in Dublin and isolated large-scale firms elsewhere found it practicable to enter the export field. Probably a third of net industrial output originated in Belfast or its immediate hinterland; and roughly two-thirds of total industrial exports including processed food and drink.

In the rest of the country industry was thinly spread, organised largely in small firms catering for a local market. Malting, brewing, distilling and milling, to some extent re-organised in larger firms, survived in the grain-growing regions. In the dairying regions of the south, bacon curing, and to a lesser extent condensed milk, were commonplace with the major firms to be found in the ports. There was little variety in industry in the towns. Instances such as jute in Clara, hosiery in Balbriggan, fertilisers in Wicklow, explosives in Arklow, cement in Kilrane (co. Wexford), farm machinery in Wexford, roofing felt in New Ross, were uncommon.

Nevertheless, some evidence of industrial recovery in the towns was visible even before the end of the century. Enterprise in wholesale trade had always displayed itself, and where opportunity was present enterprise for industrial development did not prove wholly lacking. There appears to have been a decided interest around 1900 in technological developments in light industry at that time and in the promotion of companies to exploit them. A very early instance of enterprise was the expansion of plant making aerated or mineral waters. By the end of the century, most towns had a firm engaged in their manufacture; those in Dublin and Belfast were large-scale businesses with a substantial export trade. Tobacco did well also with some 17 firms in 1920, of which four were large. While the doubling in exports between 1904 and 1914 reflected the progress of the industry in Belfast, the relatively secure hold the industry had on the home market testified to the success of the industry generally. Significant too was the recovery of the woollen industry: the number of power looms rose from 307 in 1874 to 925 in 1889; factory employment from 1,374 in 1868 to 3,443 in 1899. The quality of Irish woollens improved; as a distinctive product they had a well-defined appeal; they commanded a small but rising market abroad. Of the comparatively small output of the Irish woollen industry, exports accounted for a substantial proportion and showed no sign of tapering off: they doubled between 1904 and 1914. The evidence of a modest reversal of the unfavourable industrial fortunes of the Irish country towns became more definite in the relatively prosperous first decade of the century. Bootmaking factories had already appeared in a number of towns before 1900. The number of factories increased further in subsequent years, and imports of footwear grew rather little between 1904 and 1914 despite the high level of rural spending on drapery and footwear. Imports dominated the market for ladies' shoes and quality shoes for men. In these lines, Irish factories were unable to compete, one shopkeeper, for instance, simply keeping ' a few pairs to satisfy hot Gaelic Leaguers '. In the cheaper end, especially in men's wear, however, Irish footwear did well on the home market. Recovery in bootmaking boosted the tanning industry, employment rising from a mere 193 in 1907 to around 500 in 1920. A small export trade in quality sole leather existed at the beginning of the century; by 1920 a much increased proportion of output was exported. The fortunes of the paper industry recovered too, employment rising from 530 in 1907 to 800 in 1920. Several other industries showed expansion in a modest but definite way. Significantly they sometimes succeeded in exporting part of their production. Between 1904 and 1914 exports of margarine, preserved meats and hosiery doubled.

The first world war boosted the trend, partly by the inflated demand in England and more importantly by prosperity among the agricultural population boosting the home market. Another factor which was by no means insignificant was the emergence of conscious support for Irish industry. This interest existed from the early 1880s: it was enhanced by the growth of national consciousness associated with the Gaelic League in the 1890s, and by the propaganda in favour of domestic industry conducted by Arthur Griffith and Sinn Fein. The interest in Irish industry was reflected in the establishment in 1903 of the Cork Industrial Development Association, the first of many such local bodies. The Cork Association was responsible for the holding in Cork in 1905 of an all-Ireland Industrial Conference. As a result of the conference, an Irish Industrial Development Association was established. It secured legal recognition for a distinctive trade market for Irish-made goods, took legal action against foreign goods described as Irish-made, and sought to create a greater public awareness of Irish industry and Irish industrial products. Interest in Irish industrial revival in the 1880s had not in general been protectionist. Parnell, it is true, had been seriously interested in the prospect of using tariff protection to encourage industrialisation. However, much of the support for the industrial and political movements came from the trading classes in the towns who, like their counterparts in England, were sceptical of the benefits of protective tariffs. An interest in tariff protection in Ireland stems in part from the growing questioning of free trade in England evident in the fact that it was an issue in the general election of 1905. In Ireland, of course, the obvious inferiority of Irish industry to English, and the close association of the tariff issue with the fiscal aspects of home rule helped to obtain a wider forum for protectionism and to win a greater measure of support for it after 1905. But tariffs, or how a policy of tariff protection might be implemented in detail, was never thought out, partly because contemporaries thought that Ireland's inclusion within the United Kingdom had of itself stultified the country's economic development. They tended to overestimate Ireland's natural advantages and resources, and hence, as a rule, assumed optimistically that under altered political arrangements much of the country's industrial recovery would be spontaneous.

The towns fared relatively well in the 1890s and early 1900s. Even in towns where population had declined sharply in the two preceding decades, population remained relatively stable or even increased. The building industry flourished in the first decade of the century – a sign of a relatively high level of economic activity and itself a particularly significant source of income for the unskilled or casual labourer. Belfast was the best-off of Irish towns. While conditions in the mills were hard and children tended to be neglected because of the absence of women of working age from the home, the earnings of women in the mills supplemented the wages of unskilled male workers. In other towns, a higher proportion of male workers was likely to be unskilled, and except in Derry their earnings were less likely to be supplemented by female earnings. Unskilled employment was also casual and irregular – perhaps as much as one-fifth of the male labour force was at any point of time out of work. Nevertheless, urban living conditions had improved over recent decades, a sign not so much of satisfactory conditions as of an even more appalling situation in the past. Tea, white bread and sugar lent variety to the diet, and on the whole the families of unskilled labourers were better clothed and shod. The aspect in which there was least sign of improvement was in housing. Unskilled labourers on a wage, if regularly employed, of 12s a week could not afford to pay more than 1s-2s a week in rent. Because a room could be rented at this price and because the location was central, the poor crowded into tenements in the decaying districts, formerly fashionable, in the centre of the towns. Mortality rates were much higher than in the countryside. Even as late as 1901-11, the death rate in Dublin averaged 24.7 per 1,000 compared with 17.3 for the country as a whole. In the 1870s the death rate in Dublin and other major towns was no higher than many British towns. In 1874 the death rate in Dublin was in fact only 26.0 per 1,000 compared with 28.7 in Belfast, 32 in Liverpool, 30.4 in Manchester and 31.2 in Glasgow. The prevalence of epidemic diseases, however, meant that death rates fluctuated rather widely from one year to another, or in a particular year, between different cities. A downward trend was, however, less noticeable in Dublin and other Irish towns than in major British cities. This made comparison between Dublin and British cities, with the exception of Liverpool, very invidious by the early twentieth century. One reason was that major sanitation works were undertaken more slowly than in England; another that public drainage schemes of themselves did not greatly ameliorate the sanitary state of families living in crowded tenement houses rather than in isolated dwellings. Dublin had the worst slum conditions of the British Isles, its slum population like that of another notorious example, Glasgow, being largely a tenement one. Nevertheless, though more belatedly than in other major cities, the death rate and the infant mortality rate did decline in the first decade of the century. If Dublin conditions showed signs of improving more slowly than those of other cities, there were other factors involved. The Dublin marriage rate was 50 per cent higher than that of the country as a whole, and its birth rate about a third higher. This had two effects – one, an uncommonly high dependence rate adding to the poverty of labouring families among whom marriage was earliest and families largest, and two, in consequence of the high birthrate a disproportionately large part of the population in the age groups most vulnerable to epidemic disease.

Roughly a third of the population of Dublin within the boundaries of the Grand and Royal Canals lived in slums. This somewhat exaggerates the dominance of the slums because new townships inhabited by the better-off were growing rapidly beyond the city boundaries. By 1911 they added almost 100,000 inhabitants to the 300,000 living within the boundaries of the city as extended to the circular roads in 1900. With its great central slumland and prospering suburban townships, Dublin produced an unusual phenomenon of unskilled workers seeking cheap tenement accommodation in the centre and travelling out to work outside the city. In 1891, when the population of city and suburbs amounted to 349,594, only 8,952 of its 44,881 labourers and dependants lived outside the boundaries. On the other hand, half of its 18,611 clerks and dependants and two-thirds of its 15,847 gentlefolk and dependants lived beyond the city boundaries. Outside the slum districts, and especially in the townships beyond the canals, a large, prosperous and expanding middle class existed.

Despite its large slumland, Dublin revealed all the characteristics of a relatively prosperous city. Its large and expanding aggregate purchase power was reflected in an impressive growth in the city's retail trade. As an example, one may instance Mrs Purdon of Dundrum whose weekly household account, in the early 1870s, came to £2 a week with regular purchases at three shops including a grocer and butcher, and a weekly 'bill at little shop'. Domestics living in were paid as little as 10s a month. Compared with the weekly household account, the cost of domestic service was low, and comfortable suburban ladies such as Mrs Purdon could afford to employ several. The total number of female servants in Dublin city and suburbs in 1891 was 23,726.

Given this comfortable community in the city and in the suburbs, retail trade developed rapidly, competition was keen and led to developments such as deliveries to the house and more extensive and sometimes ingenious advertising. Findlater's opened 10 branches of their grocery and wines and spirits business in the late nineteenth century. In 1890 they introduced, in conjunction with Hartnells, a magazine entitled *The Lady of the House* in which the last eight pages advertised their range of wares. They distributed 3,000 copies at 1d each to their customers.

Ireland was in many respects a highly developed country by the end of the century. About a half of its output – industrial and agricultural – was exported. Its major industries had an international renown, Belfast liners and linen, Irish whiskey and Dublin beer and biscuits having an unrivalled name. The country had an extensive banking and transport system. The paradox to contemporaries was that, despite these circumstances, Ireland was not as prosperous as they would like to see it, and incomes compared with England and Scotland were relatively low. The fact of population decline seemed to lend emphasis to this impression. One explanation, popular in the late nineteenth century, for this paradox, was that the country had long been overtaxed. Between 1853 and 1860, Irish taxation was at last brought up to the British level: income tax was introduced to Ireland for the first time, and whiskey taxation was trebled. When home rule was a live issue in the early 1890s, a commission was appointed to examine the financial relations between Ireland and England since the Union. Its report in 1896 seemed to bear out the nationalist contention that Ireland had been overtaxed. The Commission's report, in line with the evidence before it, largely concerned itself with revenue alone. The conclusion that Ireland was overtaxed was based on a comparison between actual tax revenue and an equitable share of United Kingdom tax revenue based on Ireland's estimated taxable capacity relative to Britain. A fundamental difficulty in this approach is the fact that no reliable estimates existed of the relative incomes of the two countries, and the Commission's conclusions were based therefore on premises which would warrant only very tentative deductions. The Commission did not concern itself at length with government expenditure, although if revenue and public expenditure within Ireland were compared, the case for overtaxation would have been weakened. While a significant proportion of such expenditure was incurred for imperial rather than local purposes –

and it was for this reason that the Commission chose not to take expenditure into account – the effect of such expenditure – e.g. army and naval expenditure – on incomes and employment was as beneficial economically as many other forms of public expenditure. It remains true, of course, that taxation relative to income was higher in Ireland than in Britain. This was a consequence of the fact that indirect taxes on consumer goods such as tea, tobacco and whiskey were relatively high and that in relation to income the poor consumed relatively large quantities of these products. In other words, as was said by one contemporary at an earlier date, Ireland was not poor because she was overtaxed, but overtaxed because she was poor. Regional contrasts in the incidence of taxation are also concealed by generalisations about Ireland's or Britain's relative share. Within Britain itself, the poorer regions were overtaxed relative to the richer parts. In Ireland, the eastern half of the country was, given higher per capita incomes, more lightly taxed than the poorer regions which, on a per capita basis, consumed as much or more whiskey, tobacco and tea than other areas but purchased much fewer untaxed goods. In the 1850s there probably was a rise in the amount of money remitted from Ireland on government account. This was probably offset by a significant rise in government expenditure in subsequent decades, and government expenditure in Ireland very definitely exceeded revenue in the decade or so before 1914.

Another feature often quoted as a source of Ireland's economic deficiencies was the amount of capital invested outside the country. This would not have applied to the eighteenth century which had been characterised by a net inflow. Even in the first half of the nineteenth century, there was no marked outflow. Government loans on which interest was payable at the Bank of Ireland rose from £21 million in 1818 to £41 million in 1851. But this was offset to some extent by private borrowings in England by Irish landowners and by British investment in early Irish banks and railways. In fact, in the third quarter, Irish investment outside the country may have fallen. Government stock on which interest was paid at the Bank of Ireland actually fell to £37 million by 1875. While some stock may have been realised to purchase British or foreign railway stocks, it seems likely that some of the sums realised and much new saving was attracted into Irish railway construction and into the purchase of existing Irish bank and railway stocks from British investors. It is only from the 1870s or 1880s that a definite capital outflow emerged. Government stocks at the Bank of Ireland fell to £24.5 million in 1893. Remunerative railway building in Ireland had virtually ceased. Of the 1,039 miles of railway constructed between 1880 and 1913, little was remunerative, about 605 miles being subsidised in one way or other from public funds. In this period much Irish investment capital went into the purchase of overseas railway and colonial stocks. The papers of Irish businessmen in this period show an active interest in the purchase of such stocks. The decline in government stocks at the Bank of Ireland seems to suggest that much of the holdings were realised for investment elsewhere.* As a result of the wartime inflation, the amount of government stock on which interest was paid at the Bank of Ireland rose by £64.6 million between 1914 and 1921. Allowing for the fact that the rising funds of the Irish banks were also held on the London market, it is not unlikely that Irish investment abroad rose by £100 million during these years. As the total value of Irish foreign investment was sometimes estimated as being in the region of £250 million in the early 1920s, it is not unlikely that total Irish investment abroad around 1914 was of the order of £150 million.

The significance of foreign investment was in part that income on it constituted an important new source of earnings which increased the annual income of the community. Only less important were remittances from emigrants and migratory labourers – earnings from these sources remitted through banks and post offices amounted to £2 million in 1906. The emergence of these sources of income and their rise to significant proportions in the late nineteenth century was bound not only to increase income but to influence the disposal of income. Some additions to income were likely to be saved or deposited in banks – some income also financed further purchases of foreign securities – but much of the increase was likely to be spent on consumer goods and hence ultimately on imports. In consequence imports rose more rapidly than exports in the late nineteenth century. This relationship between imports

* The apparent rise in government stock between 1898 and 1910 is accounted for by the land stocks issued to landowners as compensation for land purchase and does not represent true foreign investment. In fact, stocks payable at the Bank of Ireland masked a continuing decline in non-land stocks. Of government stock of £36.4 million in 1905 land stocks held in Ireland amounted to £23.3 million.

and exports by increasing the total availability of goods within the country was behind the improvement in living standards from the 1890s. The trend was facilitated by the static nature of rents in the nineteenth century. Rents did not alter much after 1815. They probably amounted to £10 or £12 million pounds per annum, and rents remitted to absentees probably remained relatively stable at £2 million or so. The consequence of relatively stable rents was that they declined as a proportion of national income throughout the nineteenth century. The incomes of farmers rose from mid-century; traders' incomes rose, and incomes grew spectacularly in the Belfast region. In 1815 the total value of exports was little larger than the rent roll of Irish landlords; by the 1890s the value of Irish exports was probably twice the size of the rent roll. Viewed in this way, the economic crisis of the land-owning class in the 1880s seems to emerge as a late stage of a long-drawn-out relative decline of landed income and landed investment in the economy. In the eighteenth or early nineteenth centuries imports amounted to only 75 per cent of exports, the balance being necessary to finance remittances to absentees and interest on English capital invested in Ireland. By the late nineteenth century, on the other hand, remittances to absentees, though they had not declined in absolute terms, were much smaller relatively to national income or to foreign trade. There was also a growing excess of interest payments from overseas over those to creditors abroad. At some point, probably in the 1890s, in consequence of the steep rise in interest on capital invested abroad and in emigrants' remittances, and the sharp relative decline in remittances to absentees, imports came regularly to exceed exports. As early as 1904 imports exceeded exports by 11 per cent. Along with its large foreign trade, its export-oriented industries and its highly developed infrastructure of banking, commerce and railways, extensive foreign investment yielding a sizeable income made Ireland comparable in some respects with a handful of highly developed nations. At the same time the comparison heightened the paradox of Ireland's position.

7

Stagnation and Growth in Ireland
1922-1971

The first world war, and especially the two years after it, were the
most hectic period of agricultural prosperity in Ireland's history,
surpassing even the best years of the Napoleonic wars. Agricultural
prices trebled from a base figure of 100 in 1911-13 to 288 in 1920.
The rise was roughly paralleled by bank deposits. The terms of
trade favoured Ireland, export prices rising more rapidly than
import prices. The value of exports exceeded imports in seven of
the eight years between 1914 and 1921. Prosperity was pronounced
in the farming community. The high earnings were achieved
despite some decline in the quantity of exports in 1918 and 1919.
At one and the same time, therefore, farmers greatly enlarged their
earnings and increased their own consumption of agricultural
produce either by consuming more or by substituting better-
quality Irish produce for the inferior imported bacon they often
used. The volume of imports fell from an earlier date, although
sharply only in 1917 and 1918. The combination of high earnings
in agriculture and some shortage of imported goods meant high
prosperity for the trader. As one merchant in an Irish country
town wrote in retrospect 50 years after, 'the years 1915 to 1921
were really legendary'. The businessman's large profits were in
part the product of the effect of inflation on stocks purchased at
one price and sold in conditions of relative scarcity at a higher
price. High profit levels and a decline in outside competition gave
local manufacturing industry a boost. The modest recovery evident
even before 1914 in several industries was accentuated during these
years. Farmer, trader and manufacturer did well. The urban and

rural wage earner did less well, as wages lagged behind rising prices. Emigration virtually dried up during the war years. As most emigrants came from rural rather than urban centres, the pool of underemployed increased in the countryside: underemployed young men who in peacetime might have emigrated supplied the rural recruits for the Irish Republican Army in 1918 and later. Social disaffection was rife among the rural labourers in several parts of Ireland in the early 1920s.

The great agricultural boom collapsed in 1920. Prices slumped. The index of agricultural prices fell from 288 in 1920 to 160 in 1924. Economic dislocation was considerable. Businessmen or farmers who had borrowed money were in great difficulties; the banks themselves were gravely embarrassed by the fall in the value of shares or land pledged as collateral for loans; and unemployment increased. The economic difficulties were overshadowed by the treaty negotiations and by the civil war in 1922-3. But they were substantial, and the years 1921 to 1923 were years of economic contraction. In one large business in a southern town, for instance, turnover fell in each of the three years.

Ireland was able to absorb the shock of the economic difficulties to a large extent by virtue of the enhancement of her creditor status during the war and post-war inflation. Already a creditor country before 1914, her creditor standing improved enormously during the war. The export surplus from 1914 to 1921 amounted to £76.6 million. To this sum should be added an unknown sum in respect of net invisible earnings (interest on existing investment, pensions, emigrant remittances, earnings in HM forces). The large surplus financed the purchase of many additional stocks and shares in this period. Government stocks alone on which interest was paid at the Bank of Ireland increased by £67 million between 1914 and 1922, a figure approximating to the size of the trade surplus from 1914 to 1921. In consequence of the growth of investment holdings at this rate, the interest accruing to residents in the Irish Free State alone in the early 1920s was larger than the interest accruing to the whole island in 1913. The increase in investment income ensured that the economy could increase its imports without a corresponding increase in exports. In 1904 exports had financed 90 per cent of imports; already as early as 1924 exports financed only 74 per cent of the imports of the Irish Free State. The standard of consumption of the population at large had on the whole risen in the war and postwar years. The ability of the economy to maintain a higher level of imports than its exports alone would have warranted appeared to some either extravagant or even immoral. A censorious critic who adverted to the gap between exports and imports, Sir James O'Connor, wrote in 1925 :

> The visitor to the Irish Free State today will find the capital city displaying a luxury and extravagance unparalleled in any city of the same size in the world. Motor cars, well-attended horse races, theatres and cinemas, great consumption of alcohol, all the indicia, of wealth are there.

There was some economic recovery in 1924. Turnover, for instance, recovered sharply in 1924 in the southern business already referred to. Exports and imports were both at a high level too. A bad harvest in 1924, however, proved a set-back. Worse still, the fall in agricultural prices which had seemed to even out in 1925 was sharp in 1926. The volume of exports declined steeply in 1925 and 1926, and imports fell also although less sharply. There was something of an economic crisis in these years. They saw the end of economic difficulties, however. The impact of a high and rising level of international economic activity helped to restore the economic fortunes of the Irish Free State. The fall in agricultural prices slowed in 1927, and they rose rather definitely in 1928 and again although less firmly in 1929. Net output in agriculture rose by 5 per cent between 1926/7 and 1929/30. Between 1926 and 1929 the volume of exports rose by 20 per cent. The terms of trade also improved. Export prices actually rose between 1927 and 1929 by about 1 per cent; import prices fell by 4 per cent. The national income of the Irish Free State rose from £154.1 million in 1926 to £161.4 million in 1929. As prices fell by 3 per cent, income rose in real terms by 8 per cent. The volume of imports rose substantially and in 1929 had surpassed the relatively high level of 1924. Some rise in real incomes allied with a plentiful supply of raw materials was favourable to the progress of industry. Between 1926 and 1929 industrial output rose by 9 per cent; employment in industry rose from 102,515 to 108,870. In the years 1926 to 1929 per capita incomes in the Irish Free State rose slightly more rapidly than they did in Britain.

The situation in the Irish Free State contrasted with that in Northern Ireland. In the Irish Free State, slightly over 50 per cent

of the occupied population in 1926 was in agriculture, in Northern
Ireland only 26 per cent. The fortunes of the north were closely
tied up with its two major industries, linen and shipbuilding. Linen,
which enjoyed a boom during the first world war, continued to do
so in the 1920s because of its dependence on the prosperous
American market. Linen reached its peak in 1927, a fact reflecting
the antecedents of the American crash in 1929 and foreshadowing
a catastrophic fall in linen exports after 1929. In this way, linen,
reaching its peak in 1927, contrasted with the south's agricultural
exports which reached a peak in 1929 and declined in volume only
marginally even in 1930. Shipbuilding sharpened the contrast
further. After the war and postwar boom, the shipyards remained
permanently depressed. Unemployment in the north had been
18 per cent of the insured population in the depth of the postwar
depression in 1923; it was still 13 per cent in 1927, the north's
most prosperous year in the late 1920s.

The underlying trends seemed to justify the cautious economic
policies of the Free State government. Its exports did relatively
well in the world economic recovery of the second half of the 1920s,
while on the other hand a specialist industrial region like the north
showed new signs of difficulty in those years. Official outlook – and
the advice proffered by economists – was that industrial protection
would harm the state's agricultural exports by raising costs. It was
believed that agricultural prosperity, if unimpeded, would gradually
stimulate wider economic development. Hence, state intervention
was largely confined to measures such as an act of 1924 regulating
the quality and marketing of dairy produce, and acts intended to
improve livestock breeding. The Currency Act of 1927 minimised
the changes in the monetary field; the Irish pound was to be maintained at an equal value with the pound sterling. The State was,
therefore, and has remained a part of the ' sterling area '. Protection of industry was sparing, and the duties themselves where
imposed very moderate. In 1924 duties were levied on boots, shoes,
confectionery, soap, candles and in 1925 on clothing, blankets and
furniture. In 1926 a Tariff Commission was established to examine
applications for tariff protection. Applications for protection were
subject to severe scrutiny, and industrialists themselves did not
seem to favour protection.

At the same time some important steps were taken to exploit
native resources. In the Irish Free State, as in England, electricity

was organised on a national basis in the 1920s: the statutory body
for this purpose – the ESB (Electricity Supply Board) – was established in 1927. The significance of the national network was made
more effective by the building, in the face of much criticism, of the
country's first major power station, the hydro-electric station at
Ardnacrusha on the Shannon whose relatively large capacity made
it possible to reduce substantially in the 1930s the country's serious
lag in electrification outside a few major towns and individual
industrial firms. Another important step was the establishment of
the Sugar Company. Its establishment foreshadowed both the
further extension of sugar manufacturing from native beet in the
1930s and with the ESB the device of a semi-state organisation
which was in the future to become increasingly important in the
sphere of both infrastructure and industry.

A corollary of the economic policy of the 1920s which sought to
keep costs down for the benefit of existing export industries was the
necessity of keeping budgetary costs to a minimum so that taxes
should not handicap rising exports. This meant that welfare
expenditure was not expanded. This policy was facilitated by
emigration which reduced unemployment from the high level of
the early 1920s. These were boom years in America; prosperity
there acted as a magnet to many in Ireland. With many who would
normally have emigrated still in Ireland in the early 1920s because
of the wartime interruption of emigration, the number of emigrants
soared. Emigration from the Free State to regions outside the
British Isles ran at a level of 25,000 to 30,000 a year: emigration
from the island rose to a higher level than in the best years of the
pre-War decade. The relatively low priority given to welfare
expenditure also meant that comparatively little was done in the
1920s to improve housing conditions in the larger towns which
inherited extensive slums from the nineteenth century. In Dublin
the housing situation was little eased compared with twenty years
earlier. Thirty-five per cent of the population of Dublin was living
in 1931 at a density of more than two persons to a room; in one
ward, the Mountjoy ward, almost half the population was living at
a density of more than four to a room.

The situation of modest but definite expansion was interrupted
by the Great Depression of 1929. The level of economic activity
throughout the world fell sharply between 1929 and 1932. Prices
slumped. In the initial stages the impact on the Irish Free State

was limited. The volume of exports fell only by the shade of a margin in 1930, and the volume of imports was the highest since statistics were first computed on a Free State basis in 1924; import prices fell between 1926 and 1930 at twice the rate of export prices. The terms of trade thus favoured Ireland. Ireland was a substantial importer of grain and animal feeding stuffs in which the fall in prices was sharpest; the prices of livestock and livestock products – the Free State's exports – fell relatively little at first. The decline in exports between 1929 and 1931 was relatively modest, mainly occurring between 1930 and 1931.

Exports (Irish Free State)

	1929	1931
£ Million	47.3	36.3
Index of volume	120	98
(1926 = 100)		

In the Irish Free State national income fell only from £161.4 million in 1929 to £150.8 million in 1931. As prices had fallen by 9 per cent real income had risen by 3 per cent. Imports fell less in volume than exports. This points to little immediate impairment of living standards and to a continuing high level of industrial activity. As most industry in the south was geared to the domestic market, it was not subject to disruption by the world depression in export markets. The volume of industrial output rose by 2 per cent between 1929 and 1931; in the same years industrial employment rose from 108,870 to 110,588. In one major wholesale and retail business with an extensive rural hinterland in Munster, turnover was at its peak in 1931, decline becoming evident only in 1932 and 1933. The southern situation contrasted with that in the north. Incomes in the north were more closely dependent on industry, and the north's industries, export-oriented, were highly sensitive to international conditions. It is likely that income in the north, in contrast to the south, fell in real terms in these years. In Belfast 20,000 were unemployed in linen in 1930. Shipbuilding fell sharply. By 1931 one-quarter of the insured workers in the north were unemployed.

By international standards the south had fared well. However, the prices of its exports were bound to suffer further as depression deepened overseas. In the Free State's case the emerging difficulties in its foreign trade were accelerated by the financial dispute with England in 1932. The cause of the dispute was the withholding by the Irish government from the British of the land annuities due under the various acts relating to land purchase prior to 1922. In retaliation the British government in July 1932 imposed special duties on livestock, dairy produce and meat with a view to recouping the amount withheld by the Freé State government. Quota restrictions also accompanied the duties. Exports from the Irish Free State fell sharply in volume. Even more seriously, export prices plunged downwards, the index of export prices falling from 86.8 in the first half of 1932 (1930 = 100) to 70.3 in the second half of the year. The volume of exports even at a reduced level was maintained only with the help of subsidies. The nadir of the situation was reached in 1934 with both the volume and prices of exports at a low level.

Exports (Irish Free State)

	1931	1932	1933	1934	1935
£ Million	36.3	26.3	19.00	17.9	19.9
Index of prices (1930 = 100)	90.5	78.5	64.5	60.9	61.7
Index of volume (1926 = 100)	98	82	74	72	77

The so-called 'economic war' was responsible for a sharper fall in agricultural prices and for a more belated recovery than would have been warranted by the simple operation of international market conditions. Irish agriculture before 1932 was highly export-oriented – some 50 per cent of output in the Irish Free State was exported. By the second half of the decade only a third of output was exported. With the decline in export outlets, a policy of self-sufficiency was pursued in the 1930s. A policy of minimum prices and market regulation promoted the production of wheat, sugar and feedingstuffs. Outlets for cattle were limited; in 1934 a bounty on calf skins was intended as a subsidy to encourage the contraction of the cattle industry. Limited foreign markets and high costs of Irish produce made for a fluctuating volume of exports of dairy produce, eggs and butter with a tendency to decline. In fact, some recovery in exports in 1935 was tied up with a cattle-coal pact with England. In return for an increased quota for cattle in

England, English coal to an equivalent value was admitted to the Irish Free State. The retaliatory duties on both sides were left untouched. The pact was renewed in 1936 and 1937, foreshadowing the more far-reaching Anglo-Irish Trade Agreement of 1938 which restored Anglo-Irish trade relations to normal. There was no overall rise in agriculture in the 1930s : some decline in cattle and a rise in tillage in the first half of the decade; a fall in tillage acreage and a recovery in cattle in the second half.

In the Irish Free State industrialisation accelerated in the 1930s. The main reason for the advance was the protectionism which emerged in the 1930s. In the early years of the Great Depression (1929-31) no new protective duties were imposed on manufactured goods; the only duties introduced were to protect Irish butter, oats, oatmeal and bacon from foreign competition. When England departed from free trade at the end of 1931, the Irish Free State was one of the last countries which was still on a substantial free-trade basis. In a situation of general protectionism in the world at large, it was inevitable that the Irish Free State would move in the same direction. The move was all the more inevitable as the Fianna Fail Party which came to power in 1932 had been critical of the existing policy for years and favoured protectionism. The budget of 1932 imposed 43 new duties. The Anglo-Irish 'economic war' accelerated the resort to higher tariffs. In retaliation for the English duties, duties and quotas were imposed in Ireland on coal and other goods from England. The Emergency Imposition of Duties Act of 1932 gave the government power to impose new or increased duties without prior sanction. From 9 per cent in 1931, the level of duties rose to around 45 per cent. The decline in emigration added to the forces making for higher protective tariffs. In consequence of the American recession emigration to the United States virtually dried up. Emigration 'overseas', i.e. to areas other than Britain, fell to 1,462 in 1931. By 1935 unemployment at 133,000 was double the level of 1926. In consequence of the decline in emigration population stabilised for the first time in any intercensal period since the Famine. The rise in industrial employment eased the situation somewhat. Employment in industry rose from 110,588 in 1931 to 166,513 in 1938. Industrial output rose by 40 per cent between 1931 and 1936. The rise was sharpest in footwear, hosiery, bricks, glass, paper, metals, leather, where domestic output had been relatively modest to start with. Clothing and confectionery were the only large categories to experience a nearly comparable rise. In tobacco output rose little. A policy of import substitution had definite limits. The small size of the domestic market limited the prospects of expansion. While imports of finished goods fell, imports of raw materials for industry rose. The value of imports in consequence fell less sharply than the value of exports. But for the country's substantial earnings from previous investment, the cut-back in imports would have been much sharper. In 1933-5 imports ran at twice the level of exports despite the fact that the amount of external disinvestment was small. The country's strong creditor position meant in effect that the Free State's ability to import was not dependent directly on the level of its exports; in consequence, compared with many primary producing countries, it was able to maintain its imports at a relatively satisfactory level. The country's few manufacturing export industries fared badly. Output declined in the largest of them, brewing. Total exports of manufacturers fell. Excluding tractors, food, drink and tobacco (in which exports also fell), exports of other manufactured goods – a mere £1.6 million in 1929 – fell to £0.5 million in 1935.

Once the more obvious possibilities of industrial expansion had been exploited, new opportunities were likely to be few. After expanding by 40 per cent between 1931 and 1936, industrial output rose by 4½ per cent between 1936 and 1938. Widespread protection also created many difficulties for industries themselves favoured by protection. For instance, the benefits of protection of bootmaking were in part impaired by protection of the tanning industry, which tended to limit the choice of material by the boot-makers and raise their costs. Tariff protection was not likely to make for an efficient industrial base. It also succeeded in raising industrial prices above world level, a situation whose unfavourable consequence especially for the consumer necessitated the Control of Prices Act of 1937. The Control of Manufactures Acts 1932-4 were intended to ensure that in the course of industrial expansion control of companies would remain in Irish hands.

The national income in real terms stagnated in the 1930s. Unlike Britain, it had not fallen between 1929 and 1931. In contrast to Britain where national income in real terms rose substantially in the 1930s, it fell by about 3 per cent between 1931 and 1938. As real incomes rose in industry and services, the fall in incomes was concentrated on the agricultural sector. Incomes in Northern

Ireland probably fell also in the 1930s, and more sharply. In the north, the difficulties were most evident in its industrial sector. In 1932 one-quarter of the insured population was unemployed, in the recession of 1938 nearly 30 per cent. The shipbuilding industry suffered in an especially severe manner. Its work force fell from 20,000 in 1924 to 2,000 in 1933. In 1932 some 60 per cent of shipbuilding and engineering workers were unemployed. In 1933 Harland and Wolff did not launch a single ship, and in 1934 Workman, Clark and Company went out of business. In the summer of 1938, when economic activity had fallen off sharply again, one-half of the linen workers were unemployed. Throughout the inter-war period, the north had the highest level of unemployment in the United Kingdom. Thus, northern industry fared much worse than the smaller industrial sector in the south, tariff-protected and dependent on the domestic market. By way of contrast, agriculture in Northern Ireland fared relatively well in the 1930s compared with agriculture in the Irish Free State. It benefited from the protection and market regulation introduced for agriculture in the United Kingdom. A significant growth of Northern Ireland agricultural exports to Britain may be dated back to the 1930s and to the subsequent war years.

Exports from the Irish Free State had fallen sharply during the 1930s from their 1929 level. They plunged further during the war years from 1939 to 1945. Between 1938 and 1943 the volume of exports was almost halved. Imports fell more drastically still: in 1943 they were less than a third of their pre-war volume in 1938. This was a sharp contrast with the first world war. In the first world war, exports had fallen below the 1912 level only in one year, 1918, and even then only by about 11 per cent. Imports fell more definitely, but here also the decline was pronounced only in the years 1917 and 1918 and even in 1918 the decline did not exceed a third of the 1912 level. More strikingly still, prices had soared during and after the first world war, and export prices had outstripped import prices. Between 1939 and 1945, on the other hand, export prices rose only by 89 per cent; import prices rose by 122 per cent. In the first world war, price control and centralised purchasing developed more slowly and less systematically than in the second world war. Ireland was, in consequence, a loser in the relative prices secured by its exports. The heavy price inflation of the first world war had been responsible for the rise in Ireland's overseas assets. The rise in the foreign assets of the Irish Free State in the second world war was due exclusively to the dramatic fall in imports in consequence of their virtual unavailability. Between 1939 and 1946, external earnings exceeded external payments by £162 million, a sum roughly approximating to the rise in the Free State's foreign assets during the same period. In contrast to the first world war, the rise represented a situation of weakness rather than strength. Given the shortage of goods, the economy was seriously run down during the war years. Net agricultural output rose during the war years. Gross agricultural output, i.e. agricultural output including the value of inputs from outside agriculture, fell. What this meant in simple terms is that there was underinvestment in agriculture. The level of output obtained during the war years could only be held for a relatively short period, and at a later date additional investment in the form of fertilisers and re-equipment would be necessary to make good the neglect or underinvestment of the war years. The fall in imports reduced the supply of raw materials and fuel for industry. Output fell by 27 per cent between 1938 and 1943; industrial employment fell from 166,513 in 1938 to 143,517 in 1943.

The economy expanded rapidly after the war. The rate of growth of output and employment was high. The rate was higher than in Britain; the rate of growth was, of course, artificially inflated by the extent to which output had fallen during the war years.

Republic of Ireland

	Volume of Industrial Output	Industrial Employment
	(1953 = 100)	
1943	39.9	143,517
1949	80.9	208,545
1953	100.0	228,403

The weakness of the economy showed itself in the export sector. Agricultural output stagnated; this meant in particular that exports remained at a relatively low level. The expansion in industrial output was destined largely for the home market. Superficially rapid, the weakness of the expansion in the industrial sector is revealed by the largely unchanging composition of industrial output. Manufacturing in the food, drink, tobacco and textiles categories accounting for 47 per cent of industrial output in 1938, still accounted for 45 per cent in 1950. Efforts were made to expand industry notably by the Undeveloped Areas Act of 1952 which provided special grants for areas defined as underdeveloped. Beyond attracting some firms, principally textile firms, to such areas, its success was extremely limited. Exports, in fact, never even remotely approached the 1929 level, although the volume of imports rose to record proportions. The continued failure of agricultural exports to expand adequately and the fact that industrial expansion was confined to goods for the home market made inevitable recurrent crises in the balance of payments. Severe credit restrictions made necessary by the large deficits in 1951 and 1955 resulted in stagnation during the 1950s. The crisis in 1951 was occasioned in part by the upsurge in prices of raw materials, following the outbreak of the Korean war; that in 1955 was purely domestic in origin, preceding a mild international recession by three years and revealing the full extent of the economy's economic weakness. Agricultural output failed to rise. Industrial output showed signs of stagnation also, industrial employment itself falling in the crisis that followed the balance of payments crisis of 1955.

Republic of Ireland

	Volume of Industrial Output	Industrial Employment
1953	100	228,403
1958	101.9	210,324

Emigration soared in the 1950s; between the censuses of 1951 and 1961 it was at its highest level since the dark decade of the 1880s. The years 1957-8 marked the depths of the crisis. The records of one large retail and wholesale firm in Munster confirm the lack of buoyancy in turnover in the 1950s.

The crisis was directly a consequence of the weakness of the State's foreign trade, and of the resulting large deficit in the external accounts which necessitated severe deflationary measures in 1956 and 1957. The severity of the crisis was reflected in the introduction and continuance of high import levies. Irish tariffs had reached the highest point in the history of the State. The difficulties were enhanced in 1958 by a bad season in which net output in agriculture fell more sharply than in 1947 and probably also any other year in the history of the Irish Free State. Between 1938 and 1958 despite the war years national income had risen on average by about 1 per cent per annum in real terms. Between 1952 and 1958, in much more favourable international conditions, it actually rose by less than 0.5 per cent per annum.

The stagnation of the 1950s was followed by recovery. To a small extent recovery was due to a rise in agricultural output from the depressed level of 1958. In addition, after two decades of total stagnation in agricultural output, net output rose by about 9 per cent in the 1960s. Economic recovery was, however, tied more closely to the growth of industrial output. After the virtual stagnation of the 1950s, the volume of industrial output rose by 82 per cent between 1959 and 1968. The rise in industrial output was occasioned to a large extent by a rise in exports of manufactured goods. In 1960 the volume of exports from the Republic of Ireland passed the 1929 level for the first time. In 1966 exports were 88 per cent above the 1953 level, and 59 per cent above the 1929 level. The rise in exports was in part facilitated by the boom in trade in manufactured goods, caused by the high level of economic activity in industrial countries and by a shortage of labour in many of them. Changes in Irish domestic policy helped to widen the effect of international trends on the economy. The limitations of the policy of industrial protection pursued since 1932 were evident to all in the crisis of 1956-8. The realisation that the home market was too small to sustain either a sound or expanding industrial base led to several important measures. This realisation was expressed for the first time in the Finance Act introduced in the crisis of year 1956 in which provision was made for the remission of part of the tax for a period of five years on profits of companies derived from new or increased exports. The amounts and periods of remission were extended in the Finance Acts of 1957 and 1958. In 1957 the policy of providing grants to promote industrialisation in underdeveloped areas under the 1952 act was extended to the rest of the Republic. The grants for underdeveloped areas had amounted to as much as the full cost of the plant, and half the costs of equipment and training. The grants extended to other areas amounted to as much as two-thirds the cost of plant and one-third the cost of machinery. At the same time the Control of Manufactures Acts of 1932-4 were relaxed as far as export business was concerned in 1958; in 1964 they were repealed.

The belief was also expressed that too high a proportion of the State's investment was not invested productively. The aims of the five-year Programme of Economic Expansion introduced in 1958 was to channel investment into more directly productive channels and to raise the rate of increase in national income to 2 per cent in real terms, itself a modest rate compared with the rate already experienced by most countries in the 1950s. In the event, real incomes rose in Ireland by 4 per cent per annum in the years 1959-63. One feature of the Republic in the 1950s was the relatively low rate of investment – only some 15 per cent of gross national product was invested. This proportion, to a large extent by a disproportionate rise in government expenditure, had been raised to as much as 24 per cent by the end of the 1960s. In part, the increased rate of investment has been financed by a large inflow of capital in the course of the 1960s. The outcome in terms of income and output was less a consequence of planning than of the remarkably high level of world activity in this period and of the move in Irish policy from a closed economic system to a more open one. Some of the basic decisions were taken between 1956 and 1958 in the years of economic crisis. Subsequently, the high import duties have been scaled down, in part unilaterally, in part in the context of the Anglo-Irish Free Trade Agreement of 1965. The south's economic growth in the 1960s has been closely dependent on a higher rate of growth of exports. A dilemma in the expansion of the State's exports has been its high degree of dependence on a single market – Britain. This close dependence and the traditional ties between the two countries were reflected in the trade agreements of 1938, 1948 and 1960. For a country as dependent on foreign trade as Ireland the failure of negotiations to result in a general free-trade area in Europe in 1957 heightened the dilemma. A wider market in Europe has an appeal for Ireland, especially as Britain itself has grown relatively slowly in the 1960s. Irish economic policy in the 1960s has been guided by what is regarded as the paramount necessity of admission to the Common Market if Britain is admitted as a member and on the other hand the aim of securing closer economic ties with Britain in the interval. The Free Trade Agreement of 1965 reflects all these considerations.

This has made the Republic even more dependent on international conditions. Not only is the Republic's foreign trade large in relation to its output by international standards but increased borrowing from abroad has increased the number of its foreign creditors. This leaves the economy much more vulnerable than in the past. In the depressed years of the early 1920s and in the still more severe depression of the 1930s a strong creditor position acted as a buffer against the worst effects of international crisis. Today its creditor status is relatively much weaker. The Republic's interest in free international trade and in a continued high level of economic activity is therefore greater than ever.

Emigration has fallen in the 1960s; with emigration now smaller than the rate of natural increase the Republic's population has been rising. Significantly, too, the traditionally late marriage ages have fallen and the birth rate has risen. For Northern Ireland as well as for the Republic the 1960s has been a period of relatively rapid economic growth. The north's traditional industries, linen and shipbuilding – between them linen and engineering accounted for 50 per cent of output – experienced difficulties in the 1950s. For the north as for the south the dilemma has been that new job opportunities have not expanded rapidly enough to absorb all the labour drifting from more traditional industries. In the Republic's traditional major industry – agriculture – the fall in numbers has more than outweighed the sizeable increase in employment in manufacturing industry and in services. The north by contrast was already a highly industrialised country, but the problem was the same in that there was a sharp run-down in the numbers employed in its major industry – linen – and that employment has stagnated precariously in shipbuilding and in its aircraft-building offshoot. In consequence, the impressive growth in employment in new industries, notably in man-made fibres and in light engineering, has been offset by the fall in numbers in more traditional activities. Thus, if north and south are to continue to develop, they are both dependent on a continued expansion in manufacturing industry, and on the large amount of investment that would make that expansion possible. As both states are small economies, expansion on the desired scale is feasible only in the context of exporting a major part of any additional output; that in effect means that both states are highly dependent on trends in international trade and investment and vulnerable to any changes that adversely affect these trends.

Ireland around 1913 – towards the end of the free trade era – exported the remarkably high proportion of 50 per cent of its industrial and agricultural output. It was certainly the most export-oriented small country, and one of the most export-oriented regions, in the world. This explains why the Great Depression of 1929 and later with its contraction of world trade inevitably ushered in a generation of stagnation. In Northern Ireland, decline was deepened and prolonged by the secular run-down of the linen industry; in the Irish Free State by a policy of self-sufficiency behind tariff barriers which, given the south's continued dependence on imported raw materials and fuels, led inexorably in the long run to recurrent balance-of-payments crises. For north and south, the dilemma of the whole history of their development in recent centuries has been that export dependence went hand in hand with the existence of few outside markets for linen, agricultural produce and the specialised output of Belfast's engineering. The history of linen lies in two phases; the first, the growth and decline of its English markets, the second, the growth and decline of its American market. In agriculture, markets in Europe were always few and erratic; those outside Europe barely outlived the eighteenth century; and subsidisation and protection has adversely affected Ireland's foothold in the British market in the twentieth century. The decline of other agricultural markets, and in the twentieth century of the American market for linen, has made Ireland – north and south – much more than in the eighteenth or nineteenth century a satellite of England's industrial revolution and latterly a partner in Britain's comparative stagnation as well. The attractions of the Common Market, in the eyes of the government of the Republic of Ireland and of its advisers, lie mainly in the large market for agricultural produce that industrialisation has created in recent decades in western Europe and which is at present supplied by protected high-cost local producers. Both Northern Ireland and the Republic of Ireland are, therefore, vitally interested in the diversification of foreign markets. The widening of the industrial base in the north, the growth of an industrial sector in the south, have both relied in part on an inflow of capital in the 1960s. A large capital inflow, creating liabilities, has reduced the strong creditor status which characterised Ireland in 1914. The reduced creditor status deprives the island of the buffer that could absorb some of the shock of depression, as it did so effectively in the Free State in the 1930s, when it mitigated what would in other circumstances have been the even more disastrous results of the ' economic war '. The small size of the two economies in association with their vulnerability to changes in trade or in investment means that whether or not Britain or Ireland enters the Common Market, Ireland's interest lies more than any other small country in stable international conditions, a rising level of world economic activity and ready or low-tariff access to foreign markets. Internally, in 1970 and 1971 competitiveness in costs – given wage inflation – might seem the most pressing issue, but it derives its economic significance primarily from the necessity of not only maintaining but expanding exports.

Bibliographical Note

Irish economic history has been influenced by political preoccupations deriving from Anglo-Irish political conflict. The older textbooks, all written in a period of growing political consciousness in the first quarter of the twentieth century, are ample testimony to these influences. While the approach reflected in these books is now widely questioned and in the process of replacement by new interpretations, no single modern textbook exists surveying comprehensively the economic history of recent centuries. *The formation of the Irish economy* (Cork, 1969) ed. L. M. Cullen, is an introduction to a number of aspects of Irish economic history since the eighteenth century. L. M. Cullen, *Life in Ireland* (London, 1968) and *Six generations: everyday work and life in Ireland from 1790* (Cork, 1970) survey the economic and social background. T. W. Moody and J. C. Beckett (ed.), *Ulster since 1800: a political and economic survey* (London, 1954); *Ulster since 1800: a social survey* (London, 1957) are both excellent introductory accounts, now unfortunately out of print. R. B. McDowell (ed.), *Social life in Ireland, 1800-45* (Dublin, 1963) is a useful account of several aspects of Irish social life in the pre-Famine decades.

Aspects of Irish social history 1750-1800: documents selected and edited by W. H. Crawford and B. Trainor with an introduction by J. C. Beckett (Belfast, 1969) presents a large number of documents illustrative of aspects of Irish economic and social history. No less informative than the documents are the illuminating commentaries which accompany them and which comment on the background and interpretations. The documents are especially informative on the land system, landlord-tenant relations, rural social organisation, politics and popular movements. Among the documents is a long and important letter, *c.* 1778, on the Irish woollen trade by Luke Gardiner. The Public Record Office of Northern Ireland has also in its *Education Facsimiles* series, a collection of documents entitled *The Great Famine 1845-1852*. Çollections of documents are useful : they supplement textbooks and, where the teacher is concerned, help to make study or teaching more concrete and varied. In addition to the Public Record Office of Northern Ireland publications, the Gill-Macmillan series *Insights into Irish History* also performs this role. The first two books in this series : L. M. Cullen, *Merchants, ships and trade, 1660-1830* and W. H. Crawford, *Domestic industry in Ireland,* are available.

On more recent economic and social history, the relevant chapters in F. S. L. Lyons, *Ireland since the Famine* (London, 1971) are an excellent, critical and comprehensive survey. They deal with social and economic history at equal length, and cover North and South. For the South only since 1922 James Meenan, *The Irish economy since 1922* (Liverpool, 1970) is a comprehensive and detailed account. Useful also for the survey of recent decades is D. O'Mahony *The Irish economy* (2nd ed., Cork, 1967). J. Johnston, *Irish agriculture in transition* (Dublin, 1951) is a good account of Irish agriculture. R. D. Crotty, *Irish agriculture: its volume and structure* (Cork, 1966), while theoretical in approach and highly controversial in its thesis, has a useful account of Irish agriculture in the twentieth century.

The older accounts of Irish economic history, while dated, are still of use. In many respects, the best and ablest early account of the Irish economy is in the first volume of W. E. H. Lecky's *History of Ireland in the eighteenth century* (London, 1892). This account is doubly worthy of note : because of its intrinsic clarity and because both its framework and argument decisively influenced the ' economic histories ' which appeared in the twentieth century, starting with A. E. Murray, *History of the commercial and financial relations between England and Ireland from the period of Restoration* (London, 1903, reprinted 1907). Murray's volume was one of the few to survey the second half of the nineteenth century – its account of the fiscal relationship between the two islands in the nineteenth century is still useful. G. O'Brien's books have much detail, although very uncritically presented, on Irish economic history from 1600 to the Great Famine. Chart and Burke are short surveys of Irish economic history; Burke's account is sometimes erratic in presentation and overloaded with statistical information; Chart is concise and readable.

Burke, J. F., *Outlines of the industrial history of Ireland* (Dublin, 1920)

Chart, D. A., *Economic history of Ireland* (Dublin, 1920)

O'Brien, G., *Economic history of Ireland in the seventeenth century* (Dublin, 1919)

O'Brien, G., *Economic history of Ireland in the eighteenth century* (Dublin, 1918)

O'Brien, G., *Economic history of Ireland from the Union to the Famine* (London, 1921)

The period from 1660 onwards can hardly be studied without some reference to previous history. A. Longfield, *Anglo-Irish trade in the sixteenth century* (London, 1929) is useful, although its use of sources is largely limited to port books and it applies inappropriately political concepts formulated in the eighteenth century or later to the Tudor period and background. For the first half of the seventeenth century, H. F. Kearney, 'Mercantilism and Ireland, 1620-1640' in T. D. Williams (ed) *Historical Studies I* (London, 1958) is an indispensable commentary on interpretation. Chapter II and section 3 of the bibliographical note in H. F. Kearney, *Strafford in Ireland* (Manchester, 1959) are also important. *Advertisements for Ireland, being a description of the state of Ireland in the reign of James I* (Dublin, 1923), ed. G. O'Brien, is a very informative contemporary account of Ireland.

Monographs dealing with aspects of Irish economic history are:

Black, R. D. C., *Economic thought and the Irish question 1817-1870* (Cambridge, 1960)

Coe, W. E., *The engineering industry of the north of Ireland* (Newton Abbot, 1969)

Connell, K. H., *The population of Ireland, 1750-1845* (Oxford, 1950)

Cullen, L. M., *Anglo-Irish Trade, 1660-1800* (Manchester, 1968)

Delany, V. T. H., and D. R., *The canals of the south of Ireland* (Newton Abbot, 1966)

Edie, C. A., *The Irish cattle bills: a study in Restoration politics* (Transactions of the American Philosophical Society, new series, vol. 60, pt. 2, 1970)

Edwards, R. D., and Williams T. D., (ed.), *The Great Famine* (Dublin, 1956)

Fetter, F., *The Irish pound 1797-1826* (London, 1955)

Freeman, T. W., *Pre-Famine Ireland* (Manchester, 1957)

Gill, C., *The rise of the Irish linen industry* (Oxford, 1925, reprinted 1964)

Green, E. R. R., *The Lagan valley, 1800-1850* (London, 1949)
  Industrial archaeology of co. Down (Belfast, 1963)

Gribbon, H., *The history of water power in Ulster* (Newton Abbot, 1969)

Johnston, J., *Bishop Berkeley's querist in historical perspective* (Dundalk, 1970)

Lynch, P., and Vaizey, J., *Guinness's brewery in the Irish economy, 1759-1876* (Cambridge, 1960)

McCracken, E., *The Irish woods since Tudor times* (Newton Abbot, 1971)

McCutcheon, W. A., *The canals of the north of Ireland* (Dawlish, 1965)

O'Donovan, J., *The economic history of livestock in Ireland* (Cork, 1940)

Riordan, E. J., *Modern Irish trade and industry* (London, 1920)

Woodham-Smith, C., *The Great Hunger* (London, 1962)

Irish economic history received little attention after the spate of writings appearing on aspects of Irish economic development in 1918-21. Not until K. H. Connell's book, *The population of Ireland* (Oxford, 1950) did the wider issues in Irish economic history again receive attention at any length. One reason for the neglect of the subject in the intervening decades was the belief that the necessary sources were consumed in the destruction of the Public Record Office in 1922. This view itself reflected the belief that economic development was politically determined and that economic history should be written from political and administrative sources. Modern historians, however, base their conclusions to a greater extent on private and business papers. Little of such material was housed in the Public Record Office. The obsession with the political and legislative aspects of Irish economic development has, however, deep roots in the history of recent centuries. On this aspect of Irish economic history, see L. M. Cullen, ' Irish economic history: fact and myth' in L. M. Cullen (ed.) *The formation of the Irish economy* (Cork, 1969)

In the last two decades the issue that has received most attention and stirred up the most controversy is that of population growth in the eighteenth and early nineteenth centuries. Superficially this issue is simply whether a decline in the death rate or a rise in the birth rate was responsible for the sharp rise in population at that time, and what factors were instrumental in causing the changes in the death rate or birth rate. But it is more than that because the basic assumptions in much of the discussion that people married at a very early age or that a potato diet was universal rest on the presupposition that Ireland was to a large extent characterised by a simple subsistence society. Historically, this has been reinforced by two factors, (a) the assumed existence of hostile legislative factors, and (b) a land system claimed to have been oppressive. The subsistence thesis, implicit in Connell's classic, *The population of Ireland, 1750-1845*, explicit in Lynch, P. and Vaizey, J., *Guinness's brewery in the Irish economy, 1759-1876*, has been close to the core of much modern writing on Irish economic history. The 'subsistence' concept, often formulated in terms of two economies – 'market economy' and 'a subsistence economy', does not, however, square well with the evidence of the growth of trade and use of cash and with the complex pattern of social relationships in the greater part of the country. It is weakened too by the necessity to revise the more sweeping assertions made about the effects of legislative measures and about the character of the land system. A widespread smuggling trade has often been seen as a consequence of the 'suppression' of some important branches of Irish trade in the eighteenth century. The character and limited extent of the smuggling trade is explored in L. M. Cullen, 'The smuggling trade in Ireland in the eighteenth century', *Proceedings of the Royal Irish Academy*, vol. 67, Section C, No. 5 (1969). Some of the views about rural relations are questioned in L. M. Cullen, 'The Hidden Ireland: re-assessment of a concept', *Studia Hibernica*, 1969. Modern research has tended to emphasise regional and social contrasts. This is true of the nineteenth century no less than the eighteenth. Both the Union in 1800 and the land system are emerging as more complex factors in the unfolding of Irish economic and social history than they have usually been held to be.

The list of articles from periodicals set out below is not intended to be comprehensive. Articles have been selected either because they contain a substantial amount of descriptive data or because they raise important issues of interpretation.

Armstrong, D. L., 'Social and economic conditions in the Belfast linen industry', *Irish Historical Studies*, Vol. VII, No. 28 (Sept., 1951)

Andrews, J. H., 'Road planning in Ireland before the railway age', *Irish Geography*, Vol. V, No. 1 (1964)

Connell, K. H., 'The potato in Ireland', *Past and Present*. No. 23 (Nov., 1962)
'Some unsettled problems in English and Irish population history, 1750-1845', *Irish Historical Studies*, Vol. VII, No. 28 (Sept. 1951)

Cousens, S. H., 'Emigration and demographic change in Ireland, 1851-61', *Economic History Review*, 2nd series, Vol. XIV, No. 2 (Dec., 1961)
'The regional variations in population changes in Ireland, 1861-1881', *Economic History Review*, Vol. XVII, No. 2 (Dec., 1964)
'The regional variation in mortality during the Great Irish Famine', *Proceedings of the Royal Irish Academy*, Vol. 63, Section C, No. 3 (1963)

Cullen, L. M., 'The value of contemporary printed sources for Irish economic history in the eighteenth century', *Irish Historical Studies*, Vol. XIV, No. 54 (Sept., 1964)
'Problems in the interpretation and revision of eighteenth-century Irish economic history', *Transactions of the Royal Historical Society*, 5th series, Vol. 17 (1967)
'Irish history without the potato', *Past and Present*, No. 40 (July, 1968)
'The smuggling trade in Ireland in the eighteenth century', *Proceedings of the Royal Irish Academy*, Vol. 67, section C, No. 5 (March, 1969)
'The Hidden Ireland: re-assessment of a concept', *Studia Hibernica*, No. 9 (1969)

Drake, Michael, 'Marriage and population growth in Ireland, 1750-1845', *Economic History Review*, 2nd series, Vol. XVI, No. 2 (Dec., 1963)
'The Irish demographic crisis of 1740-41' in *Historical Studies VI*, ed. T. W. Moody (London, 1968)

Goodwin, A., ' Wood's halfpence ', *English Historical Review*, Vol. LI (Oct. 1936), reprinted in R. Mitchison, *Essays in eighteenth-century history* (London, 1966)

Griffith, A. P. G., ' The Irish Board of Works in the Famine years ', *Historical Journal*, Vol. XIII, No 4 (Dec., 1970)

James, F. G., ' Irish colonial trade in the eighteenth century ', *William and Mary Quarterly*, Vol. XX (1963)
' The Irish lobby in the early eighteenth century ' *English Historical Review*, Vol. LXXXI (July, 1966)

Kearney, H. F., ' The political background to English mercantilism, 1695-1700 ', *Economic History Review*, Vol. XI, No. 3 (1959)

Large, D., ' The wealth of the greater Irish landowners 1750-1815 ', *Irish Historical Studies*, Vol. XV, No. 57 (March, 1966)

Larkin, E., ' Economic growth, capital investment and the Roman Catholic church in nineteenth-century Ireland ', *American Historical Review*, Vol. LXXII (April, 1967)

Lee, J., ' Money and beer in Ireland, 1790-1875 ', *Economic History Review*, Vol. XIX, No. 1 (April, 1966)
' The construction costs of Irish railways, 1830-1853 ', *Business History*, Vol. IX, No. 2 (July, 1967)
' The provision of capital for early Irish railways ', *Irish Historical Studies*, Vol. XVI, No. 61 (March, 1968)
' Marriage and population in pre-Famine Ireland ' *Economic History Review*, 2nd series Vol. XXI, No. 2 (Aug., 1968)
' Irish agriculture ', *Agricultural History Review*, Vol. XVII, pt. 1 (1969)

Lyons, F. S. L., ' Vicissitudes of a middleman in co. Leitrim, 1810-27 ', *Irish Historical Studies*, Vol. IX, No. 35 (March, 1955)
' The economic ideas of Parnell ' in Roberts, M. (ed.) *Historical Studies II* (London, 1959)

Monaghan, J. J., ' The rise and fall of the Belfast cotton industry ', *Irish Historical Studies*, Vol. III, No. 9 (March, 1942)

Nowlan, K. B., ' Agrarian unrest in Ireland, 1800-1845', *University Review*, Vol. II, No. 6 (1959)

O'Connor, T. M., ' The embargo on the export of Irish provisions, 1776-9 ', *Irish Historical Studies*, Vol. II, No. 5 (March, 1940)

Razzell, P. E., ' Population growth and economic change in eighteenth- and early nineteenth-century England and Ireland', in Jones, E. L. and Mingay, G. E., *Land, labour and population in the Industrial Revolution* (London 1967)

Simms, J. G., 'Connaught in the eighteenth century', *Irish Historical Studies*, Vol. XI, No. 42 (Sept., 1958)
'County Sligo in the eighteenth century', *Journal of the Royal Society of Antiquaries of Ireland*, Vol. XCI, pt. ii (1961)

Wall, M., 'The rise of a Catholic middle class in eighteenth-century Ireland', *Irish Historical Studies*, Vol. XI, No. 42 (Sept., 1958)

Walsh, B. M., 'A perspective on Irish population patterns', *Eire-Ireland*, Vol. IV, No. 3 (Autumn, 1969)

FURTHER BIBLIOGRAPHICAL NOTES

The outstanding feature of the last five years has been the appearance of three major works in a revisionist vein in Irish nineteenth-century agrarian history:

Donnelly, jr., J. S., *The land and the people of nineteenth-century Cork* (London, 1975).

Maguire, W. A., *The Downshire estates in Ireland 1801–1845* (Oxford 1972).

Solow, B. L., *The land question and the Irish economy 1870–1903* (Cambridge, Mass., 1971).

Lee, Professor J. J., *The modernisation of Irish Society 1848–1918*
(Dublin, 1973) has some very stimulating comments on economic issues. A paper by the same author, "The dual economy in Ireland, 1800–1850" in *Historical Studies VIII* (Dublin, 1971), ed. T. D. Williams, is also very useful on a controversial issue in the study of the pre-Famine Irish economy. T. C. Barnard, *Cromwellian Ireland: English government and reform in Ireland, 1649–1660* (Oxford, 1975) helps to fill in the obscure pre-1660 economic background.

In the growing periodical literature, the following are the most relevant recent additions:

Carney, F. C., "Pre-Famine Irish population: the evidence from the Trinity College Estates", *Irish economic and social history*, vol. II (1975)

Crawford, W. H., "Landlord–tenant relations in Ulster 1609–1820", *Irish economic and social history*, Vol. II (1975)

Cullen, L. M., "Population trends in seventeenth-century Ireland", *Economic and Social Review*, vol. VI (1975)

Malcomson, A. P. W., "Absenteeism in eighteenth-century Ireland", *Irish economic and social history*, vol. I (1974).

O Grada, C., "Seasonal migration and post-Famine adjustment in the west of Ireland", *Studia Hibernica*, vol. XIII (1973)

Note on Primary Sources

This note is not exhaustive; it is intended to draw attention to some of the main categories of primary source used in individual chapters.

Chapter 1: 1660-1689 (pages 7-25)
Statistical data on trade in this period are available in British Museum, ADD. MSS 2902, 4759, and in *Calendars of State Papers, Ireland*, 1663-5, pp 694-8; 1669-70, pp 54-5; *Domestic*, 1671, p 507; fiscal data in British Museum, Harl. MS 4706, and ADD. MS 18022; *Calendars of State Papers, Ireland*, 1663-5, pp 460-1; 1666-9, pp 672-3. The port books in the Public Record Office, London, also document the trade, for individual English ports.

Petty's writings in C. H. Hull, *Economic writings of Sir William Petty,* 2 vols. (Cambridge, 1899), and Marquis of Lansdowne, *The Petty Papers,* 2 vols. (London, 1927) and *The Petty-Southwell correspondence,* 1676-87 (London, 1928) and Sir William Temple, *Essay upon the advancement of trade in Ireland,* 1673, are especially important.

The *Ormonde MSS* (Historical Manuscripts Commission, new series) have much information both on administration and economic life, as have British Museum manuscripts ADD. MSS 2902, 4761. The published calendars for the *Orrery Papers* (Irish Manuscripts Commission, edited by E. MacLysaght, 1941) and for the *Herbert Correspondence* (University of Wales Press, 1963, edited by W. J. Smith) are guides to two rich collections of estate material.

The memoranda book of James Twyford of Bristol (in the possession of Lord Hylton, Ammerdown Park, Radstock) has many invoices and copies of bills of exchange relating to Irish trade between 1674 and 1681. A memoranda book of protested bills of exchange and other commercial documents in the Chester City Record Office (C/B/166) throws much light on trade with Ireland from 1639 to 1665.

Details of exchange rates – an informative source of economic trends – are scattered through administrative and business or estate papers. I am indebted to Mr T. V. Jackson of Rayleigh, Essex, for a large mass of exchange rates drawn from postal archives.

The most informative single collection of business papers are the Macartney letter books (one volume for 1660-7; the second for 1679-81) in the Linenhall Library, Belfast. The Sharp MSS in the Historical Library, Society of Friends, 6 Eustace Street, Dublin 2, have some pertinent information. A published source – *Some account of the life of Joseph Pike ... with preliminary observations, by John Barclay* (London, 1837) – has also some information on Irish trade.

The Admiralty records of French ports throw light on the movement of Irish trade with French ports at this time. Figures based on the port of St Malo have been published by J. Delumeau, *Le mouvement du port de St Malo à la fin du XVIIe siècle.*

Chapter 2: 1689-1730 (pages 26-49)
For this period, some useful early statistics are in British Museum, ADD. MSS 2902, 4761, 18022, 20710 and in *Journals of the House of Commons of Ireland*, vol. 2, app. lxxxix. From 1698 continuous trade statistics are available in Public Record Office, London, Customs 15.

Collections of papers such as the Wyche Papers (Public Record Office of Ireland, Dublin), King MSS (Trinity College, Dublin) and the Southwell MSS (British Museum) are very informative on the background. The most informative estate papers are the Egmont letter books (British Museum) and the St George papers (Public Record Office, London, c110/46, St George v. St George) while the Sarsfield Vesey papers (Public Record Office of Ireland, Dublin) are also useful. The calendar for the *Inchiquin manuscripts* (Irish Manuscripts Commission, ed. J. Ainsworth, 1961) is also useful. An invaluable merchant collection are the letter books and accounts of a Bridgwater firm in the Public Record Office, London, C104/11,12, Cleek v. Calpine. James Fontaine, *Memoirs of a Huguenot family* (New York, 1853) has some pertinent information on trade in the 1690s as well.

Chapters 3 and 4: 1730-1793 (pages 50-99)
Overseas trade, basic to the study of the eighteenth century, is documented at length in the Ledgers of Exports and Imports (Customs 15), while commodity prices, market reports, exchange rates and from 1777 the prices of stocks and government funds are reported in contemporary newspapers. J. Castaing, *The course of exchange and other things* (London University Library, British Museum and Library of the Bank of England, London), gives the London exchanges rates on Dublin continuously for the eighteenth century.

The *Journals* of the Irish House of Commons have much useful information, the appendices in particular containing, in addition to reports on the grain, linen and woollen trades, a mass of statistics relating to trade, output and revenue.

Customs and excise administration are voluminously documented in the Minutes of the Revenue Commissioners (Customs I, Public Record Office, London). Trade policy in war time and the celebrated ‘ embargoes ’ are documented both there and in the State Papers, Ireland (Public Record Office, London). Colonial aspects of the embargoes are discussed in two books by Richard Pares, *War and trade in the West Indies, 1739-1763* (Oxford, 1936); *Colonial blockade and neutral rights, 1739-1763* (Oxford, 1938).

Merchant papers are informative not only for trade but for economic fluctuations generally, harvest conditions and banking. Outstanding are the Mussenden papers (Public Record Office of Northern Ireland, Belfast), Gurney papers (Society of Friends, London), Pelet papers (Archieves Departmentales de la Gironde, Bordeaux), letter book of Alexander Oliphant of Ayr (Scottish Record Office, Edinburgh), account books and letter books of Edward Hardman (Trinity College, Dublin), Grubb papers (Society of Friends, Dublin), Lecky papers (Society of Friends, Dublin), and Courtenay and Ridgway ledger (in the possession of Mr Henry Ridgway, Mallow). There is a small but interesting collection of copies of letters captured in wartime in State Papers, Ireland, S.P. 63, vol. 408 (Public Record Office, London). In particular the immensely important linen trade is documented in the Andrews papers (Messrs Isaac Andrews and Co., Belfast), a collection of letters received by a London merchant James Hudson in the early 1730s (Public Record Office, London, C105/15, Herne v. Barber),

Greer papers, Weir papers, James Ferguson account book, and account book of a Ballycastle merchant, 1751-54 (all in Public Record Office of Northern Ireland). I am indebted to Mrs Amy Monahan of Castletown, co. Carlow, for the opportunity to consult an unpublished study based on the extensive Faulkner papers in her possession, which relate to linen in co. Tyrone, and farming in counties Wicklow and Carlow. The Andrews papers describe milling as well as the linen industry.

Estate papers touch on all aspects of economic and social life. Outstanding among them are the Egmont papers (British Museum), Downshire papers (Public Record Office of Northern Ireland), St George papers (Public Record Office, London, C110/46), Abercorn papers (Transcripts in Public Record Office of Northern Ireland), and Wandesforde papers (National Library, Dublin), while other collections such as the Blake, Fingall and French papers (National Library, Dublin) are helpful. Frequently estate papers document both inland and overseas trade and manufacturing industry, notably grain milling and textiles. The O'Connell papers (Library, University College, Dublin) document branches of overseas trade, the Townley Hall papers (National Library, Dublin, and an isolated account book in the Meath County Library, Navan) milling, and the Bellew papers (National Library) both milling and overseas trade. The Ainsworth Reports on MSS in private keeping (in the National Library) are a guide to many estate collections, while among the publications of the Irish Manuscripts Commission *The Kenmare manuscripts* (ed. E. MacLysaght, 1942), *The Shapland Carew papers* (ed. A. Longfield, 1946) and the *Inchiquin manuscripts* (ed. J. Ainsworth, 1961) are invaluable. Marquis of Lansdowne, *Glanerought and the Petty-Fitzmaurices* (London, 1937) throws much light on estate management and life in co. Kerry, based on the vast Petty-Fitzmaurice archives. Some aspects of economic life, usually at a more modest level, are documented in Quaker wills and inventories (Society of Friends, Dublin).

Estate papers and business records often illustrate banking and the operation of the monetary system. Information bearing more directly on banking is to be found in the Sarsfield Vesey papers (Public Record Office of Ireland, Dublin), La Touche accounts (National Library, Dublin), Dillon MSS (Microfilm, National Library, Dublin) and the Shaw ledgers and letter books (National Library, Dublin).

Reminiscences, personal accounts and descriptions of travel, published or unpublished, often have extremely useful information. Among such items are the accounts and diaries of Charles O'Connor with information on prices, farming and famine in the 1730s and 1740s, parts of which have been edited by S. Ní Chinnéide in ' Dhá leabhar nótaí le Séarlas O Conchubhair ', *Galvia*, Vol. I (1954), and in ' Dialann Uí Conchúir', *Galvia*, Vol. IV (1957); the Narrative of Captain George O'Malley, the first chapters of which describe his youth and early escapades in the west of Ireland (typescript in the possession of Professor Conor O'Malley, Galway); Isaac Butler's tour in 1744 (MS in Public Museum, Armagh; another portion not in Armagh MS edited in *Journal of the Royal Society of Antiquaries of Ireland*, Vol. XXII, pts. 1, 2, 4 (1892)); *carnets de voyages* by Coquebert de Montbret in Bibliothèque Nationale, Paris (*See* S. Ní Chinnéide, ' Coquebert de Montbret in search of the Hidden Ireland ', *Journal of the Royal Society of Antiquaries of Ireland*, Vol. LXXXII (1952); ' A Frenchman's impressions of Limerick city and people in 1791 ', *Journal of the North Munster Antiquarian Society*, 1948; ' Coquebert de Montbret's impressions of Galway city and county in 1791 ', *Journal of the Galway Archaeological and Historical society*, Vol. XXV (1952); six letters of Edward Willes (Public Record Office of Northern Ireland). Among published items in this category, the most useful are :

A. Young, *Tour in Ireland* (London, 1780)

Thomas Cloney, *A personal narrative of those transactions, in which the author was engaged, during . . . 1798* (Dublin, 1832)

Mary Leadbeater, *The Leadbeater Papers*, 2 vols. (1862)

R. McHugh (ed.), *Carlow in '98. The autobiography of William Farrell of Carlow* (Dublin, 1949) (first two chapters)

The Registry of Deeds, Dublin, is a rich source throwing light incidentally and directly on all aspects of economic life.

Chapter 5: 1793-1851 (pages 100-133)
Economic conditions in the first half of the nineteenth century are documented copiously in parliamentary papers, in particular the reports on the exchanges, 1804, butter trade, 1824, promissory notes, 1826, the poor, 1830s, the so-called ' Drummond ' report on railways, 1838, and the Devon Commission, 1845.

The census data for 1821, 1831 and 1841 are very full not only on population but on many aspects of agriculture and occupations. The various Statistical Surveys sponsored by the Royal Dublin Society are extremely useful, as is the indispensable *Topographical Dictionary of Ireland*, by S. Lewis, 1837.

Business and family papers are invaluable. Among the material used in this study are account book of James Carroll (in the possession of Miss Agnes Carroll, Cloneevin, co. Louth), Grubb papers (Society of Friends, Dublin), Wandesforde papers (National Library), and Townley Hall papers (National Library).

The first valuation records (Public Record of Ireland, Dublin) are of great value for the economic and social study of the 1830s and 1840s, as are the Ordnance Survey maps of the same period on account of their wealth of economic and social detail.

Chapter 6: 1851-1921 (pages 134-170)
Parliamentary papers are extremely informative for this period. Apart from the inevitable voluminous enquiries, of which those on the housing of the labouring classes 1885, industries (Ireland), 1884-5, and the commission on financial relations (so-called ' Childers Commission ') are perhaps the most widely informative, they contain a daunting array of statistical information : the rich quarry of the decennial population census, annual agricultural statistics, the industrial production census of 1907, and statistics of overseas trade from 1904. Among unofficial published sources, Marmion's *Ancient and modern history of the maritime ports of Ireland* (privately printed, 1855), *Thom's Directory* (annual), and E. J. Riordan, *Modern Irish trade and industry* (London, 1920), are the most useful for statistical data in addition to providing much other information.

Business papers are invaluable for this period, and survivals from *c.* 1850 are numerous and often rich. A fuller analysis of business material for this period will probably answer not only microeconomic questions, but even some macroeconomic questions, e.g. the important topic of the timing and scope of some of the basic trends in investment, etc. Among the private papers used in the course of this study are Malcomson papers (Messrs. Hardman, Winder and Stokes); Purdon papers (Trinity College, Dublin); diaries of Richard Hilliard, Killarney; a New Ross contractor's accounts (in possession of author); papers relating to various businesses and families in the Hardman, Winder and Stokes archive; papers belonging to a

long-established south Wexford firm. I am indebted to Mr
Alexander Findlater for a copy of a short account of Findlaters
prepared by him from the firm's archives. Contemporary director-
ies such as Stratten's *Dublin, Cork and South of Ireland: a literary,
commercial and social review, past and present* (London, 1892)
have much information on individual businesses in the nineteenth
century. *Guide to Irish Quaker records* (Irish Manuscripts Commission, 1967), edited by Mrs Olive Goodbody, calendars a number
of items relating to nineteenth-century business.

Reminiscences have often much invaluable information on economic life generally, and more specifically farming life, otherwise
rather hard to document in any intimate fashion:

M. Carbery, *The farm by Lough Gur* (London, 1937)

W. Macdonald, *Reminscences of a Maynooth professor* (London,
    1925)

P. O'Laoghaire, *Mo sgeal féin* (Dublin, 1915)

Joseph Brády, *The big sycamore* (Dublin, 1958)

E. de Blaghd, *Trasna na Bóinne*, Vol. 1 (Dublin, 1957)

Fictional accounts are sometimes useful in the light they throw on
living conditions and attitudes. Outstanding in this regard is Charles
Kickham's *Knocknagow*, a rich source for farming conditions and
attitudes at a somewhat indeterminate time in the nineteenth
century.

A series of articles by Seamus Brady, based on Lord Leitrim's
diaries, in the *Irish Press*, October 2-7, 1967, is also of interest.

Chapter 7: 1922-1970 (pages 171-187)

Official material, in the nature of statistics and enquiries or reports,
for this period is voluminous, and too well known to require any
description here.

The *Journal of the statistical and social enquiry society of
Ireland* affords many illuminating comments on statistical information and economic trends in this period. A little-quoted but often
perceptive commentary are the chapters on ' Development problems in Southern Europe and Ireland ', in the Economic Commission for Europe's *Economic survey of Europe, 1959*.

Some business material such as Richard Hilliard's diaries, Castlecomer Mining Company papers, and Locke's Distillery papers have
influenced the account given in this chapter.

Index

Abbeyleix, co. Leix, 106
Abbeyvale, co. Kilkenny, 92
Achill, co. Mayo, 116
Absentees, absentee incomes, 16, 45-7, 56, 83, 170
Admiralty, English, 56, 103; French, 197
Agent, estate, 44, 83-4, 113-14
Agriculture, 7-11, 77-81, 109, 139, 141, 148-150, 171-3, 177-8, 179-83, 185-6, 189, 200
America, Americas, 55, 57-9, 75, 103, 174-5, 186
Anglo-Irish Trade Agreements, 178, 184; Free Trade Agreement, 184
Antigua, 12
Antrim, 86; co., 48, 60-1, 122
Arigna, 89
Arklow, 162
Armagh, 86, co., 48, 60-1, 80, 122
Arnotts, Cork, 144
Athboy, 121
Athlone, 73, 85, 86
Athy, 89

Bacon, bacon curing, 162, 171, 178
Bairéad, Riocard, 63
Balance of trade, 46-7, 72, 74, 100, 104, 169-70, 172-3; of payments, 15, 95, 182, 186
Balbriggan, 94, 106, 108, 162
Ballina, 63, 81, 116, 121
Ballinamore and Ballyconnell Canal, 122
Ballinasloe, 86, 87, 121-2
Ballycastle, 96
Ballymahon, 61, 147
Ballyshannon, 86
Balrothery, co. Dublin, 130
Bandon, 86, 119, 121, 144-5
Bangor, 122
Bankruptcy, 75, 157
Banks, banking, 72-5, 85, 90, 101-2, 104, 125-9, 167-9, 172, 199; Bank of England, 126-7; Bank of Ireland, 95, 101-02, 104, 107, 125-8, 154, 168, 169, 169n, 172; deposits, 137,
138, 150, 154, 171; note circulation, 95, 102, 109, 125-6
Bann, river, 122
Barbados, 12
Barley, 68, 69n, 158
Barrow, river, 88-9; navigation, 88
Bedford, duke of, 69
Beechmount, co. Cork, 90
Beef, 8, 10, 11-15, 18, 21, 26-7, 31-3, 44, 50, 52-3, 54-9, 67, 87, 101, 103, 109
Belanagare, co. Roscommon, 69
Belfast, 19, 20, 24-5, 29, 69, 73, 85, 87, 90-1, 94, 102, 106, 107-08, 120-5, 127-8, 132, 141-3, 146-8, 157-65, 167, 170, 176
Belmullet, co. Mayo, 149
Belturbet, co. Cavan, 86
Berkeley, Bishop George, 49, 67
Bessbrook, co. Armagh, 108
Bills of exchange, 16, 30-2, 42, 56, 60, 72-3, 95, 102, 107, 125, 127-8, 196
Birth rate, 118, 166, 185, 192
Blackburne, Edward, 148
Blacksmiths, 144, 147
Blackwater, river, 122
Blakes, 12
Blarney, co. Cork, 90, 94, 157
Bleaching, bleachers, bleach greens, 61-2, 83, 93, 127
Board of Directors of Inland Navigation, 122
Board of Works, 122-3, 129, 132
Bootmaking, boots, 147, 163, 174, 179
Bordeaux, 52
Boyne, river, 143; Navigation, 89
Breen, Dan, 155
Brewing, 39, 88, 90, 91-2, 97, 123-4, 144, 147-8, 157-8, 161-2, 179
Bristol, 17, 27-8, 30, 34-5, 40
Britain, 41, 54, 85, 90, 97-8, 103, 158, 179-81, 184, 186; see England, United Kingdom
Brooke, Robert, 97
Butler, Isaac, 61

Butter, 8-12, 14, 17-18, 21, 26-7, 32-3, 44, 48, 50, 52-58, 59, 82, 87, 103, 109, 154-5, 177-8
Byrne, Edward, 92

Callan, co. Kilkenny, 86
Camac, river, 90
Canals, 49, 83, 88-9, 94, 100, 122, 166
Capital, 16, 60-1, 80, 82-3, 85, 87, 94-6, 100, 108, 125-6, 128-30, 143, 161, 168-70; inflow to Ireland, 24, 28-30, 32, 94, 97-8, 129, 168-9, 184, 186; outflow from Ireland, 22, 129, 168-70, 172, see Investment
Carlisle, 14
Carlow, 86; co., 199
Carrick-on-Shannon, 44
Carrick-on-Suir, 64
Carrickfergus, 19
Cary, John, 30
Cashel, 86
Castlebar, 63, 116, 121
Castlecomer, 88
Catholic, 60, 67, 78-9, 84
Cattle, 7-11, 14, 27, 44, 48, 52-5, 59, 67, 75, 81, 87, 101, 112-13, 177-8; Cattle Acts, 13, 15-18, 39, 55-6, 59
Cavan, 86; co., 61, 111, 120, 122
Census, 110, 112, 116, 119, 120-1, 141, 145-6, 201
Chester, 17
Church of Ireland, 35, 114, 154
Clara, 162
Clare, co., 65, 91, 111-12, 117, 142, 152
Cleeves, 156
Clonliffe mill, 157
Clonmel, 73, 86, 146-7
Cloth, 32-3, 86, 116
Clothing, 174, 178
Coal, 49, 88-9, 91, 96, 146, 177-8
Cobh, 121
Colebrooke, 74
Colello, Richard, 94
Coleraine, 86-7, 122
Colles, William, 93
Colonies, 11-12, 54-5, 57-8, 75-6
Commercial Propositions (1785), 97, 99
Commission on the Poor, 114, see Poor Law
Commission, Financial Relations, 167-8
Commissioners of Navigation, 49
Common Market, 184, 186-7
Congested districts, 150-3; Board, 152-3
Connaught, 61, 81, 117, 141, 152
Connemara, 123

Co-operatives, 155
Cork, 9, 19, 32, 38, 41, 55-6, 58, 73, 75, 85, 87-8, 90, 92, 94, 98, 103, 124, 142, 143-8, 161, 164; co., 8, 56, 64, 66, 79, 80, 82, 84, 111-12, 119, 152; Cork Industrial Development Association, 164; Earl of, 8
Corporation for Promoting and Carrying on an Inland Navigation in Ireland, 88
Cottiers, 70, 80, 81-2, 99, 135-6
Cotton, 92, 93-4, 97, 99, 102, 105-08, 119-20, 122-3, 146, 148, 159
Crommelin, Louis, 59
Currency, 13, 30-4, 42, 174; see Banks, note circulation
Customs, see Duties, Revenue

Dairy farming, dairying, 54-5, 59, 78-80, 82, 137, 139, 154-5, 162; dairy produce, 177
Dalkey, co. Dublin, 94
Dargan, William, 143
Davitt, Michael, 149
Death rate, 118-19, 131, 165-6, 192
Deeves, 94
Defenders, 84
Deflation, 101, 104, 107, 182
Denmark, 154-5
Depression, 36, 62, 75, 105, 107; see Great Depression, Recession
Derbyshire, 107
Derry, 35, 69, 122, 160, 165; co., 48, 60-1
Diet, 69-71, 77, 80, 117, 130, 136, 138, 149, 151, 165, 192
Dillon, 74, 151
Dingle, 121
Distilling, 90-2, 123-4, 144-5, 157-8, 161-2
Dobbs, Arthur, 51
Dodder, river, 90
Donegal, co., 111-12, 117, 130, 140, 152-3, 160
Donegal, Lord, 83
Doneraile, 121
Donohill, co. Tipperary, 156
Down, co., 48, 60-1, 122
Dowries, 81, 82, 101
Drainage, 129-30, 139
Drogheda, 9, 24, 85-6, 108, 120, 124, 128, 142-3, 146
Drummond Report or Commission, 108-10, 128
Dublin, 9, 14, 19, 20, 25, 31-3, 45-6, 60-1, 64, 69, 70-1, 73-4, 83, 85, 87-95, 98-9, 102, 106, 107, 121, 124-8, 141-4, 148, 157-8, 162, 165-7, 175; co., 130; Society, 49
Dundalk, 20, 24

Dundrum, co. Dublin, 166
Duties, 21, 26, 33, 35, 39, 42, 54, 59, 60, 66, 97, 105, 145, 174, 177-8
Dungarvan, 86
Dungannon, 122

Economic War, 177-8, 186
Egmont, Earl of, 51
Electricity Supply Board, 175
Emancipation, Catholic, 115
Embargoes, 57-8, 76
Emigration, 28, 40, 75, 132, 134-7, 151-3, 156, 169, 172, 175, 178, 182, 185
Encumbered Estates Acts, 138
Engineering, 124, 161, 185-6
England, English, 7, 10-17, 22, 24-5, 27-8, 30-43, 45-6, 49, 50-1, 53, 55-60, 64-5, 68-9, 72, 75-6, 91-5, 101, 103, 105-7, 119, 120, 126-9, 142-3, 152, 163-5, 167-8, 170, 177-8, 186; see Britain, United Kingdom
Ennis, co. Clare, 84, 86, 141-2
Enniscorthy, 86
Erne, river, 122
Erris, co. Mayo, 116
Established Church, 84; see Church of Ireland
Eviction, 140, 149, 150
Exchange business, rates, 13-16, 21-2, 30-4, 40, 42-3, 45-6, 72-3, 75, 107, 197
Exeter, 35, 40
Exports, 7-15, 22-4, 27, 31, 32-4, 39, 41, 43-4, 46, 48, 50-5, 58-60, 62, 65-6, 69, 71, 75, 83, 97, 100-01, 103, 108-9, 127, 157-9, 161-3, 167, 169-70, 171-7, 179-80, 182-7
Europe, 9, 12-13, 16, 27, 33, 38, 46, 50, 54-5, 60, 85, 95, 186

Fairs, 11, 13, 66, 74-5, 86-7
Famine, 7, 9, 10, 27, 43, 46-7, 50, 68-9, 104, 118, 130, 200; Great Famine, 69, 81, 131-9, 141; Famine, France, Scotland, 27-8
Farmers, 63-6, 68, 70, 80-2, 93, 95, 101, 109-14, 118-20, 130-1, 136-7, 139, 148-9, 170, 171-2; see Tenants
Fermanagh, co., 111, 120
Fethard, co. Tipperary, 86
Fever, 69, 131-2; see Plague
Ffingall, Mary, 32
Fianna Fáil, 178
Findlaters, 167, 202
Finlay, 75; Fr. Finlay, 155
Fitzgibbon, 66
Flanders, 21, 26, 32
Flax, flax-seed, 38, 75, 108, 137

Flour, 38, 68-9, 89, 91-4, 96, 99, 100, 109, 147, 157
Footwear, 163, 178; see bootmaking
Foster, John, 98; Foster's Corn Law (1784), 96
Foyle, river, 160
France, 11-13, 21, 26, 27-9, 33, 42, 46, 50-2, 54-5, 57-8
French, Robert, 61

Gaelic League, Leaguers, 163-4
Gaeltarra Eireann, 153
Galway, 9, 12, 18-19, 73-4, 93, 143, 145-7; co., 61, 111-12, 117, 121, 152
Catchells, 145
Glanmire, 90, 143
Glasgow, 38-9, 165
Glasheen, co. Cork, 94
Glass, glass making, 39, 76, 90-2, 97, 124, 145, 178
Gort, co. Galway, 121
Grain, 9, 11, 13, 22, 28, 43-4, 46-8, 46n, 50, 67-71, 74, 81, 89, 91, 95, 101, 103, 109, 117-18, 146-7, 176, 198
Grand Canal, 88-9, 100, 122, 166
Great Depression, 175, 178, 186
Griffith, Arthur, 164
Guadaloupe, 12
Guinness, 157

Haiti, 55
Hamburg, 51
Harland and Wolff, 159, 180
Hartnells, 167
Harvest, 27-31, 43-8, 50, 52, 67-74, 80, 91, 101, 103, 148, 173, 198
Hearth money, 43, 70, 86
Hely Hutchinson, John, 148
Herbert, Thomas, 14; Lord, 14
Hilliards, 156
Hispaniola, 12
Hoare, Edward and Joseph, 32
Holland, 13, 32, 56-8
Holyhead, 32
Home Rule, 167
Hops, 30, 76, 90
Hosiery, 162-3, 178
Housing, 22, 116, 165, 175
Huguenots, 32, 59-60

Immigration, 24-5, 28-30, 40
Imports, 18-19, 23-4, 28-9, 31, 40-1, 43, 46-8, 46n, 65, 67-74, 90-1, 97, 99, 101, 105-6, 116, 127, 169-70, 171-4, 176, 179-81
Industrial Revolution, 90, 97, 107, 186
Industry, 24, 90-4, 123-5, 130, 144-8,

156-64, 167, 170-1, 173-4, 176, 178-83, 185-6
Inflation, 101, 171-2, 187
Investment, 78, 115, 172, 181, 183-5; disinvestment, 179; *see* Capital
Iron, iron working, 8, 90, 100, 124, 144, 147
Irish Agricultural Wholesale Society, 155
Irish Industrial Development Association, 164
Irish Republican Army, 172
Islandbridge, 90

Jackson, Henry, 91
Jamaica, 12
James II, 22
Jeffreys, 94
Johnston, Mooney and O'Brien, 157
Joy and Co., 94

Kanturk, co. Cork, 121
Kells, co. Meath, 86, 111, 121
Kenmare, co. Kerry, 8
Kerry, co., 62, 66, 79, 80, 82, 111-12, 152
Kilbeggan, co. Westmeath, 121-2
Kildare, co., 70, 97
Kilkee, co. Clare, 123
Kilkenny, 71, 85-6, 90, 92, 102; co., 70, 84, 86
Killarney, 156
Kilrane, co. Wexford, 162
Kilrush, co. Clare, 123, 142
King, bishop, 29, 35
King's co., 61
Kingstown, 142
Kinnegad, co. Westmeath, 85
Kinsale, 9, 19, 56, 121

La Rochelle, 52
Labourer, 20, 23, 64, 66, 70-1, 80, 99, 101, 109-13, 116-20, 130-1, 135-7, 156, 164-5, 172
Lagan, river, 19
Lancashire, 107
Land, land system, 10, 19-20, 22, 25, 29, 33-4, 83-4, 138-9, 153-4, 177, 188, 192
Land Commission, 150, 154
Land League, 149-50
Landlord, 20, 42, 45-7, 61-2, 72, 77-83, 94, 113-17, 138-40, 149-50, 154, 188
Le Havre, 52
Leases, 44-5, 77-82, 84, 101, 113-15
Lee, river, 19, 90
Legislation, English, British, 36-9, 49, 59, 66, 76, 125-6, 150, 154, 156; *see* Cattle Acts, Woollens, Navi-

gation Acts; Irish, 49, 73, 88, 95, 96-8, 125, 174, 178, 179, 183; *see* Union, Tillage Act
Leighlinbridge, co. Carlow, 88
Leinster, 61, 81, 87, 89, 91, 111, 117
Leitrim, co., 111-12, 140, 152; third earl of, 140
Lewis, Samuel, 120
Liège, 32
Liffey, river, 90
Limerick, 73, 85, 87-8, 92, 143, 145, 147, 157; co., 65, 71, 111
Linen, cloth, yarn, 24, 48-9, 50-1, 53, 59-64, 66-7, 74-6, 81, 85-8, 90-1, 93-5, 97, 99, 102, 108, 117, 119-20, 122-5, 127-8, 148, 158-60, 162, 167, 174, 180, 185-6, 198-9
Lisburn, 84, 86, 91
Lismore, 121
Liverpool, 142, 162, 165
Livestock, 9-11, 13-15, 21, 26-7, 29, 59, 74, 80, 86, 109, 112-13, 117, 130, 137, 149, 174, 176-7; *see* Cattle, Sheep
London, 11, 16, 21, 30, 32, 45, 58, 83, 107, 127-9, 169
Londonderry, *see* Derry
Longford, 86; co., 61, 120, 122
Lough Allen, 91
Lough Neagh, 49, 89, 122
Loughrea, 121
Louth, co., 61, 70, 108, 111, 119-20
Lowther, Sir James, 49
Lucan, Lord, 63
Lurgan, 24

Machaire Cluain, co. Monaghan, 80
Mahony, Martin, 157
Maize, 157-8, 161-2
Malahide, 94
Malcomson, 146
Mallow, 86, 121
Malt, malting, 69n, 88, 90, 92, 123, 158, 162
Manchester, 142, 146, 165
Mansion House Fund, 149
Marriage, marriage rate, 118, 135-6, 151, 166, 185; *see* Dowries
Martinique, 12
Maryboro' (Portlaoise), 86, 121
Mathew, Fr., 138, 145
Mayo, co., 63, 80-1, 111-12, 116-17, 119-21, 123, 130-1, 135, 149, 151-2
Meal, 68-9, 116; Yellow or Indian, 132, 138, 149, 151; *see* Maize
Meath, co., 60-1, 70, 80, 86, 92, 108, 111, 113, 120
Middlemen, 78-80, 82, 114-15, 139
Middleton, 86, 121
Migration, migratory workers, 40,

149, 151-2, 169
Mill, John Stuart, 153
Mills, milling, 70, 90, 91-4, 97, 146-7,
   161-2, 199; see Flour
Mississippi Company, 46
Molyneux, William, 35
Monaghan, 86; co., 60-1, 80, 111,
   120, 122, 140
Monivea, co. Galway, 61
Montserrat, 12
Mostrim, co. Longford, 61
Mountmellick, 86, 106, 121-2
Mountrath, 121
Mullingar, 86-7
Munster, 66, 77, 80-1, 87, 102, 109,
   117, 125, 141, 176, 182

Nantes, 51-2
National income, 170, 173, 176,
   179-80, 182-4
Naul, co. Meath, 92
Navigation Acts, 12, 18, 37-8
Navan, 108, 121
Navy, navies, 56-9
Nenagh, 147
Nevis, 12
New Ross, 84, 92, 162
New Zealand, 155
Newenham, Thomas, 98, 104
Newport, co. Mayo, 120
Newry, 20, 49, 69, 80, 85, 88-9, 108;
   canal, 88-9, 96
Newtownards, 122
Nicholsons, 108
Nore, river, 88
Norfolk, 14
Norwich, 107

Oakboys, 83
Oats, oatmeal, oaten bread, 68, 70,
   178
O'Connell, Daniel, 116
O'Connor, Charles, 69
O'Connor, Sir James, 173
O'Doirnín, Peadar, 77
O'Malley, George, 63, 81
O'Maoil Chiaráin, Uilliam, 80
Orange Order, Orangeism, 98, 115
O'Súilleabháin, Eoghan, 71

Paper, paper making, 124-5, 144-6,
   163, 178
Parnell, Charles Stewart, 116, 164
Peel, Sir Robert, 131
Petty, Sir William, 8, 20, 22-4, 44,
   64
Petty-Fitzmaurice, 199
Philipstown (Daingean, co. Offaly),
   121
Pitt, William, 97-8

Plague, 7, 9-10, 27; Spain, 9; France,
   46, 50; see Fever
Plan of Campaign, 150
Plunkett, Sir Horace, 155
Poddle, river, 90
Poor Law, 112, 119-20, 132, 138, 156
Population, 7-10, 18-19, 22-3, 27, 43,
   48, 55, 60, 84-5, 95, 99, 117-19,
   121-2, 131-5, 140-2, 147, 159-60,
   166, 167
Pork, 27, 101, 103, 109
Portadown, 122, 142
Portarlington, 86, 121
Portlaw, 108, 146
Portugal, 30, 41-2, 54-5, 59
Potato, 22, 70-1, 77, 80, 82, 101,
   104, 116-18, 121, 130-1, 135-8,
   141, 149, 192
Presbyterians, 35, 84
Prices, 8-10, 13-15, 17-23, 25-6, 28,
   31-4, 39-40, 42-5, 47-53, 55-6, 58-9,
   66-8, 70-1, 74-5, 79, 82, 95-7,
   100-04, 109, 112-14, 116, 137, 140,
   146, 149-50, 152-5, 171-3, 176-7,
   180, 182, 200
Prior, Thomas, 47
Privateers, 14, 27
Profits, 62, 72, 75, 94, 143, 171
Prosperous, co. Kildare, 97
Protestants, 21, 79, 84
Provisions, 12, 30, 37, 53-4, 56-9

Quakers, 60, 146
Queen's co., 61

Railways, 142-4, 152-3, 168-9
Rebellion (1798), 115
Recession, 75, 100, 104, 107, 182, see
   Depression
Rents, 20, 22, 33-4, 42-8, 56, 63, 75,
   77-9, 81-4, 101, 112-15, 119, 138-9,
   149-51, 153-4, 170
Retail trade, 130, 132, 140, 142, 144,
   151, 156, 161, 166-7, 176, 182
Revenue, 10, 13-15, 18-20, 27, 29-30,
   40, 40n, 43-4, 44n, 47-8, 67, 75,
   85, 91-2, 96, 167-8, 198
Roads, 19, 83, 87-9, 122-3, 142, 152
Robinson, 124
Ropeworks, workers, 124, 144, 146
Roscommon, 86-7; co., 61, 69, 111-12,
   149, 151-2
Ross, see New Ross
Royal Canal, 89, 100, 122, 166
Russells, 157

Sacheverell, Dr William, 25
St. Domingue, 12, 55
St. Malo, 197
Scotland, 11, 27-9, 146, 152, 158, 167

Shannon, river, 88-9, 122-3, 142, 175
Sheep, 7, 10-11, 16, 27, 68
Shipbuilding, 124, 146, 158-61, 174, 176, 180, 185
Shipping, 12, 37, 55-8
Shirtmaking, 151, 160
Shops, shopkeepers, 116, 121, 138; *see* Retail Trade
Shorney, river, 90
Sinn Féin, 164
Slane, co. Meath, 93-4, 99
Sligo, co., 61, 111-12, 152
Smallpox, 119
Smiths, 94
Smuggling, 41, 51-2, 63, 116, 192
Soap, Soapboiling, 116, 125, 146, 174
Society of Merchant Venturers, Bristol, 17
South Sea Company, 46
Southwell, Sir Robert, 56
Spain, 9, 27, 30, 42, 54-5, 57, 59
Spinning, 82, 112, *see* Cotton, Linen, Wool
Steam engine, 90-1, 122, 124, 146; Steamer, steamship, 113, 122-3, 142, 149
Steelboys, 83
Strabane, 86
Subdivision, 81, 113, 117-18, 152
Sugar, 12, 18, 38, 55, 165; refining, 90, 92, 144-5, 175
Suir, river, 66, 88
Swift, Jonathan, 36, 47, 67

Tait's, 157
Talbot, Richard, 94
Tanning, 125, 144-6, 163, 179
Tapsome (Topsham), 32
Tariff, tax, taxation, 21, 26, 27-8, 37, 97, 105, 138, 164, 167-8, 174-5, 177-9, 182-4, *see* Duties, Hearth Money
Tea, 116, 138, 151, 165, 168
Temple, Sir William, 15, 23
Tenants, 20, 22, 42-3, 45, 47, 67, 79, 81, 83-4, 139, 149-50, 153-4, 188; tenant right, 79, 83-4, 113-14; *see* Farmers, Land system, Landlord
Terms of trade, 171, 173, 176
Tillage, 22, 47, 67-8, 70, 95, 112, 135, 137, 147, 152, 178; Tillage Act (1727), 47, 49, 67
Tipperary, co., 84, 86, 156
Tithes, 47, 67, 84, 114
Tobacco, 13, 18-19, 28, 30-1, 38-9,

116-17, 138, 161-2, 168, 179, 181
Tobercurry, co. Sligo, 152
Towns, 24-5, 84-7, 90, 121-3, 140-2, 144, 147-8, 162, 164-6
Tralee, 121
Trim, 86, 121
Tuam, 121
Tullamore, 121, 147
Turnpike, 87-8, 94; *see* Roads
Tyrone, co., 49, 61, 91, 160, 199

Ulster, 24, 29, 48, 61, 63, 66-7, 81, 111, 119; Ulster Canal, 122; Ulster Railway, 142
Unemployment, 99, 172, 174-6, 178, 180
Union, 98-9, 104-5, 115, 192
United Kingdom, 104, 158-9, 161-2, 164, 167, 180,; *see* Britain, England
United States, 38, 159
Unrest, agrarian, 83-4, 113-14, 139-40, 149-50

Wages, 23, 97-8, 137, 156, 160, 172, 187
Wales, 12, 126
Waterford, 19, 69, 73, 87-8, 92, 124, 143; co., 65, 79, 86, 108, 145-6
Weaving, 83, 112; *see* Cotton, Linen, Woollens
West Indies, 12, 30, 55, 57-8
Westmeath, co., 61
Westport, 120
Wexford, 92, 162; co., 106, 162
Wheat, 67-8, 70, 147, 157
Whiskey, 138, 158, 161-2, 167-8; *see* Distilling
Whiteboys, 83-4
Whitehaven, Cumberland, 49
Wholesale trade, 95, 121, 127-8, 140, 142, 161-2, 176, 182
Wicklow, 162; co., 65, 106, 199
Wood, William, 36
Wool, yarn, 8-11, 14-16, 18, 23, 27, 33, 39, 43, 48, 50-2, 56, 66, 75, 87, 198; Woollens, 23-4, 30-7, 39-42, 49, 53, 59, 64-5, 76, 91, 95, 99, 105-8, 119, 157, 163
Workhouses, 131, 140, 142
Workman, Clark & Co., 160, 180

Youghal, 9, 19, 32, 121
Young, Arthur, 80, 93
Yorkshire, 107